Praise for **Handbook for the Heartbroken**

"*Handbook for the Heartbroken* is a lighthouse of a book, offering solace and guidance to women navigating the labyrinth of heartache. A loving companion on our way, Sara Avant Stover reminds us through her years of experience of the gentle, steady power of self-compassion. A heartfelt and essential guide for every woman's journey toward wholeness and resilience."

ELENA BROWER
author of *Practice You* and *Softening Time*

"For anyone experiencing heartbreak, past, present, or future (all of us!), Sara Avant Stover's wise and comforting teachings will wrap you in a warm blanket of understanding and truly helpful practices that bring relief. Drink the steaming cup of tea she offers us, through the incredibly poignant and insightful stories of her own healing and those of her students. I can't imagine a better companion through grief and devastation than this book."

KAIRA JEWEL LINGO
author of *We Were Made for These Times*, coauthor of *Healing Our Way Home*

"*Handbook for the Heartbroken* is an insightful guide for women navigating the treacherous waters of all types of loss and falls from grace. Sara Avant Stover offers practical tools and healing strategies, drawing from both personal experience and extensive research. This book is a must-read for anyone seeking solace and rebirth after a challenging season of life."

SARA GOTTFRIED, MD
*New York Time*s bestselling author of *Women, Food, and Hormones*

"Recognizing the fullness and complexity of who we each are and holding this fullness in the larger container of ritual, these are essential skills if we're to navigate the rupture, ordeals, and sorrow that life brings. Sara Avant Stover's work is a kind, humble, and well-crafted guidebook for just this type of navigation through the depths."

ꓷANIEL FOOR, PHD
hor of *Ancestral Medicine*

"A healing balm for the heart, *Handbook for the Heartbroken* is a guide into the portals of awakening, rebirth, and wholeness. In a culture where we are often shamed for our suffering, this book is a light on the path towards acceptance and trust. Thank you Sara, for this much-needed gift to the world."

TRACEE STANLEY
author of *Radiant Rest* and *The Luminous Self*

"In this handbook for holding and healing through life's hardships, alongside insightful contemplations and relevant practices, Sara Avant Stover lovingly offers her own and other's experiential heartaches as a much needed feminine circle of support during our own times of despair."

SARAH POWERS
author of *Insight Yoga* and *Lit From Within*

"Handbook for the Heartbroken is a soulful companion that tenderly holds the hands of women as they traverse the dark valleys of their lives. With compassion and depth, Sara Avant Stover guides us to unearth the treasures hidden within our pain, leading us to become more grace-ful, whole human beings along the way. This is a gift to women seeking solace and a deeper connection to their own inner wisdom."

MIRANDA MACPHERSON
author of *The Way of Grace*

"Sara Avant Stover has written a wise, grounded, and thorough roadmap and companion for women, helping us to move through the world with self-compassion and grace, recognizing that our experience is important, that our losses must be tended, and that we are not alone on this feminine path. Handbook for the Heartbroken is a life pre-server in a storm."

KIMBERLY ANN JOHNSON
author of *Call of the Wild, The Fourth Trimester,* and *Reclaiming the Feminine*

"This book is like a dear friend accompanying us in our darkest hours, full of permission, wisdom, and care. Sara Avant Stover's candor and generosity about her own grief opens the door for us to compassionately navigate our own. She writes, 'Grief is trying to break your heart open. It's trying to soften you.' This book helps us do that, leaving us more loving and more whole."

HEIDI ROSE ROBBINS
author of *Everyday Radiance*

"This handbook is an elegantly and truthfully written guide to heartbreak and beyond. The book itself soothes the heart."

JENNIFER FREED, PHD
author of *A Map to Your Soul* and *Use Your Planets Wisely*

"Life is guaranteed to bring all of us to our knees at some point; this is the book to read when you're on the floor. This is a gift of a book, one that is destined to be a much-loved resource for all women when life falls apart. Whether it's the devastation of romantic betrayal and relationship breakdown, the lifelong living loss of abortion, failed infertility treatments and unchosen childlessness, chronic illness and loneliness, the terror and shame of business failure, homelessness, redundancy, financial meltdown and bankruptcy, Sara Avant Stover has been there—and survived. Presented as a totally relatable mixture of vulnerable autobiography, practical guidance, and the stories of other women Sara has worked with, it is refreshingly free of the kind of inspirational bullshit that ignores the complex, intersectional, structural realities of so many women's lives. This is a candid, helpful, honest, and affirming handbook."

JODY DAY
founder of Gateway Women, author of *Living the Life Unexpected*

"This world will break your heart—the question is what will you do with it? How refreshing to read Sara Avant Stover's Handbook for the Heartbroken and have a fierce, tender, and skilled companion for the deep walk through heartbreak who knows how to make heart medicine on this journey to live on and heal well. And though the stories Stover shares are personal, each one echoes the greater wounds and heartbreak of the feminine that we each must heal in order for her to rise from the ashes of a patriarchal time and reembody her beautiful truth."

TAMI LYNN KENT
author of *Wild Feminine*

"In these times of upheaval and uncertainty, we do not need more preachy books by self-proclaimed experts. What we need is vulnerability. Beauty. Luminous examples of what it looks like to walk through the wreckage with your heart open, your mind curious, your soul attuned. We need fearless storytellers like Sara Avant Stover. This book is generous and generative."

MIRABAI STARR

author of *Caravan of No Despair* and *Wild Mercy*

HANDBOOK
for the
HEARTBROKEN

Also by Sara Avant Stover

The Way of the Happy Woman

The Book of SHE

HAND BOOK
for the
HEART BROKEN

A *Woman's Path* from
Devastation to *Rebirth*

SARA AVANT STOVER

sounds true
BOULDER, COLORADO

Sounds True
Boulder, CO

This book is not intended as a substitute for the medical recommendations of physicians, mental health professionals, or other health-care providers. Rather, it is intended to offer information to help the reader cooperate with physicians, mental health professionals, and health-care providers in a mutual quest for optimal well-being. We advise readers to carefully review and understand the ideas presented and to seek the advice of a qualified professional before attempting to use them.

Some names and identifying details have been changed to protect the privacy of individuals.

Published 2024

Cover design by Huma Akhtar

Book design by Charli Barnes

Printed in the United States of America

BK06875

Library of Congress Cataloging-in-Publication Data

Names: Stover, Sara Avant, author.
Title: Handbook for the heartbroken : a woman's path from devastation to rebirth / by Sara Avant Stover.
Description: Boulder, CO : Sounds True, Inc., 2024. | Includes index.
Identifiers: LCCN 2023027993 (print) | LCCN 2023027994 (ebook) | ISBN 9781649632364 (paperback) | ISBN 9781649632371 (ebook)
Subjects: LCSH: Loss (Psychology) in women. | Women--Psychology. | Women--Health and hygiene. | Women--Life skills guides.
Classification: LCC HQ1206 .S859 2024 (print) | LCC HQ1206 (ebook) | DDC 155.9/3--dc23/eng/20230816
LC record available at https://lccn.loc.gov/2023027993
LC ebook record available at https://lccn.loc.gov/2023027994

FSC
MIX
Paper | Supporting
responsible forestry
FSC® C103098

To my mom, Sara Hatton,
for always being the one to answer the phone.

To my dog, Sadie, for always being at my side.

To my unborn children, Zane and Lucia, forever.

And to God, for it all.

"Nothing real can be threatened.
Nothing unreal exists.
Herein lies the peace of God."

— *A Course in Miracles*

This too shall pass.

A Note to Readers

Heartbreak can bring us to the deepest, darkest corners of our lives, psyches, and souls. With this, severe depression and suicidal ideation may be present for you. If this is the case, please seek support. Help is available twenty-four hours a day through the Suicide and Crisis Lifeline by calling or texting 988 (available to both English and Spanish speakers). You can also visit their website: 988lifeline.org.

I honor and welcome people of all genders, sexual orientations, and identities here. While this book is directed to self-identified women, anyone wanting more support along their healing paths may find this book useful. Whenever I use the terms "woman" and "women" throughout the book, I'm referring to anyone who self-identifies as a woman.

When someone's full name is used in this book, they have agreed to have their identity known. Whenever only a first name is used, that person's name and identity have been changed.

Contents

Heartbreak Story: Breakup & Betrayal 1

Introduction: Reframing Heartbreak 7
Practice: Preparing for Our Journey 20

PART I: DEVASTATION

Heartbreak Story: Abortion 27

Chapter 1: Navigating Shock 39
Practice: Ways to Navigate the Early Weeks of Heartbreak 47

Chapter 2: Bowing to Grief 53
Practice: Create a Container to Grieve Well 63

Chapter 3: Validating Yourself 67
Practice: Invite All of Your Parts to the Banquet Table* 77

Chapter 4: Asking for Help 83
Practice: Get to Know a Protective Part* 96

PART II: TRANSFORMATION

Heartbreak Story: Fertility Journey 103

Chapter 5: Allowing Anger 113

Practice: Give Your Anger Somewhere to Go 118

Chapter 6: Living with Loneliness 123

Practice: Tonglen* 129

Practice: Resource Lonely Parts with Self Energy* 134

Chapter 7: Processing Pain 139

Practice: A Practice to Feel Your Pain* 144

Practice: Contacting an Exiled Part* 151

Chapter 8: Creating Ritual 157

Practice: Create Your Own Ritual 161

Practice: Microrituals to Hold Us Through Transitions 167

PART III: REBIRTH

Heartbreak Story: Career & Finances 173

Chapter 9: Finding Forgiveness 181

Practice: The Practice of Forgiveness 189

Chapter 10: Restoring Trust 193

Practice: Cultivate a Prayer Practice 200

Practice: Map Your Mistrusting Parts* 203

Chapter 11: Coming Alive 207

Practice: Opening, Softening & Allowing Meditation* 215

Chapter 12: Supporting Others 221

Practice: Ideas for Supporting Others 228

Conclusion: Preparing for Our Ultimate Heartbreak 235

Practice: Closing Ritual 239

Acknowledgments 241

Recommended Resources 243

Notes 247

Index 249

About the Author 259

*Audio versions of these meditations are available at
saraavantstover.com/heartbreakdownloads

Heartbreak Story:
Breakup & Betrayal

Katabas. It's a Greek word that means "a blow that sets your life spinning in an entirely new direction." In February 2016, my katabas struck.

The earthy scent of olive oil filled the kitchen as I tossed thin, quartered slices of sweet potato until they glistened. Spreading the potatoes evenly across a baking tray covered in parchment paper, I dusted them with a fine layer of sea salt. The evening was dark and quiet, punctuated by the dimmed overhead lights and heat sporadically gushing out of the vents. It was an ordinary Thursday. I'd just come out of the bath and, anticipating a much-needed early bedtime, put on my pajamas before starting dinner.

The bath helped cue me to wind down in advance of taking a long weekend for myself. I needed the extra encouragement: I was finally taking my foot off the gas pedal after several months of overexertion. I had been cranking to finish my second book—which was much more challenging and took me longer to write than expected—before the extended deadline. Then I was introducing my book to the world, followed by launching a yearlong online program that welcomed one hundred women. Then I was hustling to get a business loan to help bridge the gap between finishing my book and bringing in money again, plus navigating a relationship that was becoming more and more fraught with fights and sleepless nights. Eggplant-colored half-moons framed the undersides of my eyes, which, as my mom used to say when I got overly tired as a child, were "at half-mast." I was making dinner out of duty. Going through the motions to throw something together quickly as I knew that, more than anything, my body simply needed to rest.

I longed for all the years and months when my life felt bright and shiny—when my relationship with my fiancé, Matt, wasn't so fraught with challenge. One of my friends set us up on a blind date in November of 2010. We sipped herbal tea at a high-top table in a coffee shop, and as we spoke, I was pretty sure I'd never met anyone quite like him. Despite our many shared interests, he didn't seem like my type at all, and I didn't know if that was a good thing or a bad thing. While I was in Thailand over the next couple of months, we exchanged long, witty emails, and by the time I returned home in January, I had officially fallen for him.

During the first year and a half of our relationship, I felt like I was flying. I was pretty sure that I had, at long last, found my soul mate. We quickly became the "it" couple and were looked up to by many in our community. We seemed to have it all—we were both public figures, and now we were in a great relationship. Together, we went out dancing, enjoyed dinners out over glasses of cabernet and deep conversations, and held the shared intention to use our relationship as a path to our spiritual awakening. We moved in together in August of 2012. After that, things started to change.

Matt no longer gazed at me adoringly, calling me his "sun, moon, and stars," and he often stayed out late without me while I opted to go to sleep early and catch up on rest. Things slowly began to devolve, bringing us to that Thursday evening in 2016 when our relationship was being held together by a thread. Despite all that, my love for Matt felt so deep, and the thought of letting go of my dream with him terrified me. I still held on to the hope that our challenges were all part of our spiritual path, that we could use them to help us get back to where we had been and, somehow, grow even closer.

Snapping me out of my reverie, our dog leapt to his feet from his bed. The rapid click-clack of his paws across the oak floorboards of the living room, then past me in the kitchen, signaled that Matt was home. The front door swung open, letting in a gush of cold air that smelled of the outdoors. Matt knocked the tips of his boots against the door ledge, shaking off the snow before stepping inside.

"Hi, Bug," he greeted as he bent down to rub our dog's floppy ears. I noticed he did this more firmly and quickly than usual, as though he was in a rush. Picking up on his energy, I hurried to the door, meeting him in the entryway.

"Hi, love, welcome home," I greeted, sliding my arms around the cold exterior of his down jacket. Rather than waiting our usual few moments in a welcome-home hug to feel both of our bodies relax, he pulled away quickly, offering a forced smile and vacant eyes. I returned to the stove, opened it, and slid the tray of sweet potatoes inside.

Matt pulled off his coat, unwrapped the scarf from around his neck, looked at me, and grimaced. "I need to talk to you," he said. "You might want to take that out of the oven."

He walked past me toward the dining room table while I took the potatoes out of the oven and turned it off. Following behind Matt like a robot, I felt my neocortex shutting down as I sensed a bright red danger sign flashing above us.

We sat across the table from one another, a soft yellow light beaming from the luminaire above us. My stomach clenched, knowing something horrible was about to happen. The wise voice inside told me to breathe and brace myself, warning that my life on the other side of whatever Matt was about to tell me would never again be the same.

"I've been having an affair with Lindsey," he admitted. His face remained stoic and matter-of-fact while his words shot into the quiet evening like darts. "It was sexual for a while. In recent months, it's just been inappropriate texts. My men's group found out about it and confronted me last night. I knew I needed to tell you today—before someone else did."

An icy anesthetic flowed through me, numbing everything from toes to crown. My thoughts turned black and my tongue swelled, keeping me from forming words. Lindsey was part of our inner circle. I was frozen in my chair, my hands interlaced in front of me on the table.

"You're kidding, right?" I asked, scanning his face for any sign that he was about to start laughing.

"No, I'm not kidding," he replied.

"Then I need you to leave," I responded automatically.

"I'll go get my things," he conceded. He stood up and headed briskly toward the stairs.

Hot lava started to bubble in my chest, temporarily unthawing me. It jolted me to my feet and sent tears down my cheeks. I had told him to leave, but of course that wasn't what I really wanted. How could he even consider leaving me alone after sharing news like that? A part of me wanted him to wrap his arms around me, tell me what a terrible mistake he had made, and reassure me that he would never, ever leave me. Another part of me knew that life had just answered my fervent prayer for clarity. For months I'd been contemplating leaving our relationship to have a child on my own because Matt had decided he didn't want to have children, and because our relationship was fundamentally not working for reasons I couldn't quite grasp. As one of my spiritual teachers often said when clarity struck, "The fat lady had sung."

Matt didn't say or do any of the things the clinging parts of me wanted so badly. Meanwhile the wiser part of me knew I needed to let the Band-Aid be ripped off fully and completely. I rushed up the stairs after Matt until we both stood at the top. The wood floor started to undulate beneath me. He was still talking, but I couldn't hear what he was saying. I leaned against the wall with my left shoulder, trying to find something, anything, to hold me up.

"Get out! Get the fuck out!" I screamed in a voice that didn't sound like mine.

Matt fell to his knees at my feet. This man's face, the one that I had known so intimately through all of his moods and moments, now showed something I'd never seen before. It twisted into creases of anguish as he pleaded, "I'm so, so sorry, Sara."

I don't remember all of what happened next. I do know that, at some point, Matt moved past me into the bedroom to pack a bag. Still holding onto the wall, my hand traced a path across it toward my office. Once inside, I slid my hand down until it met the floor, lowered myself, and crawled into a corner. There, I pulled my knees into my chest, tightly clutching the jersey of my pajama pants and squeezing my eyes shut until I heard the soft thud of the front door close and the faint sound of his car engine starting and then fading into the distance. Inside, a ticker tape rushed through my mind with two questions on repeat: "Did he really just leave? Is this really happening?"

All around me, the house descended into silence.

Introduction:
Reframing Heartbreak

The night my fiancé, Matt, left—February 4, 2016—my life split into two. Eight years later, I now see that moment as an impassable fault line demarcating who I was prior to that night and who I was to become afterward. That heartbreak, however, was not a one-and-done event. Far from it. Rather, it was the first of a series of several more blows that encompassed all areas of my life (health, finances, work, relationships, self-identity) that sent me spiraling down further and further into grief, depression, loneliness, confusion, and, at times, desperation.

That night, however, was not only the catalyst that unraveled me. It also planted a seed of the me who I was to become. It was, I now see, a nearly unsurvivable gift that helped me to heal, mature, and evolve. It helped me to come to deeply know the different stages and flavors of heartbreak, and, in turn, to be able to sit with and support others as they traverse the dark valleys of their own lives. In this book, I share the stories of the successive heartbreaks I've faced over the past several years, anecdotes from those my students and clients have endured, and the perspectives that helped us to make sense of the unfathomable, as well as the tools and practices I used to heal and endure the longest, most painful (and, ultimately, most fruitful) years of my life.

We live in a heartbreak-illiterate world that's obsessed with success, shackled with isolation, and ignorant of how valuable our suffering can be for our growth and evolution (not only as individuals but as a species).

It's no wonder we face a void of guidance when we experience our inevitable falls from grace. And that's not all: with the growing existential threats of climate change, the pandemic, political divisiveness, and the breakdown of long-standing societal structures and ideologies, psychic anguish of all sorts is cracking through more frequently and powerfully than any of us have experienced in our lifetimes. And we direly lack the support we need to face this.

This book offers a sacred container for your heartbreak experience. An intimate and supportive mentor, it will be with you when you struggle to survive your darkest hours. At times this book will also mother you with a gentle power, providing fiercely loving guidance to help you continue moving forward. Our initial caregivers and the media often teach us to fear challenging emotions like grief, sadness, depression, confusion, and rage. We are repeatedly told that our only option is to find happiness at all costs by getting married, having children, following our dreams, and living happily ever after. In actuality, heartbreak is an inevitable part of *everyone's* life journey (usually many times over). This book will show you that it's only through fully turning toward your heartbreak (with support, courage, and compassion) that you can heal. Not just that, but fully embracing these darker seasons of life is the only way to become a fully wise, mature, integrated human being.

Within the loving pages of this book, you'll have full permission to fall apart—and slowly, organically find your way back to greater wholeness. This book takes a holistic approach to not just surviving heartbreak but also transforming it into a life-affirming rite of passage. Yes, heartbreak is mandatory, but transformation is a choice.

Who Is This Book For?

This book is for any woman who's currently experiencing any kind of heartbreak, at any stage of her heartbreak journey.

There are many ways our hearts can break. The following are some examples of heartbreak this book can help you with:

Death of a loved one

Death of a pet

Natural disaster

Significant health challenge, illness, disability, or injury (yours or another's)

Dealing with a troubled teen/child

Baby loss (miscarriage, abortion, stillbirth, infant death)

Separation, divorce, or breakup

Betrayal

Addiction

Bankruptcy or a financial crisis

Major professional change

New empty nesters/ free birders

Saying goodbye to your childbearing years

Loss of community (one's family, religion, or spiritual community)

Failed fertility treatment(s)

Loss of a friendship

Loss of a job or a career

Abuse (sexual, emotional, psychological, physical)

Loss of identity

Violent social event (war, a shooting)

An accident (car, plane, or something else)

Also, this book is for you if you're grieving things you didn't get, like certain experiences in childhood or later in life. It's also for you if you're not experiencing heartbreak presently, but you know there are past hurts and grievances that you haven't fully healed. Even if you experienced a heartbreak ten, twenty, or more years ago, this book is for you, too. Perhaps you didn't have the time, perspective, courage, or resources you needed to heal at that time. Now you sense that, by not fully healing those past hurts, you're letting them unconsciously impact your life. In doing so, you're holding yourself back from experiencing the wholeness and forward momentum you most want.

Above all, when we don't successfully pass through our heartbreak journeys, we're limiting and hurting ourselves in a multitude of ways.

Keeping powerful emotions like grief, anger, and sadness unexpressed within us can shut down our emotional bodies, making it hard to experience positive emotions like joy and gratitude. This emotional stuckness can lead to depression and even physical illness. We also protect our hearts from future hurts, and this keeps us from moving forward with our lives and experiencing the connection and intimacy we most long for.

Because emotional and psychological injuries are much less visible than physical ones, we can more easily get away with (at least initially) stunting their healing and hiding them from others. When I was healing from my heartbreaks, one of my friends reminded me that it was like I'd had an accident and had broken both of my legs. She encouraged me to treat myself accordingly by staying at home and resting, and, above all, not expecting myself to be functioning as if I had two healthy legs. Think about it: if you had broken both of your legs and didn't do the things required to heal them, like resting, using a wheelchair, taking pain meds, going to the doctor, and doing physical therapy, your legs wouldn't heal, or, at the very least, they wouldn't heal correctly. The same is true for us when we're heartbroken. Even though we (and others) can't see the depth of the injury, it's still there. Without proper rehabilitation, it won't heal, and you won't be a fully healthy, functioning person until it does.

Also, initial heartbreaks can lead to subsequent losses (which you'll see some examples of in this book). For instance, a divorce or separation can lead to the loss of a home, pet, and one's sense of security (inner and outer); the rearrangement of friendships and community; health challenges; and even financial distress. Keep this in mind as you go deeper into your own heartbreak journey, probing for the cascade of losses you're likely experiencing along the way, and how each of those impacts you in different ways.

I've included financial and career loss in this list (as well as in one of my own heartbreak stories in this book) because crises at these levels can rock our entire material foundation as well as our self-esteem and sense of self. Financial challenges can force us to lose our homes, limit our ability to get the support we most need, and riddle us with fear, panic, and anxiety. Job or career loss and transitions rattle us in similar ways, especially if a lot of our time, focus, and identity has been linked to our work. Above all, I encourage you to expand your understanding of heartbreak and to see how it encompasses far more than just deaths and breakups. It can punctuate—and shatter—every corner and crevice of our lives.

Why I Wrote This Book

Heartbreak and I have been lifelong companions. Starting from an early age, on the outside I looked perfect, and I liked that. Beneath the surface, though, I wasn't happy. Growing up in a family with addiction, I often felt lonely, afraid, and unable to express my true feelings. By the time I was in my late teens, this inner pain expressed itself through anorexia and bulimia. I grappled with depression and anxiety, which I tried to self-medicate through overachieving at school and running several miles a day. Upon receiving a frightening diagnosis of advanced cervical dysplasia in the spring of 1999, I finally hit a wall. I was about to graduate from Barnard, an Ivy League women's college in Manhattan. Despite all of my outer achievements, I realized I didn't know who I was or what I wanted. I didn't know what it meant to be a woman, much less how to be one. I felt completely lost.

Luckily, life intervened through an out-of-the-blue job offer to teach at an American-style international school in northern Thailand. I accepted the job, and a few months after my graduation from college, I flew to Chiang Mai for what I thought would be a one-year position. I ended up staying in Thailand for nine years, and it was there that I began to heal through immersing myself in a slower, saner, healthier approach to life.

Now a teacher of feminine spirituality and certified Internal Family Systems practitioner, over the past twenty years, I've supported thousands of women through their own spiritual openings disguised as healing crises. I have sat with women whose children were born still. I've met women whose lives changed course due to debilitating illness and injury. I have spoken with women who left abusive relationships, grappled with how to heal from sexual assault, and struggled with addiction. I have met women who lost their mothers, whom they saw as a best friend. These are all moments of heartbreak and devastation.

My capacity to meet women in their suffering has grown as I've learned to be with my own suffering in greater and greater ways, with the magnitude of my own heartbreaks (and subsequent healing) increasing over time. As I began healing myself in my early twenties through yoga, meditation, traditional Chinese medicine, Ayurveda, and by living in harmony with nature, more and more women began asking me how they could do the same for themselves. So, starting in my midtwenties, in addition to providing one-on-one support, I began leading in-person retreats and trainings around the world. Starting in 2008, I was one of the very first people to stream yoga and meditation retreats online and became one of the first online entrepreneurs in the field of feminine spirituality.

I've also written two books about the cyclical nature of feminine healing and empowerment. The first, *The Way of the Happy Woman: Living the Best Year of Your Life,* grew out of my experience of getting sick in college and moving to Thailand. In it, I bring together everything I learned and then taught in my in-person and online women's events throughout my twenties.

My second book, *The Book of SHE: Your Heroine's Journey into the Heart of Feminine Power,* grew out of the challenges I experienced in my early-to-mid thirties while I was writing and publishing my first book and my eating disorders resurfaced. In it, I share the practices and perspectives I embraced during that stretch of my healing journey. It translates Joseph Campbell's story of the hero's journey into a modern-day version of this monomyth for women and instructs us that the crises we face in life aren't failures but rather portals into becoming more of who we truly are, deep down.

Throughout, my own life experiences have been my greatest teachers. Each book I write reflects my deepening understanding of a woman's journey—it's not lost on me that my first book was about becoming a happy woman and my current book is about heartbreak! At their core, all of these books work together and share a similar thread of supporting women to trust, honor, and align with the various seasons and cycles of our lives. Throughout all of this, I discovered that heartbreak is a crucial initiation for women to step into deeper maturity and wisdom, yet given how taboo falls from grace are in our culture, we have very little support in learning how to pass through them.

I also want to acknowledge that while I've experienced a lot of challenges in my life, I also have a lot of unearned privilege. I'm white, cis-gendered, heterosexual, and nondisabled. I grew up in a family that once had a lot of financial resources. As a result, I had access to some of the best education in the country. At different times in my life, I've been able to afford various kinds of therapy and support, as have the women whose stories I share in this book. I recognize that not everyone reading this will have the same privilege and access to resources. There were stretches in this heartbreak journey where I wasn't able to get the help, financial or interpersonal, that I felt I needed. Since I know this is a position many find themselves in, one of my intentions in writing this book is to offer accessible support to anyone who's going through heartbreak.

My Approach to Heartbreak

Now, you might be wondering, why is this book written for women? There are a number of reasons. First, my previous two books, as well as all of my teachings, are specifically for women. A feminist since childhood, I've always had a passion for supporting women. This began with growing up as the second oldest of four sisters, followed by going to an all-women's college where there was a strong emphasis on women's empowerment. Starting at an early age, I both saw and experienced how the dominant world culture places women (more covertly now than in the past) in disenfranchised positions. Many of the things we struggle with (eating disorders, sexual abuse, low self-esteem, and self-doubt, to name a few) stem from these cultural imbalances, though we're often erroneously led to believe that they arise from our own shortcomings. Since so much value is still placed on a woman's relationship and social status, coupled with the fact that we are relational beings who often need more connection, heartbreak can impact us more adversely than it does men. I want to give women a roadmap through this treacherous territory so we can grow stronger, rather than weaker, as a result of our challenges.

In alignment with all of my teachings, the approach to healing heart-break that I share in this book is holistic. It encompasses all dimensions of a woman's life—physical, emotional, mental, and spiritual. We need to address all of these in order to be thorough in our healing and to live integrated lives. To care for our physical selves, I'll emphasize moving our bodies in nourishing ways (like going for walks), doing adequate self-care, and spending time in nature. Nature is a physical expression of wholeness. Even just thirty minutes a day of walking outside can help to recalibrate and harmonize us when our lives are topsy-turvy.

To access and heal our mental and emotional dimensions, I primar-ily use the evidence-based psychotherapeutic modality Internal Family Systems (IFS), in which I have trained, practiced, and taught. Founded in the early 1990s by Dr. Richard (Dick) Schwartz, IFS applies family therapy and systems theory to one's internal landscape. What distin-guishes IFS from other psychotherapeutic models is that rather than seeing humans as having a single, unified mind, it perceives us as having a multiplicity of minds. For example, we've all had the experience of say-ing, "A part of me wants to do this, and another part of me wants to do that." IFS also takes a nonstigmatizing, nonshaming approach to work-ing with challenging parts of ourselves (like a part who feels depressed, or parts who use alcohol or marijuana to numb pain). Rather, it believes that all parts of us are inherently good. At their core, all parts hold some-thing called "Self" energy, which is akin to "Buddha nature" or "essential goodness" in spiritual traditions.

We're all born with Self energy, and nothing we do or don't do can diminish or take it away from us. Yet when we endure challenging expe-riences, not only in early childhood but throughout our lives, this Self energy gets eclipsed by protective parts who step in to help us endure those traumas (little "t" and big "T" ones, from being humiliated or criticized in school to being emotionally, physically, or sexually abused, and everything in between). IFS offers an incredibly effective, gentle model to help us access and heal these often hard-to-reach wounds. In so doing, we restore burdened parts of ourselves to their originally intended roles in our systems, and we experience more freedom, ease, and balance as a result. When our inner landscapes start to shift, so too do our outer ones.

Ultimately, IFS is not about the practitioner giving advice. Instead, it allows you to access your own innate, inner resources to guide you. It's our inner wisdom that heals us and restores wholeness. In this book, my job is to help create the conditions and atmosphere for you to access your Self more easily. Rather than fearing that bad things will happen to us or turning within and feeling scared about what we'll discover, when our inner wisdom (or Self energy) takes the lead in our inner and outer lives, there's nothing we can't handle. There's nothing we can't heal from. There's nothing we can't be with.

This brings us to the final dimension of our healing—the spiritual one. In my work and in this book, I weave in a feminine approach to meditation, inquiry, and devotion. Meditation trains us to get still, drop below the ever-changing display of thoughts, feelings, and sensations at the surface, and begin to rest in the vast, loving presence that holds us all. Unlike more patriarchal methods of meditation, this approach doesn't ask us to transcend our human experience. It urges us to relax, allow, and open into whatever is happening. Inquiry, or nonintellectual questions we reflect upon internally, then helps us to drop deeper into our physical, emotional, and mental experiences of our essential nature while also illuminating for us what blocks our access to it.

Finally, devotion ties this all together. To traverse the darkest valleys of our lives, we need to open to a Higher Power of our own choosing. Whether you know that to be Love, God/Goddess, the Universe, your heart, or something else, when life presses us into a tight corner, we quickly realize that our usual methods of coping or trying to escape won't work. At some point, we accept that the only sane choice (or really the only choice at all) is to surrender. When we let go of willing and controlling our way through life and invite our Higher Power to step in, grace can finally enter. Then, we begin to be shown the way through.

Our Heartbreak Journey

The journey from devastation to rebirth is the very journey we're now taking the first steps of together. I should warn you: it's not an easy journey. Not at all. Suffering is one of the greatest impetuses there is to personal growth. And the greater the suffering, the greater the possibility there is for change. If it were easy to midwife yourself into greatness, everyone would do it. Greatness—living as the highest expression of yourself and co-creating your life with the source of existence, which I call God—requires tremendous bravery, perseverance, patience, resilience, kindness, humility, and, if you can muster it (this is a hard one for me at times!), a sense of humor.

The journey of heartbreak is very much like walking on a tightrope. One end of the rope is anchored to your old life, the other to your new one. And to get from one end to the other, you must take one step at a time over a terrifying, treacherous chasm. If you want to make it to the other side of that chasm intact, your steps across the tightrope can't be rushed. For all of our sakes, I wish they could be. But that would be missing the point.

Transformation—which means you will be a different woman on the other side of this heartbreak than you were before it—demands equal parts guts and surrender. And, as you've probably noticed, it takes time. You must let go of who you were and what your life used to look like in order to walk, one step at a time, into the Great Unknown. Allowing all of your control mechanisms to fall away and trusting the timing of the eternal, you learn to relax into the alchemical process of evolution that wants to unfold within and through you.

When heartbreak comes and decimates your day-to-day reality, one of its purposes is to crack you open. At a time in history when closed-heartedness is the status quo, heartbreak hurls you into such an extreme and vulnerable state that you can't *not* feel your heart. Thus, when viewed and worked with skillfully, heartbreak can be the very balm this world needs. It can be a vehicle for living a soul-centered, rather than an ego-centered, life. It can be a catalyst to leave the life you wound up with in order to really feel and partner with your heart—the seat of the

Divine within you—and create the life you were born to live. In doing so, you can be a blessing to the world.

Let me be clear: this approach is absolutely *not* about rushing your process or transcending your pain, which is what our dominant culture would have us do. No. This is an "in and through" approach. We're not trying to get "over" our loss, which, most of the time, isn't even possible. Instead, we're getting "under" and "in" it. By fully embracing and honoring it, we start to be shown how to live *with* it—in both the short and long term.

How This Book Is Organized

This book follows the general arc of the heartbreak journey from inception to healing. While this is a nonlinear process with no exact steps or timeline, there is a general arc, patterned in nature, that everyone moves through: from death to transformation to rebirth.

It's divided into three parts, each of which begins with one "heartbreak story" and is followed by four chapters. Each heartbreak story gives you an intimate glimpse into the different kinds and facets of heartbreak that I experienced between 2016 and 2020. My hope is that within these personal stories, you will feel resonance with and validation of your own heartbreak experiences. I also want to note that this book shares my experiences only. While all stories and relationships have multiple perspectives, I can only represent my own perspective. Also, when someone's full name is used in this book, they have agreed to have their identity known. Whenever only a first name is used, that person's name and identity have been changed.

The first part, "Devastation," includes my abortion story followed by an exploration of the initial stages of heartbreak we often experience. Chapter 1, "Navigating Shock," explores what the early hours, days, and weeks of heartbreak can look and feel like when our systems are still numb to the reality of our loss. Next, chapter 2, "Bowing to Grief," educates us about the massive catalyst for change that grief really is. It teaches us how grief is in fact the very engine that will propel us into our new lives and gives us practices and rituals to help us survive its ferocity.

Heartbreak is a vast landscape that includes many components, grief included.

In chapter 3, "Validating Yourself," we look at the cultural stigma around grief, sadness, and our so-called "darker" emotions. Rather than heeding others' encouragement to hurry up and move on, you will be empowered to validate and trust your own unique, nonlinear experience. The final chapter in this section, "Asking for Help," stresses the importance of opening up to receive more support from those who don't judge or try to fix you.

Once through the excruciating early phases of heartbreak, we move into the stage of transformation. This part begins with the heartbreak story of my fertility journey. Following that, in chapter 5, "Allowing Anger," we open the door to the fiery face of heartbreak. Rather than spewing or resisting it, you'll be guided to partner with your anger and to use its fire to burn away old patterns and structures in your psyche and life. "Living with Loneliness," chapter 6, leads us into an important exploration of how to be with both our aloneness and loneliness during transitional times, when our usual support people and structures often fall away and we're left with more empty space.

From here, we start to meet the deeper layers of our loss with chapter 7, "Processing Pain." It's only through directly meeting and metabolizing our pain (present and past)—without trying to fix, avoid, or change it at all—that those wounds can be alchemized and we can create space for new life to grow. Chapter 8, "Creating Ritual," serves as the transformational nexus of the journey. Here, I introduce the power of ritual and how it can help us process change.

On the other side of our rituals, we arrive at the third phase of our journey: "Rebirth." I begin this part with a heartbreak story about my career and finances. Then, in chapter 9, we explore the often-misunderstood process that's at the heart of most of the world's great spiritual traditions, forgiveness. We'll explore not only how to find forgiveness for others but also for ourselves, life, and the Divine itself.

As we start to feel ready to take the first steps toward our new lives, in chapter 10 we'll consider trust more deeply. When you've been betrayed and gaslit, how do you trust yourself again? How do you move forward into your new life with boldness and courage, rather than playing it safe out of fear of being hurt again? Plus, when the life you had is over, and the new one you're stepping into is not yet here, how do you stay in the in-between space? How do you make decisions and navigate your reality when, still, nothing is fixed or predictable? We've strengthened our muscles of faith, surrender, and patience throughout the journey, and now it's time to take it even further and to allow Life, rather than our own wills and egos, to lead us forward.

In chapter 11 we explore "Coming Alive" again after heartbreak. The first step of this is arriving in greater acceptance. From here, we're better able to see the unexpected blessings our heartbreak has brought us, even if our losses seem meaningless and unfathomable. The final chapter, "Supporting Others," shines a light on how we can use all we've been through to be of service to others who are in pain.

Since each woman's heartbreak journey is different, you're always encouraged to be exactly where you are. You're welcome to jump around, if needed, to read about the stages of heartbreak you're currently in and need immediate support with. Another way to approach this is to read through the entire book and then go back and focus more intently on the specific stage that you're in.

I also want to acknowledge that I touch on a number of potentially sensitive, challenging topics in these pages, like sexual abuse, abortion, disordered eating, and suicidal urges. You have my blessing to pass over any part that feels like too much for you to take in. Please remember to seek out additional support if you feel overwhelmed at any point in this process. You can find resources, including where to find an IFS therapist or practitioner, at the back of this book.

Along the way, I'll share with you the practical tools and inspiration needed to not only make it through your darkest days but also to reframe them—not as failures but as sacred doorways. On the other side of your devastation, you'll be endowed with the gifts of greater wholeness and access to your essential qualities (like patience, perseverance, forgiveness, wisdom, courage, confidence, open-heartedness, trust, compassion, and humility). From there, you'll be able to share those qualities with the world—for the divisive and taxing times we're living in need an abundance of these qualities more than ever before.

Yet remember: the only way out is in and through. Let yourself be exactly where you are. Let your experience be precisely what it is and take as long as it needs to take. Healing usually takes a lot longer than we think it will (or than others allow it to). Also, let yourself accept support. We're not meant to go on these life-shaping journeys by ourselves (in fact, we can't).

And, as always, take what works for you in these pages and leave the rest behind. No one else's pain or heartbreak is the same as yours. Your own greatest teacher is, and always has been, within you.

Preparing for Our Journey

To get started, I invite you to create some space in your home (and your life) for this healing process. Here are some ways to do that.

1. Get a "heartbreak journal."

I recommend writing at least three pages in your journal by hand (if you prefer typing, that's fine too) each day, if possible. This is a practice that Julia Cameron calls "Morning Pages" and teaches in her seminal book, *The Artist's Way*. It's best to write these in the morning (when your mind is the freshest), but if that time doesn't work for you, it's fine to find one that does. Write these pages as a stream of consciousness, without censorship, editing, or even letting the pen stop moving!

2. Create a healing cocoon for yourself.

You may be spending more time alone during your heartbreak journey. This is a time of deep self-care, so really put some intention into creating a safe holding environment for yourself.

Stock your kitchen with nourishing foods—even a simple pot of rice and beans will offer you some easy, soothing meals. (The Indian dish of kitchari, which consists of basmati rice, split mung beans, and spices, is one of my favorites.) Make a cozy nook for yourself, be that with a blanket on your couch or a special pillow in your bed. Ask around for some good movies and shows to watch. Keep a jar of Epsom salt near your bathtub and add anything else to your cocoon that would feel especially nurturing and cozy.

3. Define your Higher Power.

At various points throughout this book, you're going to hear me mention "Higher Power." If you don't consider yourself a religious or spiritual person, I encourage you not to run for the hills! Stay with me. A Higher Power doesn't need to be a white, bearded man flying through the sky (that's not how I experience God). Not at all. A Higher Power can be your own creation—your own sense of what the greatest force in the Universe looks and feels like. A Higher Power is that which causes your heart to beat, your eyes to blink, for you to be born, and for you to die. Your connection to That Which is Greater Than You is one of the biggest medicines you'll receive in this book, so take some time to consider it now. For example, some people call this Source, Spirit, the Universe, God/dess, or the Divine.

On this note, you'll also hear me mention ancestors at various times in this book. Having lived for a decade in Asia, where ancestral reverence is a visible and common practice, throughout my own healing and spiritual journey I've explored how to include my own ancestors in my life. Different cultures define ancestors in different ways; the way I'm defining it here stems from the studies on ancestral healing I've done with Dr. Daniel Foor (I recommend his book *Ancestral Medicine* if you want to learn more about this). According to this model, not all deceased relatives are ancestors. I work with many women who had challenging relationships with deceased relatives, and the last thing they want is to have more connection with these people. That's okay. The title of "ancestor" is reserved for those deceased relatives (or ancestors of a place or a lineage) who are wise and well. Just like how not everyone in the land of the living who is old is an elder, not all deceased people are ancestors. When I ask you to call on your ancestors, you can call on those who are wise and well. These are loving, supportive beings who can help to guide you on this human plane. And if the idea of connecting with your ancestors doesn't resonate with you at all, feel free to omit it.

4. Set up a heartbreak altar.

I always encourage women to create a space in their homes for the sacred. This can be a corner of a room, a shelf, or a separate room entirely. On your altar, place a candle and any objects from nature or sacred images (like spiritual teachers, deities, or guides) that inspire you. Adding fresh flowers or inspiring phrases can be helpful, too.

In short, this is a physical space to reflect back the sacredness that you truly are. It brings into your cocoon the presence of a Higher Power to hold, guide, and support you through your heartbreak journey.

In this space, have a meditation cushion as well as your journal and any other supplies that feel supportive. I'll share guidance as we go on how to use and engage with this space.

5. Set your intention.

An intention is like a seed that you plant in your garden in the springtime. If you want your garden to yield heirloom tomatoes in August, you'll need to plant heirloom tomato seeds in it in May. The same is true here, now. If you want to emerge more whole, healed, and mature on the other side of this experience, set the intention for that now.

State intentions in the present tense, as if they are already happening. An example intention for this experience is, "I traverse my heartbreak journey with compassion, courage, and gentleness. I seek support when I need it, turning directly toward whatever presents itself. In so doing, I emerge from this experience more whole, healed, mature, and embodying and sharing more of who I truly am with the world."

Now, write down your intention for this journey in your journal. It's good to have that on the first page (or to keep it on your altar), so you can return to it when you feel shaky and unsure (which, you will see, is part of the process).

With these pieces in place, we're ready to start our journey into heartbreak. Remember, this isn't for the faint of heart. So, draw in a deep breath, take my hand, pause, and regroup whenever you need to. Let's begin . . .

Part I

DEVASTATION

Heartbreak Story:
Abortion

Colorado; April 2017

Climbing the blue-carpeted stairs of the two-story building, my mother and younger sister behind me and one of my girlfriends in front of me, I told myself, *I can stop this. I can turn around right now.* But I knew, whether I kept moving forward or turned back, there was no escaping this katabas. It had come for me. No matter what.

"Keep going, Mom. You're doing the right thing," my son encouraged from deep within me. "We're in this together."

So, I kept walking up the stairs. So, I didn't turn back.

Exactly two weeks earlier, I was leading a women's yoga and meditation teacher training at a retreat center just outside of Calistoga, California. It was the second day of seven. At five o'clock, I finished teaching for the day. Heading out of the practice hall and into the late afternoon mist and drizzle, I started walking back to the teacher's cottage where I was staying.

Twenty-two women from as far away as Australia had flown in for the training. Under the best of circumstances, leading a weeklong event demands my full energy and focus. Even more so at that particular training, for I was test-driving a new curriculum and didn't have tried-and-true lesson plans to lean on. Plus, I had just entered the second trimester of my first pregnancy and learned that I was having a boy, which I had announced publicly five days earlier.

After suffering from debilitating, round-the-clock nausea for the past several weeks, I was starting to feel a little bit better. Still, I was operating at only around 50 percent of my usual capacity. On top of that, I had moved into a new home with my new partner, Jonathan, and his child only a few days earlier. I felt like I was rounding a corner. For the first time, I could start enjoying my pregnancy. I could finally celebrate the blessings I'd been calling in so fervently, for so long.

When I arrived at my cottage, I switched my phone out of airplane mode so I could communicate with my on-site teaching assistant. That's when I saw it—a text from my business manager. It read, "There's a sensitive email that came in today. I know you're teaching, but you're going to want to take a look at it right away. XO"

SHIT. My intestines knotted. A slick layer of sweat coated my palms. *She never texts me. She knows I stay off of email when I'm teaching. This must be really bad.* I sat down on the loveseat and logged into my email. The message was at the top of my inbox, and the subject line read, "Personal message for Sara about Jonathan."

FUCK. I opened the email. At the top, my business manager wrote, "Sara, this came in today and I wanted to get it to you right away. Please let us know if there's anything we can do to support you."

FUCK. FUCK. FUCK. My eyes raced over her words and down to the forwarded email:

Dear Sara,

We've never met, but when I saw the recent post on social media about your pregnancy, I knew I had to reach out to you.

I've been sexually involved with Jonathan since last September. I had no idea that he was with you. I have evidence if you want it. He's the true definition of a misogynist.

The email was signed with her name and phone number. Inside, humiliation scorched me. Hands trembling and heart pounding, I heard the voice inside of me say, *This is another one of those moments. Your life won't ever be what it was fifteen minutes ago. You are forever changed.* I knew exactly what that voice meant. I had *just* had one of those rug-pulled-out-from-underneath-me, life-shattering moments only fifteen months earlier. I had *just* faced my biggest fears and deepest pain. I thought I was finally coming through to the other side. *How could this be happening to me again . . . so soon?*

Only this time, I knew it was worse. Far worse. I looked down at my belly. Now it wasn't just me. It was me . . . and my baby.

I put in my earbuds and called Jonathan.

"Hey, babe!" he exclaimed. "How's California?"

"I got an email today," I cut in. Then I shared what I'd learned from it.

"It's not true. I promise you it's not true," Jonathan replied calmly. "Sara: listen to me. It's NOT true."

His son, whom he had just picked up from school, was in the car. Jonathan told me he'd call me back once they got home.

"Do you swear on your son's life that it's not true?" I implored.

"Yes," he answered, before hanging up.

Next, I texted the woman who'd contacted me, requesting her evidence. She responded right away, saying she didn't feel comfortable sharing it anymore. Since children were involved, she didn't want to get tangled in any legal battles.

He must have just called her.

"How about FaceTime?" I texted back. "Then I can still see the evidence without leaving a record. I need to know who's telling the truth here."

We FaceTimed a couple of hours later, and I saw everything I needed to. Jonathan was, in fact, the one who was lying.

While my betrayal by Matt the previous year will probably remain the biggest shock of my life, I now recognize that a *very* subtle, subconscious part of me *did* know what was happening with him. It was the part that spoke to me in nightmares I had about him and Lindsey sleeping together, which Matt dismissed. It was the part that he led me to believe was eye-rollingly jealous and always the one at fault. Over time, that part became buried under hundreds of Matt's lies. Lies that put my mind and gut at war with one another. Lies that made me question my sanity. I now know that there's a psychological term for this: gaslighting.

A covert manipulation technique that creates cognitive dissonance by telling a person that her experience of reality is wrong, gaslighting is one of the most damaging and insidious forms of emotional and psychological abuse there is. It causes a person to question her own sanity, memory, or perception of events. Whether or not someone intentionally gaslights you, the result is that they create feelings of self-doubt and confusion, making you more susceptible to their manipulation and control.

When I began putting the pieces together, all the strange occurrences from my time with Matt started to make sense. When we first met, I felt bright, healthy, engaged with the world, and confident. By the time we separated, I felt dimmed down and drained. I hardly recognized myself. I was *always* exhausted. I hid behind black sunglasses for a few years. I stopped socializing because I felt so unsafe going out with Matt. My hair started falling out, and I developed mysterious illnesses, including, toward the end, prediabetes. No matter how much time and money I invested in myself, my health only got *worse*.

Neither I nor anyone I sought help from thought to look at the energetics of my home environment or relationship as key contributors to my distress. I thought it was just me. I viewed my relationship with Matt as a primary part of my spiritual path, so I was willing to stay in the fire in order to learn and grow through our union. Matt and I were in couple's therapy for two years with a highly regarded therapist. In our time together, the therapist never suggested they caught a whiff of what was really going on.

After the truth came out (and more women, beyond just Lindsey, came forward to tell me they'd also been sleeping with Matt while we were together), I started working with my mentor and a new therapist more intensively. For several months after our separation, I read books, took online courses, and attended weekly therapy sessions to help me heal from our dynamic. I was committed to learning from my mistakes and taking responsibility for my life. After reading Pia Mellody's book *Facing Love Addiction*, I was floored by how accurately she depicted Matt's and my dynamic. I was, I realized, the love addict, and Matt was the love avoidant. Deep down, I was terrified of being alone.

Determined to heal and move on, I devoted myself to creating a new life. I envisioned my future partner and a family rooted in integrity, security, and well-being. Every day I worked to become the woman I would need to be to live that life. My support team celebrated how well I was doing. My only frame of reference, however, was past breakups, and my separation from Matt was so much more than just a breakup. It wasn't until much later that I realized the extent of the damage all the cognitive dissonance had done. Plus, old wounds of abandonment, shame, humiliation, and worthlessness surfaced. My dominant emotional state was fear—bordering on paranoia—of future betrayal. When these factors are present, as I know now, it's very common for women to enter into another relationship with a narcissist. Now that I know more, I wish I had taken more time to heal and learn to trust myself again before I started dating. But I was enraged that I had already lost a lot of time with Matt, and I was determined not to allow my past to prevent me from living the life I wanted.

In early August, six months after Matt and I separated, I met Jonathan. I felt instant chemistry with him, and it was game on after our first date. With Jonathan, I approached the dating process with more maturity and scrutiny than I ever had before. I vetted him by bringing him around friends and family early on. I met with mutual acquaintances to ask them about him. I even ran a criminal background check on him! I was upfront with Jonathan about my broken engagement and desires for marriage, family, and monogamy. Since Matt's dishonesty robbed me of the ability to make emotionally mature decisions for my life and to have a genuine voice in our relationship, I was committed to enforcing my needs and boundaries going forward.

Jonathan's vision for his life mirrored mine. We shared the desire for a new beginning. His fun-loving nature made me smile, laugh, and feel sexy and beautiful in ways I hadn't in years. I spoke up about things that, in the past, I would have ignored so as to give my partner the benefit of the doubt. I spoke up about red flags, even yellow ones. Jonathan always had a very logical, plausible explanation for my concerns. (Now I know: always make sure a person's actions and words are congruent, and don't believe their words over their actions.)

While he drove me home from one of our early dates, I told Jonathan that he reminded me a lot of Matt and that that scared me. I had learned through reading Sandra L. Brown's book *How to Spot a Dangerous Man Before You Get Involved* that many of the qualities these men had in common were classic markers of emotional unavailability. Jonathan began to cry and had to pull over to the side of the highway. He shared how hurt he was that I would even think something like that. He vowed to help me heal from my past so I could learn to trust again.

On another car ride, he grabbed my right index finger, pressed it onto the home button on his iPhone, and gave me full access to his phone. Whenever I started to feel anxious, he said, I could look through it.

"I know time is the only nonrenewable resource," Jonathan told me, "and I know you lost years of your life with Matt. I'll never waste your time, and I promise you only a wholehearted, adventurous life."

One of the sticking points in my relationship with Matt was that, while we were both "maybes" to having children when we first started dating, a few years later, Matt became a decisive "no." For a couple of years I grappled with whether or not I wanted to leave our relationship to have a child. Ultimately, I decided to stay. The news of his betrayal, and the realization that it had been going on throughout our discussions about me staying or going, infuriated me. I wished he'd just let me go rather than stringing me along during those final few years of my late thirties, when I would have had more time to find a new relationship and have a child with someone.

So, while I'd been longing and praying to get pregnant and have a family for a long time, my pregnancy with Jonathan was accidental. From the moment I learned I was pregnant, I felt a deep sense of doom and dread inside, and I wasn't totally sure why. My inner guidance still felt incredibly scrambled after all the gaslighting with Matt. At the same time, the women I shared my news with in the early weeks reminded me that having a child is a major life adjustment, and, especially when a pregnancy is unplanned, feelings of doubt and panic are normal. Those emotions conflicted with surprise and wonder that I could even get pregnant at all. For the first couple of months of my pregnancy, I vacillated between feeling like this baby was an answered prayer and pondering whether or not I should get an abortion. I had doubts about Jonathan and about whether or not I could afford to have a child, if it was the right time in my life and career, and if I'd be able to secure the support I'd need to be able to juggle it all. I'd always envisioned being more resourced and settled when I became a mother.

With all of this swirling inside me, I'd gone so far as to meet with an abortion counselor and to schedule a surgical abortion at a local women's clinic. A few days before the scheduled procedure, I got a call from the clinic telling me that the doctor had a personal medical emergency and they needed to cancel my appointment. I took that to be a sign, so I continued onward with my pregnancy.

And, about a month later, there I was in Calistoga, on day two of the teacher training. After learning about Jonathan's lies, I was able to channel my intensity into leading the twice-daily sessions. During breaks, I stayed in my cottage, gathering information. Two choices felt strongly aligned for me: get full, legal custody and raise the baby on my own, or terminate the pregnancy.

Inside, my heart and mind reviewed the previous several months with Jonathan, trying to understand how this had happened. I thought I had been in love with him, but I realized that, like Matt had done in the early years of our relationship, Jonathan had been "love bombing" me—a hallmark phase of any romantic relationship with someone on the narcissistic spectrum. With Jonathan, this gave a much-needed boost to my self-esteem after feeling so rejected and humiliated by Matt. Yet, that over-the-top affection wasn't real love. Once I took the bait and was hooked, a switch was flipped in both Matt and Jonathan, and their behavior radically shifted. Their attention turned elsewhere (to other women), and I longed to return to the idealized state that we started in, not realizing that it had all been an illusion.

As the pieces started clicking rapidly in place, I told Jonathan our relationship was over and asked him to stay somewhere else when I came home. I also asked him for custody of the baby. With shock and disgust, he replied, "Absolutely not." Paternity rights in Colorado are some of the most progressive in the country. Courts don't care about dishonesty or infidelity. Unless there's concrete evidence of physical or drug abuse, or the two parents come to an alternate agreement, courts give 50 percent custody. I told myself I didn't need to decide anything until I returned to Colorado the following week.

I woke up on the last day of the training—a sunny, Sunday morning—feeling both relief and dread. Relief because I would soon no longer be holding space for others and could turn my attention fully to my baby and myself. Dread because I knew that whatever my final choice ended up being, unimaginable difficulty loomed before me.

In the years since, after I've shared this story publicly, many have asked me, incredulously, how I managed to teach a weeklong training in the midst of everything. The answer to this is twofold: I've been teaching events like that training since my midtwenties and have had many experiences of needing to show up and teach despite challenges (not sleeping well, being sick or jet-lagged, going through a breakup, even managing students who were having nervous breakdowns). And while the magnitude of past challenges didn't come close to what I was facing in California, I had sufficient training in showing up, no matter what, that I was able to stay present. But, above and beyond that, before I teach or speak in public, I always say a simple prayer, "Your words, my lips." I hand the event over to God and consciously allow something greater to flow through me. I remember I'm the conduit, not the source. So, each time I walked into the practice hall to teach in California, I felt bolstered. I, too, was surprised at how fully I was still able to show up.

When the training finished, I returned to our new home in Colorado. Heading into the kitchen for a glass of water, I felt all the effort it had taken to actualize that new home. It looked so ordered. So settled (Jonathan had unpacked everything while I was away). Feelings of nostalgia and doubt started to swell inside me.

Then I looked down. On the counter sat Jonathan's black iPad along with a handwritten note.

"Welcome home! Press play on the iPad to watch a video tour to help you find everything."

My tiredness lifted as my heart started racing. I willed myself not to watch the video, for I'd witnessed the power of Jonathan's silver tongue before. Instead, my intuition guided me to swipe my finger across the screen from right to left, bypassing the video and flipping over to the second page of the home screen. To the iMessage icon.

There, I saw a list of messages—some with just phone numbers, a couple with names—of women he'd been sexting with over the past few weeks, some while I'd been asleep in the other room. The texts were even more disturbing than what the woman who'd emailed me had shared. One was with a married woman, whom he invited to our new home for wine and lingerie while I was in California. Another was with a woman he had picked up, in my car, the night that he had dropped me off at the airport. There must have been a tech glitch when syncing his phone— the rest of the iPad had been wiped completely clean.

On a hunt, I looked through the app purchase history and saw dozens and dozens of secret messaging apps. Apps where messages disappear, apps for hooking up with married women, apps that I never knew existed and wouldn't have thought to look for when exploring his phone. (Now I know: when you need to play detective, you're in the wrong relationship.)

Cold tingles of fear ran down my arms and legs.

Who the hell is this person?

I had feared that Jonathan might cheat on me, but the evidence pointed to a reality that was far worse than I could have ever imagined: a life filled with massive deception, manipulation, and infidelity. I double-checked that all the doors were locked even though he had a key. I grabbed a kitchen knife to keep beside me on the nightstand, willed myself to shower, locked the bedroom door, and got in bed. I knew I needed to at least try to rest. I laid in bed alert, exhausted, and terrified until the sun and a cold dawn breeze filtered in through the white curtains.

At 6:30, I got out of bed and headed down to the kitchen. After making a French press of coffee, I took my first sip and began checking items off my list. My sisters were concerned for my safety, urging me to call the courthouse to see if I could get a restraining order (no). Then I began my search for a new home. I wanted to move out by the end of the week, so I emailed the owner of my old apartment to see if there was any way I could move back in (yes!). I emailed my new landlord to see if there was any way I could get out of my current lease with Jonathan (no).

A few hours later, the doorbell rang. Unlocking and pulling open the red front door, I welcomed Owen, a family lawyer whom I had known socially for several years. After I filled him in, Owen outlined my three options: abortion, adoption, and having the baby. I ruled out adoption. If I was going to birth the baby, I was going to mother it.

Then he started walking me through abortion.

"Have you heard of quickening?" he asked me.

I shook my head, so Owen continued.

"It's when the baby's development really shifts, around the middle of the second trimester, and you can start to feel him moving inside of you," he explained.

"If you're going to terminate this pregnancy, you will need to do it within the next week. If you wait any longer than that, it will be much harder. On a number of levels."

I was too far along to be able to get an abortion at the women's clinic.

"I'm pretty sure you can still get an abortion at Planned Parenthood. When you meet with your doctor tomorrow, she'll be able to tell you more."

Then Owen talked me through having the baby.

"Even if you're not married and don't put Jonathan's name on the birth certificate, he still has 50 percent custody since he's the biological father," Owen explained.

He talked me through different scenarios, including going to court over the next several months to try for full custody.

"That would be an expensive and stressful process with no guarantees," he continued. "Even if you *did* manage to get full custody, Jonathan could come back at any time in the child's life, up until their eighteenth birthday, to demand custody again."

Should that happen, he explained what it would be like to have Child Protective Services come into my home and inspect every nook and cranny of my life.

Then he asked me the hardest questions I've ever been faced with: "What would you do if your child looked like Jonathan? And acted like him? What if Jonathan turned the child against you? Are you prepared to stay in the state of Colorado to raise this child?"

He talked me through all kinds of scenarios and then asked more difficult questions: "What is most important to you in your life? What are your career goals? What kind of parent do you want to be? Will you really have the bandwidth to do your current work and take all of this on?"

After sweating and squirming through answering his questions about my deepest fears, weaknesses, values, and desires, I realized out loud, "If I knew for sure that I could have a child later on—either on my own or with the right partner—then I would terminate this pregnancy. I'm going to be forty in six months, and I'm now single."

"I have a healthy baby growing inside me right now," I continued. "It's my fear that I won't be able to get pregnant again and fulfill my dream of being a mother that is holding me back the most. But I don't want to make the biggest decision of my life from fear."

As we neared the end of our two hours together, Owen shared, "You know, Sara, I don't think it's a coincidence that you reached out to me."

Pausing to catch my gaze, he continued, "Many years ago, I had a run-in with a sociopath. Mine was in a different context, and I ended up far worse than you, if you can believe it. But that's a story I can share with you another time."

"For now," he continued, "I want you to know that I get how magnetic these men are. They're larger than life. And I understand what an expensive life lesson this is for you, on a number of levels. I know what it's like to get in so deep with a person like this, in such a short amount of time. They operate really quickly. It's quite a quagmire you're in after only knowing this person for eight months. I'm really sorry that this is happening."

When we hugged goodbye, Owen advised me to sit with everything we had talked about.

"No matter what," he urged, "you need to make this decision in the next day or two."

The next morning, Tuesday, marked one week since I had seen the email. I met with my doctor to discuss my abortion options. She too said I needed to act quickly and referred me to a clinic in Denver. I called them when I got home. Their next opening wasn't until the following Monday afternoon.

"You're getting in right under the wire," the clinic receptionist said. "Starting on Tuesday afternoon you'd be in a whole new category, with a higher risk of complications."

I booked the appointment, once again knowing I could always cancel if I changed my mind. As I headed to bed that night, I felt relieved that I could take the next morning to rest and connect with my baby before I started preparing to move again. With my head propped up against a mound of pillows and my journal in my lap, I closed my eyes.

Then: *clarity*. The rinse of relief when every part of me *harmonizes* and *knows*.

A warm, powerful peace surrounded me. My son, greeting me for the first time. *My son!*

He declared, "Mom, I'm not supposed to be born. You're meant to terminate this pregnancy. I came into your life to teach you some big lessons. I love you. It's okay."

His voice boomed down into my guts and through my bones. Tears began to roll down my face, as they do now, writing these words years later.

Tears of relief. Tears of gratitude for being in the presence of such a great being. Tears for my son's and my fate. Tears for ignoring red flags. Tears for meeting Jonathan. For getting pregnant. For not getting an abortion sooner. Tears for the tragedy I felt my life had become. Tears for the knowing that things can never be other than exactly as they are. Tears calling me to trust the perfection of it all.

I invited my son to stay with me in spirit and to come back in a way that was best for him—whether that was to his father through another woman, to me at a time when we could have a happy life together, or to another family. As I cried myself to sleep, I set my son free, knowing he didn't need it. He was already Freedom itself.

While the months following that night led me to some of the deepest, darkest places I've ever known, that evening, Grace allowed me to feel a sense of short-lived peace and perfection in order to make the decision I needed to.

Chapter 1

Navigating Shock

"No one ever told me that grief felt so like fear."

— C.S. Lewis

The "death" phase of grief is all about survival. There's no need to think about the so-called "new you" or your "new life" right now. Instead, all you need to focus on is how to stay alive. How do you get out of bed in the morning? Feed yourself? Face the unbearable pain that wracks not just your heart, but your whole body? Much less make it through the day?

We'll explore the answers to these questions by taking a closer look at the nascent stages of grief, like shock, obsessive thinking, and extreme disorientation. While I experienced all of these after my abortion, it was the news of my fiancé's betrayal the year prior that shocked and rocked me the most. So, let's start there.

Colorado; February 5, 2016

"Please, let it have been a dream. Please, *please*. Let it have all been a bad dream," I begged aloud when I woke up the next morning and the memories came barreling in. It had happened before—dreaming the unthinkable and waking up to the sweet relief that all I loved was still whole. Still touchable.

So, I waited for the smell of his coffee, the sound of his razor buzzing in the bathroom, for him to come in and kiss me good morning before he left for work. But the house stayed still, and I remained alone.

And, as the sky grew brighter, I knew it wasn't a dream. It was my life. As I lay in bed, my new reality pushed its way more and more into my waking consciousness. Not wanting to wake anyone up with a 3 am phone call, I'd braved the night alone. Yet, as soon as the sun rose, I called my mom. Just hearing her voice and uttering the news out loud started to make it all feel more real.

"Oh, no. Oh, Sara, I'm so sorry," my mom comforted.

Finally feeling that someone was there to hear and hold me, even if just on the other end of the phone line, I began sobbing uncontrollably.

"Why don't you pack up some things and come out here to stay with me for a little while?" my mom suggested. "I'm concerned about you being there alone right now."

The thought of venturing out into the world in my state felt far too overwhelming. I wondered if I could even make it to the bathroom— much less all the way to Chicago. So, my mom coached me through another plan. I texted my friends, Eileen and Michael, to tell them what had happened and to ask if I could come over. They wrote back immediately.

"Oh my god, Sara, we're so sorry. Yes. Please come over. You can crawl into our bed. You can take a bath. We will take care of you. Just come."

Robotically, I got dressed. Afraid I would throw up, I moved slowly, my mind willing my body to do what it said. *I have to get out of this house. I have to get out of this house.* As I made my way downstairs, my friend Julia texted to check in on me: "Don't forget to drink some warm water. Keep drinking it, your body needs it. And eat avocados so you don't lose too much weight."

I forced myself to fight back nausea and gulp a few sips of water. Then I grabbed a food bar, gathered my keys and purse, and headed over to Eileen and Michael's. For the rest of the day, I lay in their bed. Atop their white duvet, I gazed out their bedroom window at barren branches bathed in late-winter sun. They made me scrambled eggs on an English muffin, brought me back a mango-and-banana smoothie after they ran errands and picked up their daughter from school, and took turns coming up to the bedroom to sit and talk with me.

I envied how knit together their lives were. How they had their predictable routines. Their warm and comfortable home. And, most of all, how they had each other. Their lives were the same today as they were yesterday. And they would be the same again tomorrow. In witnessing that, I ached for the familiar and for the life I'd had that would never be again. Most of all, I dreaded the days, weeks, and months of aloneness ahead of me that I knew I'd need to face.

When it was Michael's turn to come and sit with me, he shared, "The thing that's going to help the most is Dr. Time. And, unfortunately, time takes time. It's going to take you at least a year to heal from this."

I knew he was right, and I dreaded the year that lay before me. In it, I saw a year of enduring pain rather than enjoying life. I saw myself hurled to the outskirts of "normal" life. I saw my loneliness and the treachery of the deep inner work that awaited me. I resented—and feared—all of it. *Why me?* I wondered. I didn't ask for this dark valley to cross. It felt to me as if my partner had died suddenly in an accident. The man I'd thought Matt was vanished the moment he told me the truth.

Throughout that day (and for many days and nights to come), I relentlessly texted him. As new memories surfaced, I struggled to piece things together and understand what had really been going on for the past few years.

"Where were you really that night? Did you sleep with her too? What was really going on there?"

Throughout the coming week, while my mind raced, working to understand what had happened, emotionally I remained relatively calm. Those around me commented on how well I seemed to be doing. Yet this seeming stability was temporary. Under the surface, the heartbreak was sinking into deeper and deeper layers, like a leak in a home making its way down to the foundation.

After spending that first day with Michael and Eileen, that evening I returned to my empty house, which I simultaneously hated and felt comforted by. I quickly learned that the twilight hours, as day dissolved into night, were the hardest for me. My anxiety during that time was so strong, I needed to either go to a friend's house or have someone come over.

One evening, my friend Cleo came over and sat on the barstools at my kitchen counter with me as I, with my appetite nearly nonexistent, attempted to eat some semblance of dinner: half a piece of bread. Another night, I called my older sister. Feeling her presence on the other end of the line, I collapsed on my bedroom floor, my body heaving with a new wave of grief. She didn't know what to say other than, "Oh, Sara, I'm so sorry." Constant motion, having somewhere to go and something to do, along with always being with someone, in person or on the phone, helped me during those early days and weeks.

Once night finally came, I barely slept. Alone and wide-eyed, I curled up on my side of our half-empty king-sized bed. I dreaded those dark and lonely hours that seemed to go on forever. Everyone was asleep, and there was no one I could talk to. Anxiously, I obsessed over all the mysterious moments in our relationship while still struggling to piece together a coherent narrative for the past several years of my life.

I learned that, along with shock and the obliteration of daily routines, obsessive thinking often accompanies the early stages of heartbreak. The freight train of scary thoughts usually visits us in the middle of the night—between about 1 and 4 am, or what was once known as "the witching hour." You wake up and your mind is racing, trying to figure out what happened and to make sense of your free fall. Since everyone else is asleep, you have to be with the terror of your thoughts and feelings alone. When you're free of your usual distractions and supports, your body, mind, and heart work to process the deep trauma you've just experienced.

Those nights were incredibly hard to endure both while I was in the midst of them and during the zombie-like daylight hours that followed. It was during the blackness of those nights that I more deeply processed what had happened, mourned for what I'd lost, raged against my life, and bemoaned how I wished I'd done things differently.

Let's look now at all the ways your shock may be manifesting for you.

Symptoms of Shock

In the early days and weeks, during the acute stages of grief and heartbreak, shock can look like:

Nausea

Dizziness

Insomnia or other changes
in sleep patterns

Obsessive thinking

Emotional numbness

Confusion, disorientation,
and/or forgetfulness

Denial or disbelief

Feeling empty, or
nothing at all

Struggling to get out of
bed and/or performing
regular, daily tasks

Low or no appetite

Not wanting to go out
or be around people

Disruption of
daily rhythms

Headaches

Anxiety

Feeling tired and achy

Sadness, anger, guilt,
despair, and/or loneliness

Dreams or nightmares

Coming Out of Shock

About a week into my heartbreak, I visited Kaitlyn, a healer whom I've seen for over a decade now. She helped midwife me through a lot of life's ups and downs—but never as far down as when I went to see her that day. As she gently poked acupuncture needles along either side of my spine, she warned me that my system was still numb and in shock.

"There's a lot of pent-up grief inside you that needs to be released," she cautioned. "It's understandable that it hasn't come out yet, but we need to start letting it. Otherwise, it will do damage by staying stuck inside you."

Then she dropped four tiny, white homeopathic pellets into my cupped palm and instructed me to let them dissolve under my tongue.

A few days later, I could hardly get out of bed. But I had to. I was scheduled to teach a three-hour yoga and meditation video retreat that afternoon. Somehow, I had to pull myself together enough to show up for everyone—and to be on camera. Even the thought of it seemed impossible. My eyes were red and swollen from tears and lack of sleep. Searing pain throbbed in my heart so strong that I winced every time I took a step. I remembered hearing about how at one time in history, people actually died from heartbreak—that's how intense the pain can be. My MO was to just keep moving. *All I have to do is make it through today.* Or when things felt really hard, I told myself, *All I have to do is make it through this moment.* Whereas my past self would wake up, practice yoga, and meditate at home before diving into the workday, now (and for months to come) I couldn't be in stillness alone, much less meditate. The storm inside was too wild, too scary.

In an attempt to pull it together that morning, I headed out for a hike. In the past, movement and fresh air had always helped me find my center. As my hiking shoes pounded the hard, brown dirt, I started to feel that with each step my skin was being torn from my body by wild animals. The tops of my shoulders and the entire front of my body pulsed with pain. People out for their morning hikes passed me, smiling, well-rested, laughing, enjoying a normal day, perhaps even a really good day.

How can they be doing so well when I surely must be dying right now? On the outside, my blinding pain was completely invisible to them. They looked at me as if I were normal, like them. My eyes squinted, struggling to stay focused on the path in front of me as the agony continued to ravage my body. *I can't do this. I can't do this. I can't do this,* I moaned to myself. Then, my phone rang. It was Kaitlyn.

"I just wanted to check in to see how you're doing," she greeted, a hint of worry in her voice. "That remedy I gave you takes a few days to kick in. How are you?"

"Not well," I groaned. "It's interesting that you called right now. This morning the shock wore off. I'm in so much pain right now. I feel like I'm being eaten alive by wolves. I honestly don't know how I'm going to survive this."

Shock, Mother Nature's anesthesia, had flooded my body right after receiving my blow. Numbing my pain and emotions, it allowed me to function enough to find some semblance of footing in my new, transitional reality. Now, as the shock—like a pain pill—wore off, the debilitating torment of heartbreak could fully set in.

Because we all feel shock a little bit differently, let's look now at how one of my friends, Krista, experienced it.

Krista's Story: Facing Shock after Her Partner's Sudden Death

On the morning of September 10, 2015, Krista Van Derveer woke up to her phone's alarm. As she lay in bed, she relished in the realization that she'd slept better than she had in years. She needed the rest. Before she'd gone to sleep the previous night, she spoke on the phone to her partner, Mark, whom she'd been dating for almost five years. While Krista and Mark had had a very challenging last year as a couple, they had made some really good breakthroughs recently and reached a place where they were both excited about doing their hard work together. On the phone, they made plans for a date the next day to celebrate their rekindled commitment. Because Krista hadn't been sleeping well recently, she told him that she wanted to go to bed early so that she'd be refreshed for their reunion. With that, she said good night and went to sleep.

The next morning, as Krista reached over, still in bed, to turn off her alarm, she saw her phone's home screen overflowing with texts and missed calls. Immediately, a jolt of panic shot through her. She knew something big had happened and automatically called the last person who had reached out. When she did, Krista asked, "What's happening? What's going on?"

"Are you sitting down?" her friend asked.

In that moment, Krista knew it was Mark. Her friend went on to share that the night before, at a social event, Mark had collapsed and stopped breathing. They couldn't resuscitate him. As this news entered Krista, she felt her blood pressure drop. She understood then why people tell you to sit down before they share hard news. Mark's death was totally unexpected. In those moments, Krista's world turned upside down as a previously unimaginable scenario became her reality.

"What do I do? I don't even know what to do! How do I even grasp this?" Krista implored her friend, feeling a mixture of panic, shock, confusion, and disorientation.

For the rest of the day, Krista felt disembodied, as if she was watching herself have conversations she never imagined she would need to have with Mark's son and some of his friends. Over the next few months, there were eerily quiet times as well as times when Krista felt flat, frozen, and confused. She couldn't taste her food much and sleep felt both choppy and lucid. "Everything was different," she remembers. "The flowers were more alive, colors were more vivid, the veil between ordinary and nonordinary had disappeared. How I was relating to the world was different. I felt like I was swimming instead of walking."

Throughout those early stages, Krista held onto a couple of organizing principles: tending to Mark's son and daughter and, after a couple of weeks, returning to work. Although she often felt herself to be half there, half not there, having some normal experiences was helpful for her. During that time, she remembers having a bodywork session where the therapist asked her how much pressure she wanted on a scale of one (lowest) to ten (highest), and she requested eleven. She was having such a hard time feeling her body through all the numbness.

Yet, about a month after Mark's passing, Krista's numbness started to wear off and the grief set in. She would find herself lying on the floor and crying for hours, or pulling it together during the day at work only to come home at night and completely fall apart. It took Krista about nine months before she felt she could be fully present and engaged at work again.

As Krista's and my stories illustrate, these early days, weeks, and months of heartbreak can be incredibly disorienting as our bodies and psyches struggle to make sense of our new, previously unfathomable realities.

Ways to Navigate the
Early Weeks of Heartbreak

Given the intense physical and psychospiritual impact of heartbreak's onset, we need to bring greater support and care to this stage of the journey. Once the chess pieces of our lives are swept away, how do we make it through the early, incredibly disorienting days and weeks of shock, and the wearing off of shock? Here are some things that have helped me and that I've offered to my clients:

- **Embrace the mantra "One breath at a time."** Rather than taking things "one day at a time," which you'll do later, during these early days, just focus on making it through one breath, or one moment, at a time. Don't try to look further ahead than that; it can be too overwhelming.

- **Know that it's okay to stay in motion.** There will be a time in your healing when it will be important to be still and feel your feelings, but that time is not now (unless, of course, that's what feels true for you). Right now, you're simply trying to make it through these early, excruciating days. Plus, our systems feel empowered when we have some sense of agency. That agency can be washing your hair, brushing your teeth, doing your laundry, etc. If you've just lived through a natural disaster, this can look like talking to your insurance company or securing essential provisions for you and your family. Even just checking little things off your list can be a big deal at this point.

- **Let yourself off the hook from sticking to your usual routine.** For instance, I normally meditate and practice yoga every day. During those first months after my betrayal, I was so rattled that I couldn't meditate, and I could only go to yoga classes (rather than practicing on my own at home). Be gentle with yourself and let things be a little topsy-turvy for a while.

- **Get outside and take walks as much as you can.** The dual medicines of walking and being in nature will help ground your body. The cross-lateral movement of your arms and legs as you walk helps your system to process thoughts, emotions, and experiences. When you're in shock, your body's working really hard to metabolize the experience of your loss and to help you make sense of it. Give your system the resources of nature's harmony and balance as well as gentle movement and fresh air. Even if you don't feel like it (especially if you don't feel like it), get outside. You can even do something as minimal as walk down the driveway or around the block.

- **Don't beat yourself up when you're caught in loops of obsessive thinking.** Remember, this is also a normal part of the process, especially in the early days and weeks. It's uncomfortable, I know, especially when it wakes or keeps you up at night. Just as walking helps your body to process your loss, obsessive thinking helps your mind to do the same. The more you allow yourself to think everything you need to think, the more this phase of the heartbreak journey will pass organically.

- **Know that sleep may be elusive for a while.** The witching/middle-of-the-night hours are when our systems process things the most intensively, especially at the unconscious and subconscious levels. Yes, you may be awake a lot between the hours of 1 am and 4 am (or thereabouts). Just as you're making space for obsessive thinking, can you also make space for disrupted sleep? This will pass too, in time. And, until that happens, see if you can let yourself just rest in bed in the dark. Even if you're not sleeping, you can still let your body rest. Or, if that's too challenging, sit up and read or listen to something that's supportive (like this book or something similar). Of course, if the lack of sleep gets too debilitating, talk to your doctor or health practitioner about getting more support, if needed.

- **Seek out the comfort of warmth.** Hot baths and showers, soups, hot beverages, and even a hot water bottle placed on your belly can be soothing during times of distress. Our nervous systems respond to warmth—whether that's through a pet or another person's emotional and physical presence, or through an inanimate object like a bath or a beverage. The warmth of a bath or a hot drink can mimic the feeling of being hugged or held by another person, which can release oxytocin, a hormone associated with feelings of safety and comfort. Warmth can also stimulate nerve receptors in the skin and muscles that can promote relaxation and reduce feelings of stress and tension, much like a hug does.

- **If you feel numb, that's okay. And, if it goes on for too long, consider getting support to help the shock wear off.** It's not uncommon to experience a tragedy and to feel completely numb for a while afterward. Some report feeling like they're having an out-of-body experience after a loved one dies, not even being able to feel any emotions until after the funeral, for example. Taking a homeopathic remedy like Nat Mur (this is the remedy Kaitlyn gave me when I was still numb) can help your system move out of shock and begin to release grief. The natural flower essence "bleeding heart" can also help your heart start to metabolize pain. Since your physical heart is made of muscle tissue, even taking a couple of aspirin can help.

While the shocking early stages of heartbreak are naturally going to feel stressful and disorienting, bringing even a little bit of awareness and support can make the process easier.

Journaling Prompts

I invite you to pause and reflect on the following questions, ideally in your journal, as writing brings clarity and can help process strong emotional and mental content. You can also take these questions with you on walks, contemplating your responses to them in a light-handed way and seeing what arises for you.

You'll notice that here, and in all subsequent chapters, I break the journaling prompts into three parts: past, present, and future. Because heartbreak is a trajectory that extends through our entire lives, this helps us to reflect on the various ways it impacts us over time. In the "Future" section, you're invited, in whatever stage of heartbreak you're currently in, to reflect on what might support you as you move forward from here.

Past

- Have you been in shock at other times in your life? If so, what was that like?

- Have you ever been around or supported someone else who was in shock? How was your experience of that?

Present

- What has shock looked and felt like for you during this current heartbreak? (For instance, have you been completely numb and disconnected from yourself and reality? Have you been unable to eat? Sleep? Do basic, daily routines?) There's no judgment here. Remember, let your experience be what it is, and simply notice how this phase has impacted you.

- Has obsessive thinking been part of how you've processed the shock? If so, what are the loops that you've been churning over in your mind?

- What has your experience been like, having your life look and feel one way in one moment and then having that all wiped away in the next? How is it to feel so "outside" of life now?

- Have you been able to tell the story of your loss to anyone? To more deeply process the experience, it can help to write it down or to tell the story to someone close to you whom you trust, like a friend, intimate partner, therapist, or counselor. Make sure you only share this with someone with whom you feel safe, who understands grief and loss and won't judge or hurry you along.

- What has helped you the most during your time of being in shock? Different things work better for different people (for example, taking walks in nature, talking/being with other people, sticking with some daily routines—or something else?).

Future

- From the list of suggestions I shared earlier in this chapter for ways to navigate shock, what would you like to implement going forward? Make a note of that now as well as a plan to give that to yourself in the near future.

Chapter 2

Bowing to Grief

"Grief work is soul work."

— Francis Weller

Within this vast and foreign landscape of heartbreak, we encounter its core language: grief. No one on this planet can escape grief. It's part of our shared humanity, whether we're grieving the fall of the Twin Towers, deaths during the COVID-19 pandemic, or a devastating earthquake, wildfire, hurricane, or tsunami. Despite how prevalent grief is, grieving is hard. A force like no other, it's a holy, alchemical process by which our souls evolve and our human selves mature. It's a transformative process that turns pain into power and your past self into your future self. It's the catalyst for change that anyone who wants a richer, truer life must endure. There are no exceptions to this.

We often find ourselves flailing after grief erases our carefully constructed lives and identities because, unfortunately, we don't have the education or perspectives we need to prepare for or navigate this process. Part of becoming a mature, strong, wise woman is learning how to grieve well and to create a support structure in your life that helps you to do this. For it's grief's engine of change that will transform your old self into your new self. Since grief, like heartbreak, will visit us many times over throughout our lives, in many different ways, if you haven't yet learned the ways of grief, it's time to now.

Colorado; June 4, 2017

Several weeks after my abortion, I attended my first community grief ritual. It had been on my calendar for the past month: Sunday from 2 to 5. I woke up that morning to a perfect June day—cerulean sky, warm air hugging my bare arms and feet, and the smell of freshly cut grass wafting in through the wide-open windows in my living room. I wasn't feeling heartbroken that day. Rather, I'd woken up feeling surprisingly light. I wondered: *Maybe I don't really need to go to the grief ritual.* I envied everyone else, brunching under umbrellas on sunny sidewalks or hiking beside cold mountain streams. Plus, my shyness resisted going somewhere new by myself, where I would need to do something as messy and intimate as cry in public for three hours.

Up until that point in my life, grief for me had been a solitary experience. As a child, I cried silently in my bed at night when I heard my parents fighting in the next room. Having trained myself not to cry in front of others, I wondered if I'd even be able to cry in front of complete strangers, or if I'd feel frozen inside my own self-consciousness. I wondered if those hours would pass slowly, painfully.

Yet, a deeper part of me knew that backing out wasn't an option. I knew from many past experiences in groups that the container truly does come alive and hold me when it's led by trustworthy and experienced stewards, and when I've set a clear intention and am willing to surrender. When all of those pieces are in place, a ritual's container can carry me into another dimension, moving (and removing) spiritual and psycho-emotional material deep within. It, along with the power of the group, amplifies my intentions and takes me further than my solitary, conceptional mind can.

What am I going to do, sit at home alone all day . . . again? I thought. So, I willed myself into motion, and an hour later I arrived at the synagogue where the ritual was being held.

Before we formally began, we sat in a long oval on a faux Oriental rug in a cool, dark room inside the synagogue. Chairs were stacked against one wall, and a few ritual "stations" were positioned around the room. Our host and founder of the Center for Somatic Grieving, Wendy, greeted us. Even though I didn't know her well, I felt comforted by her presence. We'd seen one another often in yoga and dance classes around town over the years and shared mutual friends. She began by sharing that she, too, had not wanted to come that day.

"Today is the ten-year anniversary of my son's passing," Wendy began. "He was my first child, Noah, and he died in my arms several months after he was born. While I've really moved forward with my life since then and haven't felt grief about him for some time, anniversaries, like today, are hard. I can't help but wonder who he would be if he were still here with us today to celebrate his tenth birthday. I came here to grieve with all of you, and to honor him."

"After he died," Wendy continued, "I went on a soul search and travelled around the world. I felt really lost grieving here in the United States. I didn't feel like I, or the people and culture around me, understood my grief or how to support me in my heartbreak. So I started to travel to places that did, like Bali and Thailand. And it was the rituals in Bali that really changed my life. Several years later, I met Sobonfu Somé and learned of grief rituals from West Africa as well."

The late Sobonfu Somé, whose name means "Keeper of the Ritual," and her former husband, Malidoma Somé, were instrumental in bringing grief rituals from their native Burkina Faso to the US. One of her books, *Falling Out of Grace*, was incredibly reassuring and validating to read during my heartbroken years, for, in it, she writes about the very public descent she experienced following her divorce.

She taught that grief is a collective emotion that we each carry and therefore have a responsibility to feel and let go of. In her native language, there is no word for individual grief as one is not meant to grieve alone. She said we're meant to grieve as a village, for it's only the village that has the nervous system to process the immense energy of grief. The rituals she shared are a time for communities to come together to flush out and remove pent up feelings and psychic debris. She emphasized that grief is a living, breathing being that our bodies know and need to release. I have heard, from those who studied directly with her, that Sobonfu Somé would often ask her students two questions: "Have you grieved today?" If not, she advocated that we all take time to grieve every day. The second question she would ask was, "Have you grieved enough for your loss?" If the answer was no, she encouraged you to keep grieving.

Wendy continued, "In the cultures I learned from, grief rituals are regular, community events. Everyone gathers to grieve personal losses, collective losses, ancestral wounds. Through the regular process of honoring grief in a ritualistic way, the health and happiness of each person and the village can be restored. No one is left to grieve alone."

After Wendy's sharing, we went around the circle, each of us taking a few minutes to speak to why we were there. I felt relieved at the authenticity I witnessed. Grief strips us of pretense. It decimates masks and forces us to reckon with our fragility—to reveal ours to others and bear witness to theirs. Everything that I felt inside—my resistance to going that day, my reluctance to grieve in public and to miss out on the beautiful Sunday afternoon, my wondering if I would even be able to cry—was reflected in others' sharing, even those who had been to many rituals before. It's human nature to not want to do the things that we know are good for us. I found solace in knowing that I wasn't as alone as I thought. Others near me were also trying to find their way through devastating loss and oftentimes incapacitating emotional pain.

When we stood up from the sharing circle, those who knew how to drum took their place behind their djembes, forming an area in the ritual space we were told was "the village." *Bom. Bom. Ba da ba da bom.* Standing stiff and still in the village, unsure what was going to happen next, my knees began to bounce subtly with the beat. My bones began to tingle. A timeless, familiar heat in my core started to stir. I'd met this ancient pulse in African dance classes during the semester I spent studying abroad at the University of Ghana. A beat that, as it struck the drum's skin, shattered the rigidity of the physical form I had inherited through so many generations of holding in emotion and not showing what's real. A beat that called me back to the life force inside me that knew how to move without inhibition. A beat that let me let go.

Without thought, my body marched toward the ancestral shrine. My thinking mind, wondering what I was doing, kept chattering, but a deeper part of me took the lead. I knelt before the altar and prayed to the ancestors for help. I asked them to protect me as I let the immensity of grief move through me. Then I paused and listened for what was next. *It's time to go to the grieving shrine.* With a remembered nobility, I strode toward the central cushion of the grieving shrine, at the twelve o'clock position in the ritual space.

I knelt down before the grieving shrine and bowed my forehead to the earth in a yogic Child's Pose. Without any mental cueing, my body began to heave and convulse as electric tremors of grief ran through me. I let the grief have me, and, as I did, I forgot the drums. I forgot the support person standing behind me. I forgot why I was even crying. I forgot myself and allowed myself to become grief itself. The tremors came in waves. The wiser part of me led me through them, understanding that when my body grew still between each wave—just like in the contractions of birth—it didn't mean the process was over. It meant I was to wait, staying empty for the next wave to take me, until it was time to stand up.

For the next couple of hours, we moved through the different stations as we each felt called. At the end of the afternoon, when it was time to close the ritual and reconvene in our circle, I was amazed at how quickly the time had passed and how deep we—a bunch of Americans in Colorado—were able to go within that ancient West African ritual. I went home that afternoon feeling euphoric, similar to how I felt after doing a cleanse or a silent meditation retreat. For the first time in too long, I saw a sparkle in everything around me and felt a lightness in my heart. I was starting to taste some of the mighty gifts that grief can bring us along our heartbreak journeys when we don't need to carry it alone, and when we remember how to make it a part of our lives and world.

Carolyn's Story: Allow Your Grief to Be Witnessed

About a month before I went to the grief ritual, I met the woman who had urged me to go in the first place, Carolyn Flyer. One of my friends suggested I reach out to Carolyn, a local intuitive and medium who had lost her daughter to a stillbirth a couple of years earlier.

I drove to Carolyn's office on a May morning. As I sat cross-legged on a soft, purple chair in her office, Carolyn, with her long corkscrew curls, looked at me with an empathic knowing. Even her gaze felt therapeutic. I could sense that she knew what I was feeling without me needing to say a word. Losing a baby, however that happens for someone, is a pain unlike any other. During our hour together I shared my story, and she, in turn, offered hers.

On June 5, 2015, one month before her due date, Carolyn went out for dinner with her girlfriends. She ordered mussels in red sauce, indulging one of her strange pregnancy cravings and enjoying what she believed would be her final night out before her daughter, Delaney, arrived.

When Carolyn got home that night, she settled her tired body into bed. Lying down, she grabbed her husband's hand in disbelief. "Oh my gosh, Jas! You gotta feel this! Delaney is going crazy in my belly!" The two shared a laugh. "She's a wild one," Carolyn added.

The next morning, Carolyn's body felt strangely quiet. She, her husband, and their three-year-old son went to a firehouse festival where they sprayed hoses, wore red hats, and ate hot dogs. Afterward, Carolyn put her son down for a nap, and she lay down for one as well. It was then that she noticed that the very wild child within her was suddenly very still—absent, even.

Carolyn remembered a few methods she learned in her birthing class for waking a baby in utero: she took a deep breath, laid on her left side, drank a glass of water, played music into her belly, and even ate a spoonful of honey. Still, nothing. So, she called her doctor's office apologetically and anxiously waited for the doctor to return her call.

Soon after, Carolyn, accompanied by her husband, Jason, and their son, entered the birth ward of the hospital. Carolyn was afraid that something was wrong, but she also felt embarrassed that she may have inconvenienced her doctor. In the examining room, buttons were pushed, straps were hooked up, and paddles slid across Carolyn's round belly. The thumping sound of her daughter's heartbeat was notably absent. Nurses shared nervous glances as they suggested trying another ultrasound and calling in the doctor. Carolyn asked, "Is she there? Can't you find her heartbeat?"

The doctor arrived a few minutes later, smiled at Carolyn, and sat at the edge of the bed. She turned on the monitor and glided the ultrasound paddle over Carolyn's belly once more. Then she turned to Carolyn and said, "I'm so sorry. Your full-term baby has died." The next day, Carolyn birthed her stillborn daughter, Delaney.

Carolyn's spiritual teacher, Tory Capron, attended Delaney's birth, supporting both Carolyn and her husband in bringing their once-wild, now still, and still curly-haired, daughter into the world. Throughout their heartbreak journey, Tory continued to support them. It was important to her to make sure that Jason and Carolyn continued to move toward one another in their grief rather than retreating to their separate corners, as so often happens for couples when a child dies. One of the ways Tory did this was by inviting them to her home in the mountains about twenty minutes outside of town and asking them to wear close-toed shoes.

When Carolyn and Jason arrived, Tory met them in the yard, handed Carolyn an ax, and instructed her to go to the side of the house to chop wood while Jason observed. As Carolyn chopped wood, Tory spoke to her, and, gradually, Carolyn began to notice that all the effort she had been exerting to keep her emotions packed tightly inside—so her son didn't see them, so her husband didn't see them, so that even she didn't see them—became unsustainable under the strenuous physical exertion of chopping. With a violent blow of the ax into the center of a piece of wood, cracking it open, Carolyn's mouth also opened wide. With this, she threw her head back, and she let out what she now describes as "the most feral scream anyone has ever heard"—one that spread and echoed into the wilderness all around them. Then the ax fell to the ground and her body began shaking and sobbing.

After Carolyn finished crying, Tory looked at her, smiled, and said, "I'm still here." Then she asked Jason, "Are you still here?"

"Of course," he answered. She asked him if he was going anywhere, and he said, "Of course not," adding how hard it was for him to witness Carolyn's pain and acknowledging that he had winced and shuddered when he heard his wife scream.

"Those things apparently live inside me," Carolyn shared. Being witnessed and having a space to let her usual guard down allowed them to be released. Today, Carolyn offers grief retreats for others. There, she assures grieving guests not to apologize for their tears and that, by shedding them openly, they're doing everyone a favor by inviting others to let go of their grief, too.

Grief and Your Body

Grief is an intense physiological experience. It overtakes the body, much like a fever. You can't stop, defend against, or rush it—at least, not without great consequences. Grieving is exhausting, and we must prepare ourselves for this. Just as we all experience the intoxicating hormones of falling in love when we're entering into a new relationship, we experience the inverse of this neurochemical cocktail when we grieve. Yes, grief and love are sisters. They always travel together. Whatever you love about your life, about others, and about yourself, you will one day grieve the loss of. The more we can acknowledge and accept that love and grief always walk hand-in-hand, the more we can make space for grief in our lives, too.

There is no bigger energy than grief. While sexual energy is also huge, it's pleasurable. Grief is not pleasurable. Grief feels like you are going to die. And since staying closed off to it only makes it more excruciating and exhausting, we need to know how to open to this massive, painful energy that runs through our bodies. We're born with bodies and psyches that know how to bleed, how to birth, how to breathe, how to die—and how to grieve. Grief works much like a detox. When we are supported by others to open to it, it can cleanse and rejuvenate our bodies and souls. But, as West African grief rituals teach us, the human nervous system is not designed to grieve alone. We can only grieve *well* when we do so with loving support. With all the heartbreak we're experiencing in the world—economically, environmentally, politically—we need to revive this ancient skill so we can better meet challenging situations without shutting down or getting overwhelmed.

I found trusting my body's ancient capacity to grieve to be incredibly empowering. No matter how big a grief wave was, I could surrender to a place deep inside me that knew how to simply become the pain rather than fight against it. It was just like when I swam in huge waves in Hawaii: when I dove under the wave, I'd be fine—I'd just feel the tumultuous swirl of the water crashing and cresting above me. When I stayed above the surface and tried to jump over the wave, I'd get pummeled. Similarly, when we resist grief, we deplete our vitality. A lot of energy gets locked up in suppressing its massive force. When we stop running from grief and instead turn toward and express it, a whole new stratosphere of vitality shows itself to us. Grief holds a lot of energy for us when we're willing to stay with it.

The other thing that's important for us to remember in this quick-fix world is that there's no easy cure for grief, no magic bullet. The only path through grief is grieving. Grief *will not* go away unless we grieve. Conventional grief literature says that acute grief lasts about three to six months, and, beyond six months, becomes chronic. I disagree with that; I urge you to remember that grief is a natural phenomenon that takes as long as it takes. The timing is out of our control. And the more we give into it and allow it a seat at the table of our lives, the more quickly we'll metabolize it.

If we don't give grief this space, it ends up lingering. It stays inside you, trying to find a crack through which to express itself. It can do this over time by creating illness in your body or psycho-emotional disturbances. Unexpressed grief can eventually close down your heart and harden you, the exact opposite of what grief is trying to do. Grief is trying to break your heart open. It's trying to soften you. It's trying to bring your vulnerability and tenderness to the forefront so that you can be more You. So that you can live more attuned with the suffering of others. So that you can better emulate the empathy, compassion, service, and humility of the Divine. So that you can be a holier and more whole person. But you have to open the door to it.

The more you can surrender to grief, the more you empower it to bless you. The more you resist grief, the more it can, over time, hurt you—just as any emotion does when denied. Grief, like all of our emotions, needs room and space to flow. We all have free will, so you can choose whether you allow your grief to open your heart or close it.

The number one cause of death in both men and women right now in the United States is congestive heart failure. With the way that our society is set up—to value profit over people and productivity over connection—our hearts are not being adequately supported. In fact, we're encouraged to shut them down. When there's no space for us to feel anything, our hearts become clogged and ignored, until they eventually stop beating. Conversely, our hearts renew through grief, so that we're more able to hear their guidance and to feel love and joy. Without tending to grief in a sacred, supported way, our hearts shut down, and the very center of divinity within our mortal bodies shrivels and recedes. Surrendering to grief propels us through our heartbreak journey in a healthy way, while avoiding it keeps us stuck in our journey for much longer than is necessary, maybe even forever.

How Grief & Heartbreak Impact Our Health

Florence Williams's conversation-starting book *Heartbreak* tells the story of her husband leaving her after twenty-five years of marriage and two children. Pairing her personal experience with scientific evidence, she clearly demonstrates that heartbreak is not merely histrionic, reserved for hopeless romantics. Rather, it's a bona fide trauma. Heartbreak can lead to more complex emotional duress and the dismantling of one's identity, and it can have a grave impact on one's physical health. So much so that divorce is a greater risk factor for early death than smoking, and psychologists rank heartbreak (as it relates to divorce or a breakup) as one of the most stressful and consequential life experiences one can have, just after the death of a loved one.[1]

Plus, studies have shown that women, who tend to be more focused on keeping relationships intact, are more likely than men to experience the negative health effects related to grief and heartbreak, especially if they weren't the ones to initiate the breakup.[2] Our cells start to look different. Due to the cascade of stress hormones that come on with heartbreak, our metabolism and digestion suffer, our immune systems weaken, we develop poor impulse control (which is often why we get into the wrong kinds of "rebound" relationships after a major breakup), our sleep becomes fragmented, and we feel fatigued. Plus, we have an increased risk of depression and cardiac malfunction. Over time, all of this can lead to cognitive decline, altered gene expression, and even early death.

Given the grave implications of grief and heartbreak on our health at every level, it's not only crucial that we bring a lot of care and intention to our entire heartbreak journey, but also that we give our grief outlets for healthy release and expression.

Create a Container to Grieve Well

When you're going through heartbreak, you need to be supported by people who understand grief. Often it's those who have been through an intense season of heartbreak themselves who will really know how to be there for you.

When you find yourself alone and stricken with grief, here are some things you can do:

1. Ask the nonphysical realm for support. Call to Mother Earth, Father Sky, the Four Directions, and/or your Higher Power. Call on your ancestors and any other guides (living or not) to whom you feel connected. Request that all of these larger forces be with you. These beings will create an invisible support circle, a container, to help hold and transform your grief.

2. Speak to those in your circle of support out loud if you're in an environment where that's possible. Talking (as well as screaming, crying, and even howling) really helps the grieving process. Use your facial muscles and express yourself rather than keeping everything bottled up. Grief, which often lives in our throats, chests, and necks, urges us to liberate our expressions. It wants us to be wild, messy, and raw. If you feel self-conscious doing that in front of others, explore what it would be like to let yourself make sound when you're alone.

3. If you need physical movement to help you to liberate sound and your voice, like Carolyn's wood chopping liberated her

scream, do that. If chopping wood isn't your thing, you can punch a pillow, stomp your feet, slap a dishrag against the wall, or something else. If you have people in your care whom you want to protect from this kind of release, do this while they're out of the house, go to a remote place (preferably somewhere in nature), scream in your car when you're alone, or see if there's a friend who can hold space for you at their home. Above all, let your expression be bigger (much bigger) than it normally is, bigger than you feel comfortable with.

4. When you wake up in the morning, and before you get out of bed, pray and call on your ancestors. Call on your Higher Power to help you make it through the day. As the saying goes, only what you place on the altar (of your mind and heart, in this case) can be altered.

From this foundation of more fully accepting and feeling our grief within a culture that actively denies it, we can begin to validate all of our grief-filled experiences of failure, falls from grace, and heartbreak. There's nothing wrong with any of these. They're part of the human journey. And the next chapter will support you in the important step of fully validating yourself and your experience.

Journaling Prompts

Writing about our grief can help give it another outlet. Since we often don't give much thought to this important facet of our shared humanity, taking some time to reflect on your understanding and experience of grief can be illuminating.

Past

- What was your relationship with grief like as a child? Teenager? Young adult? Now?

- How did your parents or caregivers express and relate to (or avoid) their grief?

Present

- Do you know anyone who is wise in the ways of grief?

- What about grief scares you? What do you fear will happen if you fully give yourself to grief?

Future

- What do you need in order to create more support, inwardly and outwardly, to grieve?

- What would giving grief a seat at the table of your life look like right now? Is there anything stopping you from doing this? If so, how can you address that head-on?

- What do you sense grief is wanting to teach you? Who do you sense grief is trying to help you become?

Chapter 3

Validating Yourself

"The most beautiful people we have known are those who
have known defeat, known suffering, known struggle, known
loss, and found their way out of the depths. These persons
have an appreciation, a sensitivity, and an understanding of
life that fills them with compassion, gentleness, and a deep
loving concern. Beautiful people do not just happen."

— Dr. Elisabeth Kübler-Ross

As children, many of us are told things like, "Turn that frown upside
down" or "Don't cry." Sadness, grief, anger, and depression are often
exiled from our childhood homes. We don't see our caregivers feeling
and welcoming these sobering visitors and, in turn, we learn that it's
not okay to feel them. Fast-forward thirty, forty, fifty or more years, and
we've become adult women who perpetuate the banishment of these so-
called "dark" feelings by telling ourselves, even unconsciously, that it's
not okay to feel what we're feeling. That it's not okay, especially when
we're melting down and our lives are falling apart, to be as we are.

Add to this a larger cultural milieu where we as women are often told
by society and medical professionals that, when something isn't right
with us, we're being too dramatic (the word "hysterical" stems from the
Latin word *hystericus*, meaning "of the womb") or we're imagining things.
We may also belong to spiritual communities that urge us to transcend
our suffering, to look on the bright side and be grateful no matter what,

and to raise our vibrations. We may even be taught that being in a bad mood or experiencing a life that isn't working at the moment is a sign that we're doing something wrong—or, worse, that there's something wrong with us.

Learning to validate ourselves is the remedy for this. Self-validation is the practice of acknowledging what is really true for us (even if that's the furthest thing from what we want to be feeling or experiencing) and then fully accepting it—including accepting the parts of ourselves that don't accept it. This doesn't happen overnight. It's a process, and we need to return to it regularly. We've not only been invalidated our whole lives (first by others and now by ourselves) but also mass invalidation has been endemic for women for many centuries. So, have patience. If this is new for you (as it was for me), I'll show you how.

Colorado; November 2017

I woke up to Sadie unwinding the tight ball of her body in the lower right-hand corner of my bed and crawling her way up to me—resting her head on my chest. A few months prior I'd abandoned the rule that she needed to sleep on her own bed. It felt good to have someone, something, sleeping beside me. Puffs of her warm breath landed on my cheek as her golden eyes gazed lovingly, expectantly, into mine. The thick gray blackout curtains that covered the wall of windows to my right muted the morning light, and my white-noise machine continued to fill the room with its soothing hum. Even though my surroundings were comfortable, my insides leaped from sleepiness into their familiar, anxious churn.

I hate my life. When is this ever going to end? Will I ever get to the other side of this? Am I ruined forever? As I started to rise up and out of deep sleep, my unwelcome and still unfamiliar reality returned: alone in my apartment, feeling grief-stricken and depressed, working hard to make it through each day and to believe that I would, someday, somehow, make it through all of this and be happy and normal again. Whatever that meant. I missed my old life, the one where I woke up and faced mundane life struggles. The one where the ground beneath me wasn't constantly quaking. The one where I felt like myself.

Making my way into the kitchen, I switched on the kettle and began what had become my new morning ritual. While I got dressed, drank hot water with lemon, and walked Sadie around the block, I listened to a few YouTube videos from Esther Hicks, an American inspirational speaker, author, and channeler of Abraham-Hicks, a divine entity, to help me redirect my mind.

My ears cradling white ear buds and the cool morning air washing over my face, I took in Esther's words: "Work with the laws of the universe, in concert with your inner being. Life is supposed to feel good to you. You're supposed to be having a really good time." She continued to instruct me to come into perfect alignment with my inner being by going after the good-feeling thoughts, by acting as if I were already feeling how I wanted to feel, and by doing everything I could to stay at a high vibration throughout the day.

I clung to Esther's words as if they were a life raft. Maybe if I just clung tightly enough. Maybe if I just got it right—stayed with the "high-flying feeling" throughout as much of the day as I could, that would be my ticket out of this hell. That would finally be the solution! I told myself that this was a chance to master my thoughts, my feelings, myself.

Some of my friends echoed Esther's advice. I met up with a newer friend one morning for a hike, and it happened to be a morning when my heart felt so heavy I thought I might tip over from the weight of it. No amount of positive thinking or affirmations could change it. When I saw my friend, a woman who always looked cheerful and rested, she could immediately see my heaviness and even hear it in the low, strained tenor of my voice as I greeted her. As much as I tried to appear cheerful and ordinary, there was no masking the pain emanating from me.

After the first fifteen minutes of our hike, she stopped, turned to look at me, and asked, "May I?" I nodded yes, unknowingly inviting her to coach me through breathing into my heart to help it to open more. After that lesson, she urged me to have more cadence, lilt, and lightness in my voice. Because she was older than me by a couple of decades; because I believed she knew something I didn't; because I believed I was doing something wrong since I was still feeling so incredibly depressed, and that if I were stronger and more masterful over my energy, I would be able to change my state, I listened to her. Yet doing so didn't make me feel better. It made me feel worse, which I didn't even know was possible in that moment. Her rejection of my heaviness led me to feel more shame about my condition. I mustered an even deeper conviction that I needed to change how I was feeling so that I wouldn't be turning so many people off from wanting to spend time with me.

I moved on from Esther Hicks to studying with author and spiritual guide Dr. Joe Dispenza, even going so far as to rappel down the side of the thirty-three-story Westin hotel in downtown Toronto to practice putting "mind over matter." After a tragic biking accident in his twenties, Dr. Joe, a former chiropractor, was told he would be disabled for life. Rather than accept that prognosis, he used the power of his mind to envision a full recovery—and succeeded. For a couple of years, rather than waking up and practicing mindfulness meditation as I had done almost every morning since I was twenty-one, I instead strapped on a blindfold and cupped my ears inside noise-cancelling headphones to listen to guided meditations by Dr. Joe. In some of these, I breathed forcefully, aiming to move the energy in my body so fiercely that it would pierce my brain into more wakefulness and catapult me into a new way of being. Other meditations guided me to envision the life I wanted to live, and to feel how I would feel within it. Morning after morning I felt myself walking on the beach in Santa Barbara, hand-in-hand with my beloved, a belly bulging with new life inside me. Many times during those early morning hours, I would feel the freedom, gratitude, and elation that I wanted to feel. And, many mornings, the contrast between how I wanted to feel and how I was really feeling was simply too great, and I just couldn't get there.

It started to become clear that, like Abraham-Hicks's teachings and my friend's coaching on our hike, Dr. Joe's practices were making me feel worse, not better. I felt like I was constantly falling short, that if I couldn't keep my heart open and stay in a state of gratitude throughout the day, I was failing. And I was growing tired of thinking that how I was acting and feeling was wrong. That *I* was wrong. The circumstances of my life were hard enough. I didn't need to make things even harder by raising the bar to a height I could hardly ever reach. So, I stopped.

I stopped listening to Abraham-Hicks. I stopped my Dr. Joe meditations. I stopped spending time with people who couldn't accept me as I was. And I stopped trying to get myself to feel differently than how I was feeling. Instead, I returned to my basic journaling and Buddhist mindfulness meditation in the mornings—practices that supported me in being with myself, my body, my thoughts, and my feelings, just as they were. And, immediately, I began to feel a huge sense of relief. The sadness and heaviness didn't go away, but at least I wasn't adding more layers of resistance and tension on top of them. I was beginning to let myself be okay with not being okay—and with others not being okay that I wasn't okay.

Hindsight is, of course, twenty-twenty. Yes, I wish I had stood up to my friend and the many others like her who got frustrated with or turned off by where I was in my process. I wish I had seen then that the reason my friend needed to coach me in that way, besides wanting to help me, was that she didn't feel comfortable with my sadness. And that that didn't mean there was anything wrong with *me*; rather it was a blind spot, or a growing opportunity, within herself. Likely she had not yet met her own sadness in a deeply intimate way. I realized that my true friends (who, I noticed, were becoming more and more sparse) were the ones who didn't need me to be different than how I was. The ones who could be with me even when I was depressed, hopeless, and stuck for months on end. Because me being that way was a very natural, normal, human response to the hardship and loss I had been faced with. It would have been strange if I hadn't been affected in all the ways I was.

While some of the practices I tried weren't the right ones for me, I don't regret spending so much time watching video testimonials about miraculous healings and transformations from Dr. Joe's students, or listening to so many Abraham-Hicks talks on my morning walks with Sadie. I see that they were all an important part of my journey. They gave me a lifeline, something to focus intently on for a period of time. They offered me a feeling of hope that somehow I was in charge of my process and could shift it through enough practice and will. And this brought me to the realization that, even though I was exerting more will than I ever had before (and I can be an incredibly willful person!), it wasn't going to change my circumstances. Only through trying as hard as I could, without effect, could I more deeply let go.

Above all, those practices got me to the place within myself where I could realize that it was much more painful to deny what I was feeling than to actually experience, be with, and accept the feelings themselves. I had learned the pain of invalidating myself—something I realized I'd been doing in subtle and grand ways for my whole life—and finally recognized the freedom and empowerment that came from doing the opposite.

Tasha's Story: Heal Your Self-Doubt

I started doing one-on-one IFS sessions with Tasha shortly after she made the brave choice to leave her husband of twenty-five years, with whom she had three children. Throughout their marriage, Tasha suffered from her husband's infidelity, sex addiction, and psychological, emotional, financial, and sometimes physical abuse. This ill-treatment felt familiar to Tasha, as, starting at the age of three and continuing on through her childhood, teens, and early adulthood, she experienced various forms of sexual and psychological assault.

One of the things Tasha most wanted support with through IFS was getting her inner, doubting parts under control. These were the parts of her that doubted she should have left her husband. They questioned whether or not she was really doing the right thing for her children. And they wondered whether her ex-husband was right and *she* was really the crazy one, which he was often trying to make her believe. During the first several months of our work together, Tasha regularly asked me for confirmation that, yes, she was doing the right thing and that, no, she wasn't the crazy one. After so many decades of having her experience of reality violated and negated, she was having a hard time trusting herself.

IFS stems from the premise that our personality is made up of multiple parts. It can help us with the various parts of ourselves that take on extreme roles, usually as a coping mechanism during childhood, which can cause us distress as we grow older. When we experience wounding from something extreme like bullying or abuse, or even something like emotional or physical neglect, parts within us take on protective roles with the intention to help us survive. In truth, the roles that these parts take on often do, in fact, help us survive. What we notice as we get older, however, is that those very parts who once helped us are now hindering our growth. For example, an Inner Critic who was harsh with us once kept us in line so we didn't get in trouble with our parents, but now that same Inner Critic keeps us from feeling confident in how we show up in the world, to the point where we don't pursue opportunities or experiences.

Within Tasha's system, her doubting part stepped into its extreme role to protect her when she was a toddler who was experiencing sexual abuse from one of her caregivers. It started constantly doubting her reality as a way to keep her alive, which is a common protective strategy when children experience unthinkable trauma. As a young child, the truth of her situation—that someone close to her was causing her harm—was unacceptable since her life depended on that person at times. So, to keep her from needing to face that terror, the doubting part stepped in to doubt, question, and wonder. It centered Tasha, rather than her caregiver, as the one who was doing something wrong. All of this created a haze over Tasha's reality, shielding her not only from the pain but also the truth. This helped her to survive as a child, when she was helpless, but as a woman in her early fifties, this held her back to the point of keeping her in a relationship that was hurting both her and her children.

Tasha and I spent a lot of time getting to know the origins of her doubting part and appreciating it for how hard it had been working for so many years to try to keep her safe. This validation of the parts we often try to get rid of is one of the things that makes IFS so powerful. Through this process, slowly, over time, the doubting part was able to soften and give us permission to heal the more wounded, vulnerable part it was protecting (the three-year-old who had been sexually abused). After this, Tasha's doubting part could begin to quiet down as it didn't need to work so hard to protect that toddler anymore—Tasha was now able to do that.

Above all, Tasha learned to realize that the voice inside of her that was incessantly doubting her choices wasn't *her*. It wasn't who she was. It was only a very young part of her that needed to take on an extreme role to help her survive in an extreme situation, when no one around her came to her rescue. This recognition allowed her to bring more awareness to the doubting voice within her when it arose, and instead of immediately buying into what it was saying—or, conversely, ignoring it and pushing it away—she could now see that the doubt came up when parts of her were feeling vulnerable. This was a call for her to be with those vulnerable ones, just like she would be with one of her children when they were afraid.

The more Tasha was able to be with her own doubting part rather than be overtaken by it, the more she was able to see her situation clearly. In doing this, she relied less and less on validation from me and others that what she had experienced was real and that she was doing the right thing by protecting herself. Gradually, Tasha was able to validate herself and to know that the boundaries she was setting for herself and her children—boundaries she wasn't able to set for herself as a young child— were necessary and important.

Signs That You're Invalidating Yourself

Dr. Gabor Maté, a Hungarian-Canadian physician and author who specializes in trauma and addiction, wrote a seminal book titled *When the Body Says No*. In it he explores the relationship between stress and disease and how ignoring our body's signals that it's under distress has been shown, over time, to have grave effects on our health (like developing cancer or another illness later in life). He also asserts that autoimmune diseases aren't just in our heads, but they often start with the suppression of trauma (like a heartbreak), or other parts of us (like rageful parts).[1] It's estimated that 20 percent of the population in the United States has some sort of autoimmune disease, and that, of that number, 80 percent of those individuals are women.[2] This comes as no surprise given how, for centuries, we've been conditioned to override and mistrust our bodies' signals and to look to men and other authorities to dictate for us what is and isn't true.

As I shared in my heartbreak story at the start of this section, my own body and subconscious were speaking to me very loudly during the years when Matt was cheating on me. He kept telling me that I was jealous, stressed, and insecure (which, of course, I was at some level, because I'm human, but not at the level he was leading me to believe). I bought into his perspective rather than questioning him and elevating the truth that my own being was communicating through my hair falling out, developing prediabetes, having chronic insomnia and mysterious growths on my eyes, and experiencing inexplicable levels of inflammation.

When I came out of my experiences with both Jonathan and Matt, I strongly questioned my own inner compass, especially when it came to choosing partners. Clearly, despite all the inner work I'd done, some still-untouched part of my conditioning was driving the bus. This may be the case for you, too. If so, be patient and persistent. Healing our relationship to our inner knowing takes time. We need to simultaneously develop practices to connect us with our intuition while also rolling up our sleeves and healing the young parts of ourselves that are subconsciously acting out in certain parts of our lives. This is a both-and approach to healing, and we address both of these approaches in this book.

For now, if you sense that you too may be invalidating yourself, here are some signs you can look for. These vary from person to person, but if more than one of these is present for you, I urge you to take a closer look at what you might be overriding within yourself.

- You feel high levels of anxiety (or insecurity and jealousy) and, as you look back on your life, or on previous relationships, you see that these high levels are unprecedented

- You frequently sense that you don't feel like yourself, but you're not sure why

- You're experiencing distressing physical symptoms despite the fact that you're taking relatively good care of yourself (for example, elevated blood sugar levels, inflammation, growths inside or outside the body, disruption to your sleep and/or digestion, etc.)

- You have recurring, disturbing dreams about a certain person or situation in your life

- You rarely feel a sense of inner peace and calm and often feel high levels of internal stress

- When you're feeling or experiencing something difficult, you are often hard on yourself; you have strong inner voices of criticism and self-doubt

- You find it challenging to make decisions on your own and often feel like you need to consult an "expert" to help (like an intuitive, coach, astrologer, etc.)

If any (or many) of these sound like you, don't worry: you're in good company! Again, when you recognize where you are, you can take the necessary steps to validate not only your heartbreak but also all parts of your life (including trusting your eventual joys more fully, too).

Learn to Validate Yourself

With so much cultural stigma surrounding our so-called "negative" emotions, it's important that we each learn to validate and trust our own, unique, nonlinear experiences of heartbreak. When we don't completely open and allow our experiences to be exactly as they are, our resistance keeps us stuck. Arguing with reality never turns out well. Therefore, the only true way out of any experience is "in and through" it. Yes, there may be a time at a later phase in your healing journey when focusing on manifesting and feeling good are supportive for you. Yet, like my own story that I shared earlier in this chapter, when we jump to positivity too quickly, without completely surrendering into our own suffering first, we'll likely create the opposite of what we want: even more inner distress.

Since the spiritual journey is about learning to be with life as it is, let's use whatever you're experiencing right now as an opportunity to do just that—perhaps in an even fuller and deeper way than you ever have before.

Because of our human negativity bias, things are never okay. We're never fully satisfied with how we look, how we feel, or how our lives are unfolding. Even when, for fleeting moments or days, everything seems to be humming along perfectly, there's always *something*, even if it's small, like a mosquito bite or some gas after eating a delicious meal. When we recognize and accept this about our human selves, we can remember that the path forward is not about trying to fix or control our every waking moment; rather, it's about learning to be with what will never be ours to fix or control in an open, curious, and, eventually, loving way. Thus, the pursuit to "live your best life" isn't about getting to some future scenario in which you're perfectly nested and settled again (because that won't last, either). Instead, "living your best life" is about learning to be friends with this life. Right here. The one you're living right *now*.

"Yeah, Sara," you may be saying, "but how do I do that when I hate my life? It looks absolutely *nothing* like how I want it to, and I feel so uncomfortable—and even out of control at times—that it's like I'm going to crawl out of my skin!"

My first response is, I 100 percent hear you. To bring some balm to a painful reality, I want to share an IFS visualization. This will help you to validate and include all parts of yourself—especially the uncomfortable, and even painful, ones you might want to push away.

Invite All of Your Parts to the Banquet Table

This is a meditation I created based on IFS principles. Listen to a guided audio version of this meditation at saraavantstover.com/heartbreakdownloads.

Before you begin, find a comfortable seat (or lie down) and close your eyes. Connect with your breath. Inhale space and presence and exhale stress or tension. Do this several times.

Imagine that you are in a beautiful dining room or banquet hall. Explore the room for a bit. What color are the walls? Are there any light fixtures? Is it day or night? What do you see when you look out the windows? And, of course, what kind of table and chairs are in this room? Are there any smells of food cooking or flowers in the centerpieces? Next, begin to set the table. Lay down the placemats, the napkins, the silverware. Set up the plates and the glasses. Light the candles. Trust the number of places you're setting.

As you finish that, you notice that it's time for your banquet to begin. You take your seat at one of the heads of the table, and, gradually, different parts of yourself walk through the door and take their seats. Say hello, greeting each part of you as it enters. Notice which parts show up. What do they look like? Do they say anything to you? How do they interact with you? Once you notice that all of these parts have taken their seats, ring a bell to call in any parts of yourself who may not have thought they were invited. This could include parts who hold shame, sadness, depression, anger, inner criticism, self-doubt, or other aspects of yourself that are hard to be with. Notice what it's like for you, and for them, to come into the banquet hall and take their seats right alongside all of your other parts.

Once everyone has taken their seat, welcome all of your parts. Raise a glass to toast them if that feels right. Let them know that you're going through a challenging time in your life and that, in the past, you haven't invited all of your parts to the table in this way before. Let them know that you want to do things differently now. You truly want all of your parts to know that they are welcome. You want them all to know that you value their voices, their presence, and their needs.

Take some moments to see what happens next, and respond as needed. Make a commitment to come back and revisit this banquet table with your parts. If you had a challenging interaction with any of these parts, make a note to come back to them, ideally with some support (information about how to find more support with IFS is in the recommended resources section at the end of this book). Thank all the parts who showed up, and, when you're ready, say goodbye and gradually open your eyes. Write down any insights that arose from this in your journal.

Above all, when we experience something challenging in life, it's helpful to remember that however we respond is okay. There's nothing you need to fix, change, or do, which is very counter to what you've likely been taught about being with hard emotions. Paradoxically, when we can learn to be with our discomfort in a curious and compassionate way, without trying to make it go away, the natural response is that we start to feel better. Validating is about seeing and being with, giving all of your parts a seat at the table not only during your heartbreak journey but also throughout your life.

Take a Vow of Self-Trust

After my abortion, one of the steps I took to heal my relationship with my inner knowing was to go on an "advice fast." I felt that one of the things that extended my indecisiveness about whether or not to get an abortion earlier in my pregnancy was that I consulted with too many so-called experts, including psychics, astrologers, and mentors. In retrospect, I see that getting too much input from others, especially at a time (following my betrayal by Matt) when I wasn't sure I could trust my own instincts, only made me more confused. So, for a period of time I vowed I wouldn't ask for advice or guidance from anyone but myself. That was one of the best things I did because it forced me to relearn how to recognize and trust my own clarity. These days I do consult with healers from time to time, but only because I know how to listen to myself first and then run whatever they share through my own filters.

I also want to acknowledge that while this book does offer wisdom and support, it does not offer advice. Everything I share here is meant to pass through your own inner guidance system. From there, you're invited to choose what does and doesn't feel right for you. My overarching aim, not only in this book but in all that I share, is to reconnect you with the awake, true, healing force within you—your Self.

It's important for you to truly honor your healing, your grief, and your story in a world that often won't and doesn't, so before we go any further, I invite you to join me in making a vow to trust yourself above all else. This will be your reminder to stay loyal to your own inner knowing, your body's messages, and your life. It will encourage you to trust your own experience, no matter what. Yes, there can (and will!) be inner voices of doubt and criticism, but above and beyond them, you will trust your larger Self.

Speaking words out loud brings ideas and intangible things into physical reality. With this in mind, you can read the vow that I've written below out loud, or you can write your own to read out loud.

I, (insert your name), vow, for the rest of my life, to trust my own experience of reality. I forgive myself for all the times in the past when I failed to do this, and I recognize that it wasn't my fault. From this moment forward, I commit to trusting that my own body and inner knowing are my only true guides, and I commit to faithfully following their lead despite any external consequences. I remember that, through doing this, true happiness, personal power, and freedom can be mine.

Journaling Prompts

From this new foundation of self-trust, let's explore what your relationship has been to invalidation (of yourself and others) over time. Seeing your own patterns more clearly will help you to make different choices going forward.

Past

- When you were growing up, what feelings were you not allowed to feel?

- What emotions did you see your parents express? Which ones didn't you see them express?

Present

- How has this impacted how you relate to your own emotional landscape now?

- When you experience something that's hard to be with (in your body, mind, and/or emotions), what do you normally do? Is there a behavior you engage in to distract yourself? Do you numb out? Or something else?

- In what ways do you notice you invalidate yourself or others? In what ways do you notice others, or our culture, invalidate you?

Future

- Going forward, what doubts do you have about fully trusting your own experience of reality, internally and externally?

- What obstacles do you feel may get in the way of you living in alignment with your vow?

Chapter 4

Asking for Help

"Deep grief sometimes is almost like a specific location, a coordinate on a map of time. When you are standing in that forest of sorrow, you cannot imagine that you could ever find your way to a better place. But if someone can assure you that they themselves have stood in that same place, and now have moved on, sometimes this will bring hope."

— Elizabeth Gilbert

Here's one of heartbreak's great paradoxes: this is the time in your life when you need the most support and often receive the least. You may have lost a spouse through death or divorce, leaving you financially vulnerable and unable to give yourself the space and support you need to grieve. Or, because our culture keeps everyone so busy, your friends and family may get swept up in the day-to-day upkeep of their own lives that they just don't have time to be with you in the ways you need. This, plus the fact that heartbreak thrusts us out of the flow of our lives and into limbo, often makes these in-between seasons of our lives very solitary and shaky. Still, we need human connection to help us through hard times, especially when they come unexpectedly because of the severing of some of our most intimate bonds. I'll flesh out some ways to call in more support when you need it, especially if you usually identify as being independent and self-sufficient.

Colorado; April 9, 2016

One early spring morning, two months after my relationship with Matt ended, I hurried across town to my acupuncture appointment. On the way, I remembered the name that my friends called me as a little girl when my family spent summers by Lake Michigan. The nickname spread after one of my younger sisters couldn't pronounce the "S" in my name and began calling me "Rera." My nieces and nephews, with their pudgy hands, wide, blue eyes, and freckled cheeks, now call me Rera, too.

Rera, I remembered to myself as I headed inside my acupuncturist's office: that was what Matt used to call me, too. In love notes he'd leave on Post-it notes for me to discover—on my computer keyboard, by my nightstand, tucked inside a pile of clothes in my suitcase when I'd go away on a trip without him. *Rera,* I whispered to myself as I sat in the quiet waiting room, save a fountain trickling in the corner. I felt like I was being called—summoned—to hold that small, innocent part of me more tenderly now. It wasn't just my heart that was broken—it was hers, too.

Over the past couple of months, my closest girlfriends had supported me in different ways. In the early weeks, Tara came over with a quart-size Mason jar filled with her famous green drink: Vitamixed greens blended with almond butter. Cleo and her husband invited me to spend the night. Eating a candlelit dinner and having a conversation with my friends helped me to temporarily feel normal again. And one evening, Julia spontaneously texted asking if I wanted to join her and her son, Jasper, for spaghetti.

Normally independent and self-sufficient, I wasn't used to needing (or accepting) so much support. Asking for help, usually in the form of requesting someone's company, made me wince inside. It touched on my deep fear of rejection, Rera's fear of rejection. It went as far back as grade school, when she came home from school one day and curled into a ball in the corner of her closet. A little bit later, she told her mom, through tears, that her friends had told her that they didn't want to be friends with her anymore.

Maybe that was why it was still so hard for me to ask people for help. Or maybe it went even further back than that—to the Saturday morning when my mom led my older sister and me into the laundry room to show us how to use the washing machine. Even though I had to stand on a stepping stool to reach the dials, now that my mom had four children under the age of six, it was time for us to learn how to do our own laundry. In addition to taking care of my own laundry, I helped my mom (without being asked) by vacuuming my bedroom and cleaning the insides of my windows with Windex. I microwaved bags of Uncle Ben's white rice for dinner, putting a big square of Land O'Lakes butter on top and stirring it into the plump, white grains as it started to melt.

All this passed through my mind on that spring morning. I lay down on the table and my acupuncturist, Adele, came in. With her faint Irish accent and wide, worn hands, she lifted a light fleece blanket from a neatly folded pile on a nearby armchair and gently stretched it over my thin, slightly shivering body. I'd unintentionally lost weight since the big blow-up, and my body felt more frail than usual. Adele turned on some soothing piano music and began to place needles in my inner wrists and arms, then along my inner legs and toes. Through the window, I watched the gray sky beyond the trees' brown, still-bare branches, some of which still held crinkly brown leaves.

Adele's presence soothed me. I loved coming to these sessions with her. With each visit and each sensing of my pulse, she encouraged me.

"Hmm," she uttered as she listened to what I couldn't hear. "You're getting stronger and stronger, Sara. One day you're going to need to share with other women how you made your way through this."

Anger flared in my chest, piercing its way through the near nap I was descending into from the lull of the needles. I felt comfortable with Adele, so, rather than keeping it to myself, I said out loud, "I'm tired of being strong. I'm tired of experiencing so many things in life that require me to be strong."

Adele nodded knowingly as she burned moxa above the needles on the insides of my calves, filling the room with the scent of burnt earth.

"I need so much support right now. It was easier to get that support in the beginning of all of this, but now, as the months go on, I feel like

I'm becoming a burden to people, like I'm bothering them because I'm still struggling."

I thought about my friends Eileen and Michael, with whom I'd been very close for a few years before Matt's and my separation. We often went on double dates together, enjoying glasses of red wine and decadent desserts. For our engagement party, they brought a cake from our favorite chocolatier on West Pearl Street that said, "Congratulations Sara and Matt!" Eileen and I often went for hikes and talked about our work, and, of course, they invited me over and consoled me the day after everything blew up.

But now, I hadn't heard from them since shortly after that. While it was never spoken, I sensed they had become tired of my struggles. Or maybe, as sometimes happens with divorce and separation, they felt awkward deciding if they were going to be friends with me or him. And Eileen and Michael weren't the only ones. Other friends and acquaintances who used to be part of my old life were now nowhere to be found. My circle of support had grown smaller and smaller.

Adele took a seat in the armchair next to me. "When I went through my divorce," she began, "I found myself in a similar place as you're in now."

I turned my gaze from the window to her.

"Something one of my girlfriends recommended at the time," she continued, "was to create a support train. I asked several friends, and even just people who expressed care and interest in supporting me, to be part of this. Then, each person took responsibility for one day of the week. So, on a Monday, the person who agreed to be my point person for that day would be available for me to call or text them, or for me to simply know that they were there, holding space for me."

Adele looked down at her hands folded in her lap. "There were many days when I didn't even need to reach out to anyone. It was reassuring just knowing that the option was there."

I turned my gaze from Adele back to the bare tree outside the window. She stood up and began taking the needles out while I considered who I would ask to be part of my support circle. My survival strategy over the past months had been to smoke (in secret) organic American Spirit cigarettes on my balcony, at any hour of the morning, day, or night when my anxiety had nowhere to go but to leap out of me. I also called my mom multiple times a day, two at minimum, which was a big contrast from my every-other-week Sunday phone call prebreakup. Daily spin or barre classes gave me not only somewhere to go but also a place to channel my big feelings. Also, after needing to let go of Matt's and my dog, with whom I was incredibly close, and not having adopted Sadie yet, I felt an additional, unwelcome empty space throughout my days.

Still, the incessant, dull ache of loneliness was wearing on me, especially on the weekends. Once days that I'd relished for sleeping in, doing errands and organizational projects around my house, or for going out to dinner and making breakfast with Matt, weekends became days I started to dread and needed to map out in advance. What projects could I do to fill the time? Who could I reach out to for company so I wasn't spending days on end all by myself? How would I fill all that time?

"I appreciate that suggestion," I told Adele. I swung my legs off the treatment table, reached down to slip my sheepskin-lined boots over my bare feet, and slowly rose to standing. Now, with the needles out, I could feel their effects through the weight of my feet on the ground, the smooth river of energy flowing through me, a sense of sleepiness, and a quieter mind. I again felt the gentleness of little Rera more than the roughness of the world, as if she were curled up like a kitten in my chest. And, saying goodbye, I closed the door behind me, heading home to email my seven women. It was worth a try.

Ari's Story: Receiving Support as a Refugee

The kind of help we each need (and have access to) may differ depending on our situation and the kind of heartbreak we're experiencing. This story shares an example of how one might go about seeking support when she's thrust out of her home, community, and even her country.

In 1987, at the age of fourteen, Ari Honarvar, now an author and activist, left her birthplace of Iran and arrived in the US. Like many teenagers in Iran at the time (as well as now), Ari was enraged by all the injustices, including that she didn't have the same rights that her best friend, who was a boy, had. The government controlled every aspect of her existence—both in and outside of the home. In response to this, like many of her peers, Ari often went out at night to write antiregime graffiti on walls around her home city, Shiraz. Because Iran is a theocracy, and renouncing the government is akin to renouncing God, the punishment for this was severe and could include the death penalty. When Ari started to get in trouble with the morality police, and sometime after her sister's classmate, a senior in high school, was executed, her parents felt that the only way to keep Ari alive was to get her out of Iran. They accompanied her to the US, and after a few weeks they left her to return home, an experience that was painful for everyone involved.

After her parents' departure, Ari was left in a heartbroken and delirious state. She felt the exhilaration of living in a land without restrictions: no morality police, no ration lines, no one telling her that she couldn't curse the government or sing at the top of her lungs in a bikini in the middle of a square. It was a shock to her system. Plus, Ari was reeling from the gut punch of living in a strange new world without her parents, sister, or friends. At the same time, she carried within her the rubble of a demolished childhood. Because she had lived almost her entire life amidst war and oppression, Ari felt traumatized by what she had experienced, heard, and witnessed in Iran. So, when she arrived in her new home in New Mexico, Ari began searching for something to comfort her, something to make her feel like she was at home. Amidst all of this, the hardest part for Ari was that she didn't feel like she could fully express herself because she didn't speak English. In so many ways, she felt depressed and bewildered because there were no anchors to make her feel at home.

Her older brother, whom she hardly knew, had come to the United States when Ari was only four, and he had been there for the past ten years. While they were strangers to one another at that point, he helped to secure a family for Ari to stay with for a few months while she acclimated to her new country. This family was very kind to her, giving Ari food, her own room, and presents on her birthday and Christmas. Still, Ari felt the vast cultural differences. To help her cope, she started dancing to MTV in her bedroom—something she loved, especially because dancing was forbidden in Iran. She attended ESL classes at a local church and went to school, both of which provided Ari with some structure. Even though her new reality was incredibly challenging on many levels, just having something to do every day and interacting with people in ways that weren't threatening or negative felt like steps in the right direction.

Today, while Ari lives in San Diego, California, she feels that she's ultimately made a home inside of herself. She recognizes that, if she went back to Iran at this point, she wouldn't feel at home there (especially because she would be arrested and imprisoned upon her return). Also, with the uprising that happened there in September 2022, she noted that the global Iranian community felt the heartbreak of what was happening. A part of her is still there, and she can viscerally feel the injurious ways the government is treating its own people.

As a way to help other refugees mitigate the effects of their own heartbreak and dehumanization, Ari joined Musical Ambassadors of Peace. Through this organization, she can bring what was denied to her as a child—music and dancing—to refugees, along with a sense of community. She regularly dances with thousands of refugees from all over the world in San Diego, Tijuana, and London as a means to help them to heal PTSD and support them in integrating into their new realities, for they all have similar stories of how they had to flee their homes when they didn't want to.

Ari's story reminds us that heartbreak can strike at a far grander scale than the personal. One can lose her home, her family, her community, and even her own country. Amidst it all, we need immense support—practical as well as psychological, emotional, and spiritual—to help us through. While Ari had the support of her host family, music and dancing, school, and her ESL classes when she first arrived in America, she lacked a deeper level of support that she needed to navigate the level of heartbreak and trauma she was experiencing. This void was what led her to devote much of her life to supporting refugees in the ways she had once so desperately needed and wanted.

Why It's So Hard to Ask for Help

A common adage amongst healing professionals is that trauma isn't what happened to you, it's what your body and nervous system do with what happened to you. It's also what others do (or don't do) with what happened to you—most of our wounds develop because we're left to cope with our difficult experience all alone.

In my case, growing up in a home with addiction, I spent a lot of time in deep terror, not knowing what was going to happen next. And, since addiction survives through secrecy and isolation, I was always alone with my fear and feelings of being unsafe—even though I lived in a house with five other people. I quickly learned that in order to survive, I needed to keep my feelings in and act like everything was normal, just like everyone else in my family was doing. Asking for help didn't appear to be an option.

The same is true for many women I work with who experienced deep wounds in childhood. By the time we're adults, we've become experts at keeping our feelings locked inside and having our own backs. The protective parts of us that stepped in many decades ago to help us survive our childhoods are still working hard to keep us upright and functioning at all costs, and some parts of us still feel that asking for help is risky.

Add to this our culture's harmful ideal of hyper-individualism at all costs, where we're each expected to make it on our own—and are lauded for doing so. We feel shame and resistance around needing anyone else's support since those whom we might reach out to have also been conditioned with this mindset and may hold judgments around our vulnerability and neediness. Society has set us up to view failure and falls from grace as character defects. Then, once we do inevitably topple over, we expect ourselves to be able to pull ourselves together and carry on (and if we can't, well, that's another character defect). There's no room in our society for those who are struggling. Even if we don't want to admit it, we harbor unconscious biases toward people who are down-and-out and in pain.

Ways to Ask for Help

It's important to remember that while grief is a universal human experience, the ways in which people express and cope with it can vary greatly depending on cultural, religious, and personal beliefs. As we explored in chapter 2, ritual is a common way that many cultures have supported grieving individuals. For example, indigenous cultures have specific ceremonies, which can include feasts and dancing, to honor the deceased and to support the heartbroken. In some Asian cultures, people may express sympathy by giving a gift or a donation, helping with tasks, providing meals, or holding a traditional memorial service. In many Western cultures, support is often expressed through flowers and cards, as well as through practical means like lending helping hands and bringing meals.

Living in a secular culture that doesn't center rituals around grief and heartbreak, plus the fact that many of us are groomed to be self-sufficient, it can be challenging to even know what to ask for when we're hurting. Amanda Palmer, a singer, songwriter, and musician with the Dresden Dolls, wrote a popular book called *The Art of Asking*, in which she encourages creatives to break away from the model of worrying and scraping by on their own. Instead, she proposes that we ask for help. Through doing this herself, Amanda has shifted out of being a struggling, solitary artist and has leaned on support from others (like finding places to sleep while traveling, recording new albums and going on tour, and raising up to a million dollars in a month).

In many parts of the world, the time and permission to grieve is a privilege that only some have. Most places of employment offer only a few days for bereavement leave, which, as we've seen, doesn't even cover the amount of time someone is in shock, let alone grieving. As you'll read later in this book, when I started experiencing financial challenges, I didn't feel like I had anyone I could ask for help. The need for money is not only common, but it's valid and necessary during times of heartbreak.

I have a friend who had very little financial resources. When her husband left her, she didn't have the ability to fall apart because she had to work to simply make ends meet. There was a tremendous load on her shoulders, and she certainly didn't have any extra financial resources for time to grieve, go to therapy, or get support for her body like massage and acupuncture to help her cope with the huge amount of stress that she was under.

I also remember hearing the story of Parker Palmer, an American author and educator, about a time when he was going through a deep depression. He shared how one of the things that helped him the most was when someone came and sat with him in silence, and, at times rubbed his feet. He could simply be as he was, stay in silence, and receive loving, tactile support. During my heartbreak journey, I did a lot of digging to find a therapist to work with me weekly on a pro bono basis, and I paid her $30 a session. I also had friends who were massage therapists and acupuncturists, and they each gifted me a session when I was deeply struggling both physically and financially. I acknowledge that all of these were tremendous gifts that aren't accessible to many. In some cases, we may not have anyone we can ask for help. When that happens, I encourage you to anchor deeply in the support of your Higher Power and ancestors.

Above all, when the option is available to us, it's helpful for us all to know the different kinds of things we can (and need to!) ask for during times of heartbreak—and then have the courage to make the request.

You can ask for someone to:

- Bring you a meal (let them know what you like and request they make enough for at least a few meals).

- Walk your dog.

- Come sit with you.

- Go for a walk with you.

- Give or loan you money (to buy groceries for the week or month, to pay your rent or mortgage for the week or month, etc.) and/or to start a GoFundMe for you.

- Give you a massage or an acupuncture session.

- Work with you pro bono or on a sliding scale. I recommend asking around for this. People who are very well established in their careers may sometimes keep a space or two open for pro bono clients. Otherwise, you can look to online mental health services, a student through a local university program, or a recent graduate from either a master's program or an IFS level-one training who is willing to offer a lower price in exchange for gaining more experience.

- Watch your children for a couple of hours so you can do some self-care.

- Give you a one-month pass at a yoga studio or gym.

- Grant you a scholarship for a course or program that will help you with your heartbreak.

- Pay for someone to clean your home (or ask a friend to clean it for you).

- Help you with moving or pay for movers. When I unexpectedly needed to move out of my home with Jonathan right before my abortion, my three sisters paid for movers to pack up all of my things and move them to my new home. This was a life-saver.

- Do errands for you.

- Come over and hug you, hold your hand, or even lie down and hold you (provided, of course, that you feel safe with this person). Compassionate human touch can be the most potent way to regulate our nervous systems.

- Come visit you and stay for a week to be with and support you (or ask to go visit them and stay for a week, or more).

- Check in on you and/or spend time with you on holidays, birthdays, and anniversaries (or any days that feel especially hard).

- Call on the weekends to check in on you.

- Give you more time off from work.

Of course, there are many more things that can be added to this list. What else might you add? Which of these feels like something you could use support with right now?

I also want to acknowledge that sometimes, someone close to you may try to help, but in ways that don't feel good. For example, you call your mother for emotional support, but she starts giving you advice when all you need is for her to simply be there and listen to you. If this is the case, first notice where you are in your heartbreak journey—this will help you determine your bandwidth. If you're in the early stages of your process, your bandwidth is likely very limited. When your mother starts giving you unsolicited advice, you could get off the phone by saying something like, "Thank you, Mom. I know you're trying to help. This isn't feeling like what I need right now, so I need to go. I don't have the energy to explain why right now, but I will at some point in the future when I do."

Then, when you do feel up for a conversation with your mom about this, you can say, "Thank you again for trying to help, Mom. I really appreciate it and feel your care. And I'm noticing it doesn't feel good to me when I call you in distress and you give me advice. Unless I ask for it, I don't need advice. What I do need is simply for you to listen to and be with me in whatever I'm feeling. I just need a compassionate presence to witness me. Does that sound like something you could do? I know you want to help, and that would be the best way to help me right now."

If your mom isn't able to do that, then you could think about a way that she might help you (using the list in this section for ideas, or adding your own), and pointing her in that direction. Above all, know that if what someone is doing isn't helpful, you can let them know that, kindly and courageously. And, if someone wants to help but doesn't know how (or you don't know how to ask for it), you now have some ideas and options to choose from and to see what feels right for you both.

To help bring more understanding about why you may have resistance to asking for help, let's return again to IFS. In particular, we'll revisit protective parts since these are the ones within us that can keep us from feeling connected and getting the support we need.

IFS: Two Kinds of Parts

Remember that IFS exists to help those parts of us that took on extreme roles, usually when we were young, to become unburdened and more integrated into our systems so we can live with a greater sense of harmony. In IFS, "unburdening" is equivalent to healing. When our parts become wounded, they take on the burdens of strong feelings, extreme behaviors, and limiting beliefs. In the healing process, which we call unburdening, we help them to release these defenses so they can be restored to their natural state.

There are two main kinds of parts that can become extreme: protectors and exiled parts. As I've shared before, protectors step in during risky times in our lives, when we don't have the external or internal resources we need to make it through a hard experience. They step in to guard exiled parts, which are usually young, wounded aspects of us that now hold many burdens in the form of overwhelming feelings (like sadness, despair, anger, shame) and limiting beliefs about themselves and life.

For me and also for many of the women I support, because of the environments we grew up in, we harbor little girls (Rera, in my case). These little ones are our exiles and can hold bottled-up big feelings—like fear, confusion, sadness, anger, and unworthiness—that they didn't feel they were welcome to express in their families of origin. Protective parts stepped in to keep those feelings hidden, so those little ones could stay safe. As we grow older, however, that protection prevents us from having the intimate connections we long for. It also leaves us feeling hijacked by our exiled parts' big feelings when they break through the surface.

While there are two main categories of parts in IFS, protectors and exiled parts, there are also two kinds of protectors: managers and firefighters. Managers are preemptive. Their expertise is in keeping your internal and external environments under control, so that exiled parts don't derail you by flooding your system with their bottled up feelings. Examples of managers include inner critics, task masters, perfectionists, and people pleasers. Firefighters, on the other hand, are reactive. Just like a real-life firefighter doesn't discern where she points her hose in a building that's on fire, our inner firefighters do whatever it takes to douse the flames of our exile's feelings, regardless of how much damage they do to ourselves or others in the process.

For example, when shame floods your system, one of your firefighter parts could pour a drink, smoke a cigarette, or shop online. It could take over and encourage you to overwork or doom scroll, even though those things make you feel further and further away from yourself. The next morning, a critical manager will likely step in, get angry at the firefighter part for doing what it did, shame it, and vow "never again," reinstating a strict protocol to help keep you on track. Round and round these two protective parts go, doing whatever they can to protect the one who is exiled. And round and round they'll continue to go until that exiled part is healed and the protectors can relax their extreme strategies, which they've likely been enacting for many decades.

Let's take a closer look at how this kind of protective strategy works in your own system.

Get to Know a Protective Part

This is a meditation I created based on IFS principles. If strong feelings come up while doing this meditation, I recommend coming out of it, opening your eyes, looking at objects in the space you're in, and doing some deep belly breathing.

Listen to a guided audio version of this meditation at saraavantstover.com/heartbreakdownloads.

1. Come into a comfortable position, either sitting up or lying down. You might also find it helpful to do this exercise with your journal and a pen beside you. Gently close your eyes if that feels comfortable for you.

2. Now, feel into your relationship with asking for help. Do you hold fear around that? Resistance? The belief (or past experience) that no one is there for you or that you're a burden? That your needs don't matter? Or something else?

3. Choose one aspect of your relationship with asking for help, the one that feels most prominent right now, to focus on, such as the part of you that thinks you're being too needy. (You can write that down in your journal. This is the part we'll be getting to know.)

4. Next, feel inside and see where you can find that part in or around your body.

5. How do you notice it there? Are there certain sensations, textures, colors, temperatures, or something else? (Write down what you notice.)

6. See if you can get a sense of how you're feeling toward this part of you right now. Are you feeling annoyed, angry, confused, neutral, curious, or compassionate (or something else)?

7. If you feel anything other than curious or compassionate, that means that another part of you is standing between you and this asking-for-help part you're exploring. Say hello to that new part and ask if it would be willing to give you a little bit of space. If it will, say thank you and return your focus to the original part. If the part who's standing in the way won't step aside, shift your focus to that part instead and continue this process with it.

8. Whichever part is the center of your focus now, ask it what it wants you to know about itself. (Listen, and then write it down. Parts can speak to us in voices, images, sensations, thoughts, or through a felt sense.)

9. Ask it how old it is and how old it thinks you are.

10. Ask it what was going on in your life when it started to do this job.

11. By this point, you may be getting a better understanding of how and why this part who protects you from asking for help developed. Continue journaling any insights from this part.

12. Once you've learned a little bit more, ask the part you've been focusing on if it would like to stay connected with you in some way (maybe by you checking in with it, either in your journal or in meditation, each day for the next week, or something else).

13. Thank this part for all that it has shared and gradually come back to the space you're in.

This practice of getting to know your own protective system helps you to build up a field of internal support, where, slowly, over time, you can begin to hold the young, vulnerable parts of yourself. In the meantime, you can also build up a field of greater external support through the examples shared earlier in this chapter. All of these components need to be in place to move to the next stage of our heartbreak journey: transformation.

Journaling Prompts

Let's do a deeper inquiry into your relationship with asking for help and what your next steps might be in this area. I know resistance can come up around being vulnerable and asking for support, so please don't skip this step. The heartbreak journey is too treacherous to endure alone. To set yourself up for success, take some moments to reflect on the following questions in your journal.

Past

- What did you learn about asking for and receiving help when you were growing up?
- What has been your relationship with asking for (and receiving) support in your life so far?

Present

- Can you identify specific ways that you need help right now? (For example, for someone to call you, go for a walk with you, bring you a meal, do an errand for you, or give you money.)

- What coping mechanisms do you turn to when you don't feel like you have the inner and/or outer support you need in a challenging moment? What are the repercussions of those in terms of both internal backlash and external impact?

Future

- If you were to gather a circle of three to seven people from anywhere in the world, like Adele advised me to do, who would you ask to be a part of your circle, and why? If that feels prohibitive to you, see if you can find one or two.

- Is there professional support you can also seek out, like a therapist or mentor? If that's cost prohibitive, ask if they offer a sliding scale or take on pro bono clients. There may also be group programs available.

Part II

TRANSFORMATION

Heartbreak Story:
Fertility Journey

Chicago, Illinois; October 2018

On a crisp late-October day, the Chicago sky sparkled blue while orange leaves danced inside it. My heart thumped in my chest and my insides buzzed as if I'd drunk a cup of coffee—which I hadn't. I knew I'd hear back from my doctor at any moment. So, I drove to a yoga class before work, still needing GPS to point me where to go in a city I doubted I'd ever become familiar with. Yoga always helped settle my nerves, at least a little bit.

Some of the women supporting me—those who'd been through similar journeys of trying to get pregnant—sent texts of encouragement: "I'm thinking of you today!" "I don't want to bug you. Just know that I'm here!" They, too, had endured nail-biting moments like these. Only now they had a baby swaddled to their fronts, or a little girl with pigtails to drop off at pre-k.

Back outside my mom's apartment building, which was also my home for now, I drove around the tree-lined block until I found a parking space. *If they did it, so could I,* I reassured myself, even though all of me didn't quite believe that. *Stop, Sara,* another part of me chimed in on top of the doubts. *I have to stay positive. This HAS to work. There is no other option if this doesn't work. I've put everything I have into this. Failure is not an option. I AM getting pregnant. Maybe there will be two . . .*

They felt so close. My daughter: Lucia would be her name. A name I first heard in my twenties, when I was dating a Swedish man while living in Thailand. At Christmastime, we'd hang silver and red ball ornaments on the tropical potted plant in our living room and stockings on the Thai wooden shutters. He told me about the festival of light, his favorite childhood holiday in Sweden, when everyone would dress in white and walk through the dark night, candles in hand. It was a solstice celebration to honor St. Lucia, the patroness of light. I could already see my daughter's brown, curly hair and oval, brown eyes with the most delicate lashes that would kiss her cheeks, plump like peaches, each time she blinked. Or my son, Zane, whom I'd had to say goodbye to though I didn't want to. My son whom I hoped so dearly would choose to, would be able to, return.

As I was putting my car in park, my phone rang.

"Hello," I greeted, trying to sound normal while the drumming of my heart made it hard for me to focus.

"I have some good news, Sara," my doctor congratulated me. "You have two viable embryos. I'm really pleased with this outcome. It's more than I thought we'd have. I'm going to connect you with the front desk so we can schedule your transfer later this week. We're going to transfer both embryos with the hopes that at least one of them sticks."

A shaky finger smushed itself into the red end-call button on my phone. Squeezing my eyes shut, I whispered out loud, "Oh thank God, thank you, God!" Now feeling as if I had multiple cups of coffee pulsing through my electrified body, I stuffed my phone into my pocket, grabbed my purse, and hurried down the sidewalk and up the two flights of creaky stairs to my mom's apartment.

I exploded through the front door and ran toward my mom as she sat knitting under the yellow light of a table lamp in her living room. She, too, had been nervous about the news today, although I knew she didn't want to make things harder by letting me know that.

"I have two embryos! I have two embryos!" I exclaimed with a wide smile as I bounded toward her.

"Phew!" she exhaled, standing up to hug me. "We did it! We made it this far!"

After we both settled down, I told her that I'd need her to come with me in a few days to have both the embryos transferred. I told her how we could watch it happening through a microscope that would project the process on a big screen beside us; and how the nurse told me I'd need to take a Valium before I arrived, to help nerves.

"You're going to get to see your grandchildren for the first time." I smiled, feeling relief beginning to soothe my jittery insides.

Ten Days Later

"I don't think I'm pregnant," I texted my older sister's friend, Clarissa, who had introduced me to my doctor. Several years earlier, at the age of thirty-eight, when she'd decided to end a relationship that didn't seem to be going anywhere and to have a child on her own, she did one round of IVF and got pregnant with her daughter, Kate.

"I didn't think I was pregnant either," Clarissa texted right back. "It's such a nerve-wracking experience that it's hard to trust your own instincts right now. You won't really know until you get the bloodwork back. Hang in there. I know everything's going to be fine."

I wanted to believe her. I was so very willing for her to be right. But a couple of days before, nine days post-transfer, I caved and went to the bodega several blocks north of my mom's apartment and bought a pregnancy test. Even though the pamphlet I'd taken home the week before explicitly said: "Don't take an at-home pregnancy test. They often aren't accurate in these instances. We encourage you to wait for your bloodwork to get your results." The test came out negative.

The day after taking the home pregnancy test, I went in for blood-work. Back at my mom's, I awaited the call with the results. Sitting on the side of the bed in the guest room, I ran my hand over the crisp, white cotton duvet cover and looked at the makeshift altar I'd set up on a bedside table. The altar included a leather pouch that held ashes from a goodbye ritual I'd done for Zane in a kiva with a small circle of women and a dried, pressed pink geranium that I'd plucked from the flower box on my Colorado balcony. An intuitive once told me that my daughter communicated to me through pink flowers, and I'd planted bright pink ones last spring, in honor of her. My altar waited expectantly for them.

A woman named Nadine, who I knew only through our shared experiences of fertility treatments, had sent me photos of her baby altar a few months ago. She and her husband had tried for years to get pregnant naturally. When, inexplicably, that didn't work, like me they moved on to intrauterine insemination (IUI). When that didn't work either, like me, they packed up their car, left Colorado, drove across the country, and settled into a new, temporary home where IVF would be covered by insurance. (For them it was Cape Cod; for me it was Chicago, living with my mom.) In their temporary seaside home, Nadine decorated a table with flowers, candles, sacred images, and even bottles of the various pills and injections she needed for the process. She was lucky. She'd gotten a dozen viable embryos after her first egg retrieval and now had an adorable little girl. She and her husband were planning to have at least one more with their now-frozen collection of embryos. Gazing at my altar, it seemed puny in comparison to hers.

The phone rang. It was the fertility center. I darted to close the door and slipped in my ear buds. I could already sense the disappointment in the split second between my "hello" and the nurse's response. Before, when it had been good news, my doctor had called. Now a random nurse was calling. I knew it was bad news before she even said a word.

"I'm so sorry," the nurse lamented, "you're not pregnant. But you can make an appointment for bloodwork if you want to schedule another round."

When I hung up, I didn't leap into the living room as I had a couple of weeks prior. Instead, I sulked out of my temporary room, and, immediately, my mom knew. I sat down on the couch and stared vacantly at the bookshelf in front of me, our dogs wrestling at my feet. I'd received difficult blows before. And I knew that the best way to receive a blow was to let it have me. To give into it like a punch in the gut, to let the air get knocked out of me so I could get it over with and the next moment could show or bring me whatever was next.

"I need to trust that life is trying to take me somewhere," I told my mom, tapping my feet nervously on the carpet. The wise part of me knew that was right, yet the wounded parts of me weren't ready to go there yet. I had to think—and act—quickly.

I'd already reached my out-of-pocket maximum with my health insurance, so if I wanted to do another round of IVF before the calendar year ended and my insurance reset, I didn't have time to dwell in my disappointment. I'd give my body a rest during my next menstrual cycle and begin another round in early December. That would mean that, during my post-Thanksgiving trip to Tulum, where I was going to lead a weeklong women's yoga and meditation teacher training, I'd need to start giving myself injections. Yes, that would be a little risky since I wouldn't be able to get any initial ultrasounds to monitor the follicle growth on my ovaries, but time was of the essence. Then I'd come home from Mexico, have another egg retrieval, and hopefully would find out I had multiple embryos.

More clarity came during those moments on the couch at my mom's: I knew that I needed to leave Chicago. I had been there nearly five months, and lately my soul had been telling me, when I woke up to wintry gray skies, that I needed to leave by Christmas or I would die. Even though it felt scary and far-fetched, I knew I needed to follow my heart to California, where I'd wanted to live for many years. I'd drive out to Santa Barbara, stopping in Colorado for a couple of days over Christmas. Then, once I'd gotten settled in Santa Barbara—possibly the following spring—I'd fly back to Chicago to have the embryo transferred. Even though my plan to get pregnant with the first round of IVF didn't work, at least I had a new plan. There was still hope.

Mid-December

It was the week before Christmas, and I was still in one of the last places I wanted to be: gray, cold, gloomy Chicago. I stood in the lobby of the Palomar Hotel, gripping my gloved hands into fists inside my coat's pockets.

Inwardly, I coaxed myself, *Sara, hold it together. Breathe. Feel your feet on the ground. You can do this.*

Behind me, people whooshed through the revolving doors, ushering with them streams of bitterly cold air. They swung shopping bags spilling over with brightly colored tissue paper, smiling and chatting to one another as they turned the corner. They seemed so happy. So alive. So normal.

Frozen in their sea of movement, I fixed my eyes on the arrangement of silver ornaments and evergreen boughs that sat atop a table below a large, ornate mirror. I looked into the mirror and saw my reflection.

Who am I right now? I don't even recognize myself, I thought. *How can this be my life? Why is all this happening to me? How am I going to make it through this one?*

My mom came up behind me, offering, "Oh, sweetheart, I'm so sorry." She could see the tears starting to build around the edges of my eyes and the tremor in my lips as I tried to hold them back.

"I think it will be good for you to be here with us right now," she continued. "The kids are around the corner, waiting for us."

She had made reservations for holiday tea as she had done many years prior with my older sister and her children, who lived in Chicago as well. This was my first time joining them. Feeling a thunderstorm raging inside me, unable to form coherent thoughts, I struggled to know what to do. I was about to either implode or explode there in the center of a busy lobby of a fancy hotel. I needed someone to scoop me up, wrap their arms around me, usher me into a car, take me home, put me to bed, and hold me as I cried and cried and cried. I needed support and space to completely fall apart.

But that wasn't what was offered, and that wasn't what was happening. So, like a robot, unsure what else I could possibly manage on my own in that state, I followed my mom's cue and let her lead me around the corner and down the hallway to the left, where my older sister and her children eagerly awaited us.

"Hi, Rera!" they chimed when they saw me.

And then the river of tears started flowing. "I'm so sorry, I can't do this right now. I need to go home," I admitted to myself and them. Several minutes later, an Uber arrived to take me back to Mom's apartment.

When I had arrived in Chicago in early August, the air was sticky and warm. My mom's garden bloomed with roses, hydrangea, and irises. I'd go for long strolls with Sadie on the 606, an elevated walking trail several blocks from my mom's apartment. Instead of the pine trees and dirt paths of the hiking trails we'd frequented in Colorado, we walked on asphalt and beside tall apartment buildings with rooftop decks and barbecues.

I'd left my life in Colorado behind for what I thought would be forever. I'd said goodbye to my friends, my apartment, the hiking trails, and all the pain and heartbreak I'd experienced there. Most of my belongings got packed up and carted off in a POD, to be tucked away in a storage facility in Colorado until I got clear on my next move. Into my car I packed Sadie and whatever belongings I thought I'd need until I found a new home. Maybe that would be in Chicago or Charleston, near family. Maybe in California, where I'd been wanting to move for years. Or maybe somewhere entirely different. I didn't know yet. All that I knew was that I was ready to continue moving forward, full throttle, with trying to have a baby.

Since the previous spring, I'd been doing monthly intrauterine inseminations (IUIs) in my home in Colorado with a local midwife. As each ovulation window approached, I transported a vial of donor sperm, which was stored in a liquid nitrogen chamber that I'd fasten into the front seat of my car like a passenger, from the sperm bank back to my apartment. As it sat expectantly in a corner of my bedroom, I obsessively peed on ovulation test sticks and texted updates to my midwife. "Not yet, maybe tomorrow." "Will you still be able to come then?"

When the flashing smiley face finally came, it was game time. The midwife would come over, I'd lie on my bed, and she'd find my cervix and position it in her cold speculum. After she left, I'd lie still, burning moxa over my womb, telling my baby all the wonderful things we were going to do together. For the next two weeks I'd wonder whether each food craving or slight cramp meant that I was pregnant, only to receive a string of negative pregnancy tests. Scared and heartbroken, I lamented that it had been so easy for me to get pregnant accidentally. Now I had to jump through hoops and pay large amounts of money each month to even try.

When I arrived in Chicago over the summer, I was just a few months away from my forty-first birthday, and I was starting to panic. In the realm of fertility doctors, I was considered geriatric. There was little hope or encouragement that another pregnancy was even possible for me. Yet most of my friends weren't having children until their late thirties or early forties (and I had just gotten pregnant myself the year before), so I wasn't willing to give up. IVF was my next step. I did some research and learned that, unlike in Colorado, health insurance in Illinois covers fertility treatments. My sister's friend, Clarissa, got pregnant and had a child on her own through working with a fertility doctor there that she highly recommended, so after much deliberation, I decided to head to Chicago. The plan was to stay with my mom, get Illinois health insurance using her home address, and try one (maybe two) rounds of IVF—as much as I could before the end of the calendar year.

When I got to Chicago in August, I did all my preliminary tests. And, in late September, I dove in. In the early mornings I'd bundle up, drive downtown, and brace myself against the icy winds coming across the river as I made my way from the parking garage to the front door of the clinic. Once inside I'd split my time between receiving an ultrasound to monitor my follicle count and growth and having blood drawn (Clarissa had warned me: "You'll start to feel like a human pin cushion"). Once back at my mom's house, I'd spend the day working, maybe go to yoga class or for a walk in the evening, and start the whole thing over again the next day.

As September turned to October and October turned to November, the blue skies and sticky air of summer turned into icy drizzle and a gray sky. It felt like a steel trap had descended over the city, locking us all in. Used to the open spaces and sky of Colorado as well as the sunshine (even in the depths of winter), as that steel trap descended, a depression started to descend over me. Each day I felt I was sinking deeper and deeper into a hole. Deeper and deeper into fear that this wasn't going to work and anxiety about the huge logistical and financial investment I was making—all on my own.

So, on that mid-December afternoon, as an Uber delivered me back to my mom's apartment building, I was reckoning with the end of a very difficult chapter. Earlier that day I had learned that, despite my second egg retrieval having yielded several fertilized embryos—five more than I'd had during my first round—inexplicably, none of them had made it to day five of gestation. I had thought I'd had it in the bag. My doctor had, too. I was planning on freezing them all and coming back in the spring to transfer a couple of them. I celebrated that I'd still have several left over to freeze for the future, should I decide I wanted another child.

The story I'd mapped out in my mind featured a successful round of IVF and an ensuing pregnancy as the happy ending to what had felt like an insanely challenging and unfair few years. So, before I went home in the Uber, as the news that none of that was going to happen began to sink in and the vision for my life dissolved, I told my mom through sobs in the Palomar lobby, "This is my rock bottom. This is my lowest low. I don't know how I'll survive this."

At other times in my life, when I'd given everything I'd had and then some, I'd always triumphed. Since I was a little girl, I knew the experience of giving my all and getting rewarded on the other side of that—whether that was through acing a course in school or knocking it out of the park with a work project. But this was different. I'd read all the books. Talked to all the people. Done all the research. Bought all the donor sperm. Visited all of the healing practitioners. Envisioned all the positive outcomes. Spent all of my savings, and then some. I'd left no stone unturned. I'd done it all. The women I knew who'd come out the other side of this successfully had, too, and they told me it was so worth it. Yet they had their children, and all I had was a body whacked out on too many hormones, debt and a depleted bank account, and a heart that, once again, felt irrevocably broken.

A few days later, following the instructions from my soul that I needed to leave Chicago, I once again packed up my car. Early in the morning, on the solstice, my mom and I hugged in her cold garage as orange started to light up the dawn. We sobbed in one another's arms, feeling not only the new loss I was grieving but also the truth that, most likely, we'd never spend so much time together again. Despite how hard those months had been, they were also precious in how much more time I was able to spend with my mom. My body heaved with sobs as I backed out of her garage, saw in my rearview mirror as she blew a kiss, and began the long journey toward my new life in Santa Barbara—one that already looked nothing like how I had envisioned it.

Chapter 5

Allowing Anger

"Feeling angry signals a problem, venting anger does not solve it . . . Those of us who are locked into ineffective expressions of anger suffer as deeply as those of us who dare not get angry at all."

— Harriet Lerner

When some of the frozenness and shock of heartbreak wear off, we often start to feel the more fiery dimensions of our anguish: anger. We can feel angry because of a rift or a betrayal—by ourselves, a partner, a friend, or life itself. Yet anger can be tricky for us women. We're either afraid to express it, which leads us to unleashing it internally and being incredibly harsh on (or even hurtful to) ourselves. Or, at the other end of the spectrum, we spew it, usually on those closest to us and against our higher intentions. Given that anger is a healthy, natural, and normal part of both being human and the heartbreak journey, and that so many women get stuck in their healing by stewing in toxic bitterness and resentment, it serves us to pause and spend some time here. Even (especially!) if we'd rather skip this stage entirely and jump forward to the next chapter. Yes: if healing is our aim, then opening the door to the raging face of heartbreak is our necessary next step.

Colorado; August 2017

Anger was never an emotion I felt comfortable expressing. In my family when I was growing up, there was a line drawn down the middle of us. My father and two of my sisters expressed their anger outwardly. And my mother, myself, and one of my other sisters repressed it and unleashed it internally. Since my father's rage often took up so much space in our home, I developed a strategy very early on in life to stay as calm, quiet, and collected as possible. While on the outside I was a very demure child, inside there was a lot of chaos, which, I now see, manifested physically in the form of various illnesses. Then, as a teenager, I discovered the incredible release valve of sticking my finger down my throat.

I first made myself throw up one early spring evening after a fight with my father. I was sixteen or seventeen and had come home from boarding school for the weekend. We got takeout, as we often did, from one of my favorite Italian restaurants in town. My father, mom, and I were in the kitchen, and I ate my rigatoni all'arrabbiata from a foil takeout dish. While I was eating, my father started criticizing my mother while I sat between them. As his voice rose, I started eating faster and faster, fury beginning to boil inside as I swallowed big gulps of tomato-drenched noodles. "Stop it!" I yelled, surprising even myself with my outburst. "Don't talk to her like that!" I commanded.

My father turned his line of fire from my mom to me. Robotically, I finished forking the rigatoni into my mouth, ran to grab the car keys to the left of the front door, and sped out the driveway, shifting from first to second to third gear in our rusty red Rabbit convertible. When I got to the end of our street, I pulled over before turning onto the main road. It was the spot where my sisters and I used to wait for the bus on early mornings before school. Yanking up the parking brake, I left the car running and the round headlights shining in the dark. I leapt out of the car, slammed the door behind me, and ran into the woods. There, I bent over, stuck my finger down my throat, and threw up the entire dish of rigatoni I'd just eaten. Relief immediately buzzed through my body. I ran back into the car and sped onto the main road, feeling some shame and confusion about what I'd just done, but also knowing I'd finally found something that could make me feel better, emptied, relieved of all the turmoil I so often felt inside.

Rage started knocking on my door during the summer after my abortion. This time I didn't make myself throw up to help relieve me of all that pent-up energy. Instead, I knew I needed to learn how to feel the rage. I was angry at everything and everyone. Matt and Jonathan for screwing me over. Myself for letting them. The friends who had turned their backs on me. Life for dealing me such a shitty hand that I struggled to make sense of. And the unfairness that continued to roll in, such as the letter from the IRS I received, a month after everything blew up with Matt, telling me that I was under investigation.

They said the CPA I'd been working with, the one a friend had recommended to me and nearly every other entrepreneur I knew in town went to see, had filed my business in a way that the IRS had deemed illegal in a court case against this CPA a few years before I started working with him. Even though he had filed for countless other businesses, I was the only one who was called out. I ended up owing $36,000 in back taxes on top of a $50,000 business loan I'd taken out to help me finish my second book a couple of years before, when I thought the loan was the only debt I was going to need to contend with.

The summer before Matt and I separated, I'd had two surgeries, one on each eye. Several years earlier, a pterygium—a raised growth on the white of the eye—had begun growing in each eye. There's no real cure for this condition. It's said that it may be caused by UV exposure, but likely mine were also generated by my own unexpressed emotion, mostly anger. They were not only red and painful, but they were also beginning to cloud over part of my irises. A woman I knew shared with me that she, too, used to have pterygiums on both eyes. She'd had them surgically removed by a doctor in town. And, while there's a 20 percent chance that they'll grow back (and worse) after surgery, her eyes were now white and clear. Despite the financial expense and physical hardship of having two back-to-back surgeries, I too wanted pain-free eyes again. So I went ahead with the surgeries.

In the months afterward, I launched my book, then launched an important year-long program, and then Matt shared the fateful news with me of his infidelity. With one stressor after another, my eyes weren't healing, and the pterygium in my left eye started growing back even worse.

I was having a hard time keeping my head above water at every level. I started to fear leaving the house each day. It was like I was one big open wound, and every interaction with the world felt harsh, like sandpaper being rubbed into and over that wound. When I needed to leave the house to do errands or go to a spin class, rage simmered right at the surface, like a pot with boiling water inside that keeps rattling the lid. I'd scream in my car until my voice got dry and hoarse, and at home I'd scream into my pillows, which always caused Sadie to scamper into the other room.

During a virtual IFS session with my therapist, I told her about the nearly blinding rage I was feeling. I shared my fantasies of shooting, stabbing, punching people.

"Good," she said, nonplussed. "Why don't you close your eyes and just let yourself imagine doing all of that."

"Really?" I wondered.

"Yes. Go ahead, take as long as you need."

That off-the-charts level of rage stayed pretty constant for a few months. Sometimes it was so strong I knew it wasn't wise to leave the house—I might blow up at anyone, at any moment, for any reason. Many nights I lay in bed feeling the fire pulsing through me, demanding me to feel it. To allow it. To give it space to be a part of me. And, given that I often teach and support other women in making space for their anger, I knew that I was not only feeling anger toward Matt, Jonathan, my friends, my life, and God. I was feeling all the anger I'd locked away up until then. Rage from years, decades, that had nowhere to go. Until now.

Martina's Story: Tend to the Rage that Hurts Others

Martina joined one of my IFS women's circles after a painful breakup with a man she really cared about. Through her work in IFS, she realized that her own "rage part" was keeping her from having the kind of intimate relationship she wanted. Whenever she started to get close to someone, this part of her would come out at unwanted and unexpected times, sabotaging her attempts at partnership. In her early forties, she realized with great sadness that she was never going to be able to find a life partner and have a family unless she was able to get to the bottom of this fiery part of herself.

"I saw my mom treating my dad this exact same way when I was a little girl," she shared through tears during one of our sessions together. "I would see her criticizing my dad, yelling at him for doing something wrong—basically emasculating him. And he would just sit there. He would just take it," she said. "I think a part of me learned that it was okay to treat my partner that way. Only now that I'm older, all the times I've done that, I've only pushed men away. And I'm so lonely now. I know I need to stop doing this if I want to have a real, lasting relationship."

Martina also shared that she often felt this rage simmering below the surface at other times. It lurked while she was in business meetings when she felt impatient. Or sometimes even with friends or strangers if someone said or did something that felt upsetting to her.

"When people meet me, they think I'm such a kind, happy person," she added, "which I am! But then I also have this other part of me that just kind of takes over sometimes. And I have no idea what to do about that."

Martina's rage part, we discovered over time and with patient investigation, learned its ways from her mother, who was not only a heavy drinker throughout Martina's childhood and present life, but also had the tendency to be cruel to her. As a small child with limited internal and external resources, the best way her internal system could find to protect her from her mother's unpredictability and harshness was to be cruel herself.

Understand Anger's Messages & Power

While we can view anger as a nuisance, ultimately its healthy function in our lives (just like all of our other emotions) is to communicate something important to us from our depths. While sadness tells us there's a loss to process and anxiety informs us that there's something about the future we need to address, anger delivers us the message that an important boundary has been crossed, or that one (or more) of our core values has been violated. Given this, our anger is an important partner in helping us to live our truth and integrity. Its hot, energizing presence gives us the fuel to speak up and act. During times of heartbreak, it can give us the energy we need to blaze through old patterns and structures in order to create new foundations in our lives.

If, however, we don't acknowledge the messages that anger is delivering and we don't partner with its activating energy to advocate for ourselves (or another) by reinforcing boundaries, that supercharged life force doesn't have anywhere to go. When we ignore its signals and don't express and act on it, our bodies and psyches suffer. As we explored in an earlier chapter, Dr. Gabor Maté's book *When the Body Says No* clearly spells out the correlation between stress, emotional suppression, and illness.

He writes that, "several decades ago, David Kissen, a British chest surgeon, reported that patients with lung cancer were often characterized by a tendency to 'bottle up' emotions." Kissen found that the risk of lung cancer was five times higher in men who "lacked the ability to express emotions effectively."[1] More and more research shows us how deeply connected our emotional states and immune systems really are. A study from the National Institutes of Health demonstrates how four fundamental emotional responses (anger, anxiety, mirth, and relaxation) modulate cellular responses within a variety of immune functions.[2] Also, autoimmune disorders (which you'll remember occur amongst women at a rate of two to one compared with men), tend to affect women during periods of extensive stress, such as pregnancy and other great hormonal changes,[3] which I would argue includes heartbreak. Given the grave, long-term repercussions of ignoring our anger's signals, let's explore healthy ways to express and release it.

Give Your Anger Somewhere to Go

Anger is one of the many things we aren't taught how to express (much less relate to skillfully), and it's often during life crises like heartbreak when we're forced to reckon with these bigger feelings. We recognize that the parts of ourselves that get angry are often young, using outdated and ineffective strategies to deal with big, fiery feelings.

To help with this, here are some perspectives and practices we can try to cultivate a more conscious relationship with anger. Doing this will help keep us from getting stuck in bitterness and resentment on our heartbreak journeys.

1. Speak for, not from, your parts.

This is a core tenet from IFS that we use when we're in groups together, and it turns out it works wonders when we apply this to the rest of our relationships as well. Here's an example: when anger comes up toward your partner for not taking the trash out for the umpteenth time, rather than getting passive-aggressive or lashing out at them (which is speaking "from" your angry part), try speaking "for" it by saying, "A part of me feels really angry right now that you didn't take out the trash again. It wants to start yelling at you or giving you the cold shoulder, but I know that won't help things. This part is wondering how we can change this dynamic." Speaking for, rather than from, a part helps us to stay in our center, from which we can more skillfully navigate a conflict.

If your anger is directed more at oppression or the unfairness of life, let yourself give voice to your anger. Speak to life (or your Higher Power) directly, either out loud or in your journal. Even in these instances, it's important to give your anger expression.

2. Take a pause when anger comes up.

See if you can give yourself a moment (or a few) to first just notice that you're angry. When we feel uncomfortable with anger, we bypass it and go straight to numbness or some other form of evasion. Just notice that anger is here, and get curious about where and how you feel it in your body. Is it a hot ball in your belly? Energy in your chest? Doing this allows you to first validate your anger and then to insert a little space between the arising of a thought or feeling and your reaction to it. This pause is what can transform a reaction into a response. This pause may need to be for a minute, an hour, or a day. Taking space to first be with the strong energy before speaking for it to another can help diffuse it.

3. Feel and relax into the anger.

This one also takes practice. A daily meditation practice of pausing, noticing, feeling, and relaxing into our emotions (rather than immediately reacting to them) prepares us for the times when bigger storms move through us. What is it like when you feel your anger, relax into it, and let it be here, exactly as it is, without doing anything to fix, change, express, or repress it? (This doesn't mean that you don't advocate for your needs. It means that you start with first allowing what you're feeling to be here, so the feelings don't get stuck inside of you.) Where do you feel anger in your body? What's it like to stay with that, even for a breath or two? What do you feel in your heart and mind when you're angry? Can you be with that, too, dropping any story about the anger and just being with the pure energy of it?

4. Find healthy ways to move and express your anger.

In my early thirties, I attended a weeklong healing immersion, the Hoffman Process, that helps resolve family-of-origin issues at their root so we can live as our true selves. For the better part of a couple of days, I beat pillows with plastic baseball bats and screamed from deep in my belly. When I got home, I bought myself a similar bat and kept it in my practice space for when I needed to give my anger more expression. When anger comes up, we can scream into our pillows, in our cars, or out in the woods. We can punch pillows, slap dishrags against the wall or pieces of furniture, or pummel couch cushions with a plastic bat. We can also turn on intense music and stomp our feet, moving our bodies in sharp, staccato movements. Make whatever sounds you need to. If you're a visual person, you can express your anger through art, intensely scratching and scribbling on paper or canvas.

5. Get curious about your anger.

Anger almost always has roots deeper than present circumstances. Without taking time to get to know the parts of us who are angry, we can't fully tell if the anger we're feeling is from the present or if it's more historical. Usually, it's a combination of both. However, trying to parse that out without a deeper dive would only be speculation. We need to take the time to get curious about our angry parts and to learn what their intentions are for us, as well as when and why they started in their roles. When we probe into the world of our parts, we often discover unexpected things that our conceptual minds can't pick up.

Dr. Dick Schwartz, the founder of IFS, refers to our parts as sacred, spiritual beings. They each have their own personalities, histories, and even their own nervous systems. Through this, we may learn that our angry parts internalized messages from our own caregivers, and/or that they protect vulnerable, wounded parts of ourselves that didn't feel it was safe to express their anger when we were young. Freeing up frozen anger from our youth can and will help us to metabolize and process our present-day anger in mature ways.

Giving our anger outlets of healthy expression is a key part of helping us to keep from getting stuck during our heartbreak journeys. While I wish I could say where we're going next is more pleasant than anger, it's not. Yet, like anger, loneliness holds valuable wisdom and lessons for us to become more whole, mature women.

Journaling Prompts

Writing is another avenue by which we can decode our anger's messages. I found that journaling the things I felt angry about helped me to gain more clarity. I could see the boundaries I'd allowed others to cross, and, more importantly, I could understand the boundaries that I had crossed within myself.

Past

- Consider the timeline of your life and what role anger has played during various seasons and stages. What was your relationship with anger like as a child? Adolescent? Teenager? Young adult? And now?

- In your childhood, how did those closest to you express (or repress) their anger? What did this teach you about relating to your own fury?

- If you don't feel like you relate to anger at all, consider the possibility that you may suppress it so habitually that you don't recognize either having or feeling it. If this is the case for you, that's okay. Get curious about how, when, where, and why this aversion to anger may have developed for you. Did anyone around you model this behavior? See what you can discover about this.

Present

- Take an honest inventory: what do you do when you're angry now? Consider what you feel in your body and what emotions arise as well as what you say and how you act.
- Since heartbreak brings us face to face with our anger in a more confronting way, what are you being called to notice, express, and/or heal in terms of your relationship to rage and anger right now?

Future

- Which of the healthy outlets that I've shared here speak to you? Is there one you can commit to trying within the next week?
- What new structures in your life do you want to use anger's energy to help you create?

Chapter 6

Living with Loneliness

"I wish I could show you when you are lonely or in
darkness the astonishing light of your own being."

— Hafez

In many ways, being with loneliness is even harder than being with rage.
While it's not as combustive as anger, its challenge comes through its
dull, omnipresent ache—one that overtakes your entire body and makes
it impossible for you to forget that it's there. Scientific studies have shown
that it's neither a good diet nor regular exercise that most influences our
health and longevity. Rather, it's our social connections and our sense of
belonging to a community of others who care about and support us that
impacts us the most.

Loneliness plays a central role in heartbreak. Living in a culture that's
incredibly judgmental of so-called failures, it's not uncommon for us
to lose social connections and status during these times. This, added to
the likelihood that a central attachment was ruptured during heartbreak,
makes loneliness one of the biggest things we need to contend with.
While reaching out for support is important, it's equally important to
grow our capacity to meet our loneliness. Given that three out of five
Americans are lonely (and likely other places around the world reflect
similar statistics), learning how to live with loneliness is a crucial life skill
not only during times of heartbreak but also beyond.

Colorado; November 2017

Sitting on my white sofa, I cradled my iPhone in my lap and clicked on the yellow square for the online dating app Bumble. For the past week, I'd hidden my profile. For the past couple of months, after I'd decided to start dating again, I'd gone through cycles of being on dating apps and then, when the feelings of overwhelm and despair became too great, I'd hide my profile, delete the apps, and regroup.

At thirty-nine, I'd never really dated before. I'd always met someone in passing, through work, yoga events, or a friend. Yet, since I met Matt in my early thirties, the world had changed, dating included. Now, everyone was using the apps: Tinder, Bumble, Hinge, Match. Feeling rejected by Matt, my self-esteem was at an all-time low. Even though men sent messages with comments like "Whoa! You're gorgeous!" or "What's a woman like you still doing single?," it never seemed like the men saying those things were the men I wanted to be saying those things. Maybe those strangers had intended for their comments to be compliments, but they only made me feel worse. I was left wondering, "Yeah, what *is* wrong with me if I'm still single, when all of my friends are either partnered or married? Why can't I make a relationship last?"

I didn't feel as attractive as I used to. I felt self-conscious that my eyes (still healing from surgery) often got red and inflamed and that I had dark circles under them from months of heartbreak-induced chronic insomnia. Plus, I wondered if I was "damaged goods"—if my life had gone too far off the rails for anyone to ever want to be with me again. Finding a suitable partner on the apps also felt like hunting for a needle in a haystack. So when someone who seemed to meet what I was looking for—relatively good looking, accomplished, and kind—appeared (and actually liked me back), a zing of aliveness shot through my otherwise depressed system.

On that particular Sunday morning on the couch, I matched with a man named Ryan. His profile photo showed him standing confidently with arms crossed over his very fit chest. He also appeared to be successful in his career and was interested in spiritual growth as well. We even had some friends in common. Ryan and I exchanged a few back-and-forth messages, met up for tea at an outside cafe, and, since that connection felt like a green light, we made plans to meet for dinner once he was back from an overseas business trip in a couple of weeks.

Even though my girlfriends who had been initiated into the ways of online dating warned me not to get my hopes up early on, I had a hard time reining in my imagination around Ryan. It had been almost a year since I'd had sex. The last time was with Jonathan, when I was pregnant the previous winter. Since not only my body but also my entire being felt so different than I did pre-abortion, I wondered what it would feel like to be intimate again, both emotionally and sexually. Would it feel the same? Or was I now forever altered?

Ryan and I met for dinner one early November. It was the first really cold night of late autumn. Smells of burgers on the grill and the sounds of sizzling frying pans, chattering diners, and clinking dishes filled the warm, candlelit dining room. I felt unsure and self-conscious. *How much should I tell him about my past?* I wondered, a question I'd never needed to ask myself before I had so much baggage. *Is my pain obvious,* I questioned, *like a neon sign above my head flashing "damaged goods"?* Men had always fallen for me pretty easily in the past. Yet, as I sat there, I wondered if I'd lost my mojo.

I tried to appear as normal as possible. I ordered a steak and fries. An avid CrossFitter, Ryan ordered steak and sweet potato fries, to stay inside his paleo diet protocol. Inside, I winced, as I was used to being the one with more dietary restrictions than the man I'm with. I always enjoyed being with men who were more relaxed about all of that stuff. Still, our conversation flowed. We talked about our work, how long we'd been living in Colorado, ways we enjoyed spending our free time, and what we were looking for through our online dating adventures. Quickly we discovered that we had a lot in common, and by the time we'd finished eating, we'd had a lovely evening together. Given all the disappointing coffee meet-ups I'd had with men in recent months, many of which I walked out of early, I felt an inner sigh of gratitude that I'd met a man with serious partner potential. The awkwardness I'd felt at the start of the date had faded, and I was beginning to feel things inside I hadn't felt in a long time: resonance, connection, and attraction. I could tell that he was feeling it, too.

When we finished, Ryan walked me back to my car. When we arrived there, we stood on the sidewalk, feeling that awkward, first-date moment. I wondered what was going to happen next.

"Can I hug you?" Ryan asked.

"Sure," I answered, and he leaned in to wrap his arms around my back, pulling my head into his broad chest.

We stayed there for a few moments, acclimating to one another. I breathed in the smell of the outdoors that emanated from him as he nuzzled his nose into the top of my head. Then, he gently moved one hand to guide my face toward his, letting first his lips, and then his tongue, meet mine. A tender kiss quickly transformed into a more passionate one as our bodies, within a few moments, realized they liked each other. A lot. I began to feel a warm burning in my pelvis, the first time I'd felt that in many months, and, instantly, I felt like a former version of myself. A woman who felt sexy, sensual, desirable. A woman who wasn't alone, depressed, and grieving all the time. A woman who enjoyed being with a man.

"We have two choices," Ryan instructed as he gently pulled away. "It's really cold out, so we can either say goodnight now, or I can come back to your place."

My mind started to short-circuit. In all my envisioning of our evening together over the past couple of weeks, I'd never factored that option in: *Or I can come back to your place.* I had a new dating policy to take things slowly, which, by necessity, included never going back to anyone's place after the first date. Yet, the stirred energy in me was starting to compete with the voices in my mind urging me to use caution. *Yeah, but, Sara, you need to live! Who cares! This guy is hot, and you have amazing chemistry! You know how hard it is for you to find a man you're attracted to. Just go for it. You don't have to have sex with him.*

"Hmmm," I replied, pausing to take in the surprise of this new option. "You can come back to my place, if you want," I finished, surprising myself with my choice.

"Okay, I'll follow you there," Ryan said. "See you soon."

As I led us uptown to my apartment, my heart pounded with the excitement of our kiss. My mind tried to interject, *Are you sure you should be doing this, Sara? You don't even know this man!*

A few hours later, I kissed Ryan goodnight and watched him disappear down the steps as I closed my front door. Like a giddy sixteen-year-old, I couldn't stop smiling. The fresh memories of our bodies moving together—just making out, no sex—with our shirts off and pants on. The feeling of our skin sliding against one another and Ryan whispering, "Damn, your skin is soooo soft." When he left, he excitedly promised to text me the next morning. He wanted to have me over the following afternoon for tea. Lying in bed, I tried to calm my buzzing system to a place where it could sleep.

The next morning, I was still flying high. Yet, as nine became ten, ten became eleven, and then midafternoon arrived and I still hadn't received that text from Ryan, my exuberance morphed into anxiety. *What the hell?* I wondered. *Is he ghosting me? How could I have been so naive as to have him over here last night?* At five o'clock, Ryan finally texted.

"Thanks for a great night. I just went for a hike with a friend, talk later this week?"

My heart dropped down into my guts like a bowling ball. *Fuck. I fucked up.* It seemed like I'd had all the green lights that this man was available, but he was quickly proving to be otherwise. After a few more dates over the next few weeks, Ryan confirmed my suspicion as he became more and more avoidant. He was the one who eventually ended things, and I was left with an even deeper feeling of rejection, shame, and loneliness than I'd had before I met him.

Still, it was nice to have had at least a short-lived reprieve from the unrelenting, agonizing burn of loneliness, the whole-body ache and tension of being deprived of touch, connection, and care. Sure, I had Sadie. I had my mom on the other end of the phone line. I had my connection to myself, God, and nature, but I needed more. I could feel the truth that loneliness is more deadly than smoking a pack of cigarettes a day. I could feel the days, months, years being shaved from my life each day I woke up and was forced to wearily face the relentless beast of loneliness.

A couple of years later, when I was still single but living by then in Santa Barbara, the pandemic hit, and I was living alone. The loneliness I'd been feeling for years became so strong that my hair began falling out. During a Zoom call with my IFS mentor, she shared, "Loneliness is a part of the human experience. Even though I live with my husband, there are still many times when I feel lonely. My daughter, who's on her own living in New York City, is struggling with loneliness now, too."

"How would it be," she continued, "to practice tonglen? You would breathe in the knowledge that millions, even billions, of other sentient beings are feeling loneliness right now, and breathe out compassion for them, as well as yourself."

My mentor also encouraged me to seek out pleasure even though I was sheltering in place alone, in a town that I was not yet fully landed in. That looked like taking online dance classes, buying a bottle of wine, playing music, and cooking a nice meal for myself. Inviting a friend over to have dinner in my garden. Or riding my bike to the farmer's market on Saturday mornings to buy fresh flowers.

While having Sadie's companionship, practicing tonglen, and pushing myself to curate pleasant, solo experiences helped me to endure the months and years of loneliness, there was nothing that could make that starvation for human connection go away. And that's true for all of the features and flavors of heartbreak we're exploring here together. They're part of the experience no matter how much we wish otherwise. Our task during these grave times is to not only be creative in learning how to live with them but also to grow the faith that things won't be this way forever.

Tonglen

Listen to a guided version of this meditation at saraavantstover.com/heartbreakdownloads.

This meditation and visualization practice, which I've adapted from Tibetan Buddhism, translates as "giving and taking." It's a powerful remedy for when we're feeling separate because it reminds us, in a very visceral way, of our inherent interconnectedness.

1. Come into a comfortable resting position. You can either lie down or sit up (in a chair or on the floor). If you're sitting on the floor, make sure that your hips are higher than your knees and that your spine is elongated.

2. Close your eyes or have a soft gaze on the floor a few feet in front of you.

3. Relax and begin to become more aware of your natural breath. Stay with feeling and witnessing the breath flowing in and out for a minute or two.

4. Now, consider what you're having a challenging time feeling in this moment. Maybe it's loneliness. Maybe it's physical discomfort. When I was pregnant, I did this a lot when I felt around-the-clock nausea. I'll guide the following steps using loneliness as our object of focus, but see what you're struggling to be with, within yourself, right now.

5. With your next inhale, breathe in the recognition that so many others around the world are feeling loneliness right now, too.

6. As you exhale, breath out the sentiment of "this too," that "I, too, am experiencing this loneliness with you."

7. Continue like this with your natural breath. Breathing in the loneliness of the world and breathing out the recognition of your own loneliness.

8. If this becomes overwhelming at any time, just come back to step 3, being aware of your natural breath.

9. Continue the practice for a few minutes, or for however long feels right.

Next, let's look at some of the different coping mechanisms we often resort to in order to help us manage the incredible pain of chronic loneliness.

Elizabeth's Story: Ways You Cope with Loneliness

On the cusp of her fortieth birthday and a few weeks before moving into her new home (as an excited first-time homeowner), Elizabeth met with me for her first IFS session.

She shared that despite having a job she loved and excelled in, and despite being very friendly, worldly, attractive, and motivated to develop herself and explore new things, she still felt like what she wanted most in life—a partner and a family—were beyond her grasp. No matter how hard she tried to meet men and create a more settled life for herself, nothing seemed to be working out. She found herself alone in her new home, night after night.

"I feel so ashamed to tell you any more," she continued, squinting her eyes shut as tears leaked from them, "but I know that, if I want help, I need to tell you."

"It's okay," I coaxed. "Take your time. I acknowledge your courage right now."

"Thank you," she whispered as she drew in a big breath. "Okay, so, at night, when I feel so much loneliness, I feel like a part takes over me. It makes me drink a whole bottle of wine, even when I don't intend or want to. It makes me smoke cigarettes. Basically, it encourages me to do all the things I enjoy doing with other people when I'm having fun. Only, since other people aren't around, it forces me to do those things by myself. Then, when I wake up the next morning to go for a run before work and I have a headache and feel like shit physically, I feel so bad about myself. It makes me feel like even more of a failure. It's this cycle that, no matter how hard I try, I can't seem to break out of."

"I'm going to take off my IFS hat off for a moment, Elizabeth, to tell you that I acknowledge you for showing up here today and asking for help," I offered. "And I know how hard that can be. I haven't been in the exact same situation as you, but I've experienced something similar, in my own way. I understand how painful loneliness is, and how painful the addictive cycles we can get caught in to help us manage our loneliness can be."

"Thank you for sharing that," she replied softly, through sniffles. "I'm sorry you've experienced this too, because it's horrible. And that also gives me some hope."

Elizabeth is still in the midst of healing these parts of herself, but the parts of her that felt cut off from her own essence now feel more connected to her, helping to decrease the sense of loneliness and isolation Elizabeth had been feeling. She also joined one of my IFS women's programs to be part of a community of other women going through similar things.

Because Western psychotherapeutic traditions focus so much on the individual, even the ways that we seek support can exacerbate our loneliness and isolation. Traditionally, we gathered in communities for healing circles and rituals to help us through hard times. Thus, if we have a chance, as Elizabeth does, to join a healing circle of other kindred spirits, this not only helps to hold and support us through whatever heartbreak we're nursing but it also helps to feed our deep need of belonging.

Fearing Loneliness

As women, a very primal part of us is terrified of being alone. If our distant female ancestors were abandoned—estranged from their communities and those who provided for them—they'd perish. In more recent generations, if a woman didn't get married and have a family (or at least be in a long-term relationship), she was considered a spinster at best, a useless outcast and failure at worst.

Thus one of the scariest parts of heartbreak is that it often thrusts us to the sidelines of societal ideals. We're depressed even though we just birthed a beautiful baby. We're widowed when we're supposed to be in the prime of our lives. We're still single when all of our friends are coupled. Or we're broke when everyone around us seems to be thriving. Our initial response is to buffer ourselves. We want to turn to wine, cigarettes, shopping, Netflix, carbs, the wrong relationships, comparing and despairing on social media, or working too much (amongst other things) to shield us from feeling our estrangement from the flow of "normal" life. When we do this, we hurt ourselves. The inner pain—whether that shows up as anxiety or depression or anything in between—mounts. The more we run from it, the bigger it gets. We reach for all of these things outside of us to feel some sort of connection and to ease the pain.

I have no judgment about turning to substances and/or activities to help take the edge off when we're inside some of life's most excruciating passages, like heartbreak. I've been there and done that. Yet I also know that, like me, you want true freedom and fulfillment. And this means being able to meet life on its own terms, crutch-free. Building up the inner resources to do this takes time, and one of the aims of this book is to help you get there. One of the blessings of heartbreak is that, when we engage consciously with the suffering it brings, as you're doing now, our capacity grows. So that the next time the shit hits the fan, you have more space and tools inside to face it. Not only that, but you also have the muscle memory from the past. You recognize, "If I could survive the hell I was in then, I can certainly survive this now, too."

Just like going to the gym and lifting weights builds and sculpts our outer muscles, consciously meeting challenging feeling-states, like loneliness, helps our inner emotional and attitudinal muscles to grow. In doing this, one of the things that helps us the most is growing our awareness of and relationship to the part of ourselves who can hold, meet, and be with anything and everything we ever have or ever will experience. The part of us who can never be tainted or destroyed. The part of us who holds the power to heal all of our other parts—even, and especially, those parts of ourselves that feel the most wounded and broken.

Tapping into the Part of Us Who's Always Connected

As we've explored earlier, in IFS, this aspect of us is known as our Self. Self energy exists in each of us—as well as in each of our parts (yes, our parts also have their own parts and Self energy). Self always knows what's best for us. It's connected to our intuition, and when we listen to it, it can lead us to experience the divine unfolding of our own unique paths.

Ideally, Self operates within each of us like an orchestra conductor. It's not the only one onstage, but it helps to harmonize and guide all of our other parts to create one coherent melody that is our lives, well-lived. Self helps us to live an inspiration-led, rather than a fear-led, life. And its presence is deeply healing not only to our own parts and inner system at-large but also to others and to outer systems. When there's a critical mass of Self energy present, our nervous systems feel regulated, even if we're simultaneously being with challenging experiences and dysregulated parts of ourselves.

Because Self energy needs to be embodied in order for us to feel and sense it, there are eight "C" words that we can look for to help us begin to identify the presence of Self energy in ourselves and others. These are:

Courage	Connectedness
Confidence	Curiosity
Creativity	Clarity
Compassion	Calm

Just as the sun is ever-present, even when clouds, storms, and fog prevent us from seeing it, Self energy is always available within each of us. It's here even when other parts (which can include our thoughts, inner voices, feelings, sensations, images, and a felt sense) cloud over our experience of the eight Cs. We may feel extreme parts taking over us (like anxiety, depression, loneliness, self-doubt or criticism, etc.) to the point that we forget or doubt that our identities include anything other than that. Thus, over time, there can be a deep rift and distrust between Self and our parts, creating feelings of fragmentation and loneliness inside. One of the gifts of IFS is its ability to help us to mend these rifts and to restore our system to its innate, harmonious, connected state.

Remembering that Self is who we truly are, no matter what we are experiencing in life or weathering right now, can be incredibly reassuring and empowering. While we might not be able to access our Self during times of great distress, we can remember that, like the sun, it's always here. And we can seek out the company of others who are able to rest in their own Self energy, and, in turn, can help guide as back to ours.

Resource Lonely Parts with Self Energy

This is a meditation I created based on IFS principles.
Listen to a guided audio version of this meditation at
saraavantstover.com/heartbreakdownloads.

I'm going to lead you through a short meditation to help you feel the relationship between one of your parts and your Self energy. Often when our parts feel disconnected from our Self, we experience feelings of loneliness and fragmentation in our inner worlds. You can choose a lonely part to explore, or, if there's another part of you who feels really dominant in your system that you're curious about, you can go with that one.

1. Come to a quiet resting position, either sitting up or lying down.

2. Allow your body to relax into the tug of gravity, and feel the places where your body is touching the floor or whatever surface you're sitting or lying on.

3. Become aware of your breath. Welcome fuller, deeper, more conscious inhales and exhales while you also begin to let your mind rest inside your body.

4. If you feel comfortable doing so, close your eyes and interiorize your awareness. As you do, get a sense for which part(s) are present. Is there one you feel more curious about getting to know right now? It could be a lonely part or another part who could benefit from some connection.

5. Once you've chosen the part you want to spend some time with, see if you can locate where you sense that part right now in or around your body. Trust your experience. In IFS, "first thought, best thought" is a good practice to help bypass the parts of us that overthink or overanalyze.

6. When you locate that part in or around your body, briefly sense how you're noticing it. How big is it? What sensations do you notice? Are there any colors, textures, or temperatures associated with it?

7. Next, feel inside and notice how you're feeling *toward* this part. Do you feel frustrated with it? Annoyed? Angry? Confused? If so, these are other parts of you. Say hello to them. Let them know that they're welcome to feel exactly as they do, and invite them to give you a little bit of space inside so you can have more of a direct connection with the part you set out to connect with.

8. If those other parts won't step aside and give you space, that's okay. Then you can shift your focus and follow the remaining steps in this practice with them.

9. If they do step aside, thank them. And once again, tune into how you're feeling toward that initial part. A question that can help: How open does your heart feel toward this part?

10. What we're looking for here (and it's important to be honest about your experience and not try to rush to the "right"

answer) is even a little bit of openness. Some feelings of heart-centered curiosity and compassion may also arise.

11. If and when any of those feelings are present, extend them toward the target part. No words are needed here; this is simply an energetic exchange.

12. As you do that, see how the target part responds. Is it able to take that energy in?

13. If it is taking it in (even if it's reluctant to), stay with it for some moments in this way, until it can trust you a little bit more.

14. After some time of sharing this Self energy with your target part, thank it. If it feels right, you can make a commitment to come back and spend some more time with it.

15. Afterward, journal any insights that came up for you as a result of doing this exercise.

If you felt blocked and don't feel like this meditation worked for you, notice what parts were present and leading you to feel that way. Another mantra in IFS is "What's in the way, is the way." You can't do one of these exercises wrong. They're simply opportunities to notice new parts of you who may step in and be present during different times (like a distracting part, a sleepy part, a doubting part, etc.). Welcome them all as a chance to get to know yourself better.

———————————————

As we grow our capacity to be with our loneliness, one of the things we may notice is that we're feeling a lot of pain. This is likely pain from your present heartbreak as well as pain from the past. In the next chapter we'll explore how to process your pain in ways that don't overwhelm or shut you down.

Journaling Prompts

Whenever I feel disconnected from myself, one of the ways that I reestablish connection is by journaling. When we're feeling lonely, we can feel more of our own presence and companionship simply by putting pen to paper in an honest, unedited way.

Past

- What has been your relationship with loneliness during different seasons of your life (childhood, adolescence, young adulthood, now)?

- How have you related to it during these different stages? Consider both internal and external strategies (for example, drinking, smoking, eating, reaching out to others, joining group activities, etc.).

Present

- Do you have any fears about loneliness? Do you have judgments toward your own loneliness or others'?

- Which of the eight Cs do you find is easiest for you to access? (One of my IFS trainers shared that "curiosity" is often the lowest hanging fruit. Simply becoming curious about what's happening inside or what part is present can start to bring a little bit more Self energy into your system.)

Future

- What parts within yourself do you sense feel lonely and cut off from other parts in your system, and from your own essence, or Self energy? How can you give further support to those parts?

- Do you sense new ways to try being with your loneliness going forward? What are they?

Chapter 7

Processing Pain

"Pain is not punishment and pleasure isn't a reward.
Both are ordinary occurrences of being human."

— Pema Chödrön

G rief, anger, falls from grace—these are all, in various ways, taboo in our society. Underlying all of them is yet another, even larger, cultural aversion: pain. Even our medical model rests on the philosophy that pain is bad and that we need to do everything we can to avoid it. Certainly there are many cases, such as extreme, chronic pain, where taking measures to control pain is necessary. Yet there are many more cases of individuals moving through acute growing pains, either physical or mental/emotional/spiritual, where medicating away the pain delays the process of healing. We've all heard the adages, "You have to feel it to heal it," and "The only way out is in and through," and both of these are true when it comes to healing from heartbreak.

Feeling and holding our own distress requires a kind of strength that most of us aren't taught how to cultivate. When we're faced with the overpowering psychic and emotional anguish of heartbreak, we lack the skills we need to fully meet it. Yet it's never too late to grow these skills. If we learn them now, we'll have them with us for the next challenge we face.

Colorado; June 2017

I sat cross-legged in my desk chair staring at the black, empty screen of my iMac. Midafternoon sunlight illuminated the lines recently left by the vacuum cleaner on the beige rug in my office. I closed my eyes and winced. *I have so much to do today,* I thought. *And I'm already so behind. I'm in so much pain. I don't think any amount of willpower will make it possible to concentrate right now.*

It was two months after my abortion, and I felt like I was struggling just to survive. One pain was piling on top of another: my betrayal by Matt, then Jonathan; losing my son; reckoning with the fact that I had chosen that loss; searing loneliness, humiliation, and shame; and financial strain while I struggled to work amidst all I was contending with. I opened my eyes, logged into Skype, and, about a minute later, the concerned and caring face of my IFS mentor filled the screen.

"How are you, Sara?" she asked, tilting her head slightly with concern as she seemed not only to see through me, but to feel me.

"Not good," I replied, my face contorting into heaving sobs as my body and voice tried to modulate the dam that felt ready to burst inside of me.

"I'm just in so much pain right now," I cried, cupping my face in my hands. "I don't know if I can or will survive this amount of pain. I can't think. I can't eat. I can't sleep. And I certainly can't work. The pain is just too big."

My mentor breathed with me, and that breath felt like her hand reaching over to touch my hand, communicating, *You're not alone, Sara. I'm right here.*

"I know it feels like you won't survive this pain," she said gently, "and I'm here to tell you that you absolutely will. Would it be okay if I help talk you through how to do that right now?"

I nodded, feeling my cheeks wet with tears and the outer rims of eyes starting to swell and redden.

"Okay, so, forget about trying to work today. Forget about trying to do anything right now. When we get off this call, your assignment is to get back into bed. Draw the curtains and get in your pajamas. Invite Sadie to join you, if you want. Just get into bed—see what feels best, either keeping your eyes open or closed—and you can even place one or both hands on wherever you're feeling the most pain. Right now, where are you feeling that, Sara?"

"In my heart, right here," I replied, pointing to my chest.

"Good," she said. "Then put your hands on your heart and start with just noticing what you're feeling there for one breath. Bring your meditation practice into this by dropping the story about the pain. Just get curious about the actual, physical sensations that are present. Do you feel heat or cold? Contraction or expansion? Is there a color or a texture? Do the sensations stay the same or change? How big is the area you're feeling the pain in? You get the idea."

I nodded.

"Then, maybe you can stretch to feel it for two, three, or more breaths. Just little bits of feeling the pain. Little bit by little bit. Let yourself off the hook from needing to do anything else today. This, this pain right here, right now, is the most important thing. This pain needs you to be with it. Can you do that, Sara?"

I nodded again, even though I wasn't convinced yet that the magnitude of the pain wasn't going to kill me. But, given the circumstances, I didn't really have any other choice but to try.

"Taking time to feel this is what's going to help you actually get through it. I know that sounds counterintuitive," my mentor counseled, "but give it a try and you'll know what I mean."

After our call, many voices inside me rebelled, telling me to check my email, eat a snack, call someone, but I knew that none of those were going to make me feel better. In fact, given the amount of pain I was in, they would likely only make me feel worse. So the deeper, wiser part of me led me into my bedroom, pulled on a pair of sweatpants and a sweatshirt, closed the curtains, and got under the covers. Immediately, I began to cry harder, my whole body heaving. Like my mentor suggested, I placed my hands on my heart. No one was there to hold me in my pain, but my own hands could be with me.

For a breath or two I felt the pain directly, without thinking about anything else. *Okay, I did it, I'm still alive.* So I did another round.

Okay, I did it again. So far so good. Over the next couple of hours I stayed with the process. I was slowly metabolizing my own pain, bit by bit. And, like my mentor said, it wasn't killing me, much to my surprise. It was actually helping. I was giving the pain somewhere to go by holding it, meeting it, and feeling it. I realized the pain wasn't just from recent events but was, like my anger, grief, and loneliness, a backlog of pain from my entire life. Pain I hadn't had the outer (or inner) support to feel. Pain that didn't have anywhere else to go but to freeze in my tissues until another pain came along that was so great it seemed to break me open, revealing all the old pains, telling me, "You can't move forward without feeling this. You can't move forward continuing to ignore this pain."

If You're Experiencing Suicidal Ideation

Before we move into a practice of feeling our pain, I want to first normalize that it's not uncommon to have moments (or longer periods of time) along your heartbreak journey when you think about taking your own life. I definitely experienced this, as have many of the women whose stories I've shared in this book. From an IFS perspective, this suicidal ideation is coming from a protective part of us. As I shared in an earlier chapter, there are two kinds of protectors—managers, who are preemptive and try to keep us from feeling pain, and firefighters, who are reactive and try to eliminate pain once it's become too great for managers to suppress. A suicidal part is a firefighter. Just like a part who drinks, smokes, or dissociates is also often a firefighter, the part that holds suicidal urges is trying to soothe your agony. This part believes that, when nothing else is working, suicide is the last resort to help you get out of pain. When we understand this, we see that although society demonizes firefighter parts, they are actually incredibly heroic; they're even willing to end their own lives in order to protect us. When other firefighters, like parts who drink, aren't able to keep the pain at bay, a firefighter who's higher up in the hierarchy kicks in—a part that feels suicidal. Oftentimes simply noticing that this is a part who's trying to help us manage our pain can give us some space from and perspective on it (rather than believing we are that part and acting on its directions).

Of course, if the suicidal ideation is overwhelming, I urge you to reach out for support. Help is available twenty-four hours a day through the Suicide and Crisis Lifeline by calling or texting 988. You can also visit their website: 988lifeline.org.

Now, let's talk through some of the steps you can do on your own if the suicidal ideation you're experiencing isn't too strong.

Protective Parts Who Can Keep You Stuck

You may have other strong protective parts who take over. If they stay in charge, they can keep you stuck in your heartbreak journey because they're preventing you from being with the pain and discomfort of your experience. Remember: you have to feel it to heal it.

Examples of these parts include:

- Parts who want to drink, smoke, shop, scroll the Internet, or have sex in excess

- Taskmaster parts who constantly keep you in "go mode," with no time to rest and be

- Highly analytical parts who keep you thinking about, rather than feeling, your experience

- Parts who are afraid of grief, anger, sadness, etc., and try to keep pushing them away

- Lone-ranger parts who try to do everything themselves and don't ask others for help

- Parts who judge you for your heartbreak and tell you to "hurry up" and "get over it" as soon as possible

We all have these parts within us, in different degrees. Again, we're not saying any of these parts are wrong. We simply want to notice when one (or more) of them takes over. When that happens, you can turn to the different IFS practices and meditations interspersed throughout this book. This will help you come into relationship with these parts, because if you keep letting them run the show, you'll stay stuck at various places along your path through heartbreak. The first, and most important, step forward is to be able to see that these parts are not you. They are simply protective parts of you who are afraid something bad will happen if you feel your feelings. When we lean into our strong emotions in small doses, we can gradually show these fearful parts that we actually do have the capacity to be with our pain.

A Practice to Feel Your Pain

I adapted this practice from the one my mentor
guided me through in the previous story.
Listen to a guided audio version of this meditation
at saraavantstover.com/heartbreakdownloads.

Begin this practice by getting really comfortable. If you're a caregiver, consider doing this before bed, when you first wake up, or during a window of time when you're home alone. Even little bits at a time add up and are very effective. Wear comfortable clothing, and lie down in your bed or on your couch. Cover up with a blanket. Keep your phone on silent in another room.

1. If it's helpful, like we did in chapter 2, call in your invisible circle of support. Remember, this can include your ancestors who are wise and well, friends and loved ones whom you trust and are supportive of your healing process, your Higher Power, and anyone or anything else that you feel a safe and soothing connection with. The more we feel like we're being held within a safe, benevolent container, the more we'll feel able to open up to painful feelings.

2. Clarify your intention for doing this practice. This can be something along the lines of: My intention is to meet and release past and current pains so I can feel more present and at-home in myself.

3. Next, if it supports your process of inner exploration, you can close your eyes. If that feels uncomfortable, rest your gaze softly somewhere in the space around you.

4. Turn your attention toward your body. Notice what sensations are here. Which are pleasant? Unpleasant? Neutral?

5. Gradually start to narrow your focus on those sensations that are unpleasant, painful even.

6. Where do you feel those in your body?

7. What do you notice about the sensations? (How much space do they take up? Do they have a temperature/color/texture?)

8. Stay with your curiosity about how the sensations feel and where you find them.

9. When your mind goes into thought or story, either about those sensations or something else, just bring your attention back to the experience in your body.

10. Take breaks when you need to by bringing your attention to your breath, or to areas in your body where you feel pleasant or neutral sensations.

11. Repeat this as many times as feels comfortable for you. Don't overdo it, but know that each time you meet your pain with presence, warmth, and curiosity, you're digesting and unfreezing that pain, creating more space inside for who you truly are to dwell and shine forth.

Like with our anger, grief, and loneliness in previous chapters, **our current pain also has its roots in the past.**

Daria's Story: Heal Past Heartbreaks
Along with Your Current One

Daria had just turned thirty-five and felt like her life was falling apart. Just over a year ago, her mother, who was also her best friend, took her own life unexpectedly. Her mom was the one whom Daria would speak to most every day about most everything, and now she was—quite suddenly—gone. On top of that, Daria and her now-wife had recently moved from Boston to a new home in the Berkshire mountains, with a wedding date that happened to fall just a month after her mother's death. With a new home, a new wife, a deceased mom, and homesickness for her friends and city life, Daria came to me heartbroken.

While almost a year and a half had passed since her mother's death, Daria struggled to get out of bed in the morning. She and her wife were hardly speaking, and she found herself staying up late at night, searching online for studio apartments in Boston to rent. Although her father and sister lived only a short drive away, she didn't have the same close bonds with them as she'd had with her mom. Amidst this all, she wanted to get her mojo back—to feel like herself again.

In our first session, Daria shared her story with me, often stopping to cup her face in her hands, sometimes wincing, sometimes crying. Once she had told me all she wanted to about her history, I guided her to go inside and to start noticing the parts of her—thoughts, feelings, and sensations—that were present. Immediately, Daria placed a hand over her heart and clutched it.

"There's this pain in my heart," she offered, "and I wake up every morning clutching it, just like this, because it hurts so much."

"Good," I guided. "How would it be for you to leave your hand there, just like that, and to really let your heart take in the presence of your hand right now?"

Daria nodded as I watched the grip of her hand on her chest soften.

"Now, what are you feeling or noticing there, in that space under your hand right now?" I asked.

"I feel sharp, throbbing pain," she shared, "concentrated in this tight ball in the center of my chest."

"Is it okay for you to feel that right now?" I questioned. Daria nodded "yes."

As we slowly started to create enough space between Daria and her heartache, enough for her to be with it rather than be overtaken by it, the heartache began to reveal more about itself to us. It was here, it said, because it wanted to keep Daria from experiencing even more heartbreak. She had reached her limit, it believed, so it was working hard to make sure she didn't surpass that by experiencing even more pain, disappointment, and loss. We learned that this part of her was seventeen years old and had first stepped into its role of blocking her heart when Daria was that age. At that time, her best friend betrayed her, and subsequently Daria had a breakdown, started abusing her ADD meds, and struggled with suicidal ideation.

By the end of our first hour together, the pain in Daria's chest went from a one-dimensional experience that she felt overpowered by each day to a three-dimensional part of herself, complete with its own history, personality, needs, and intentions for Daria's life.

The Parts Behind Our Pain

My session with Daria revealed to us that the part behind Daria's heart pain was a teenager. She's a part who experienced something very challenging—the betrayal of a close friend and an ensuing emotional breakdown—yet who didn't have the inner and outer resources she needed to pass through that experience without accruing wounds that became frozen in time within Daria. In IFS, this teenage part of Daria is an exiled part, and the pain that blocks Daria's heart is a protector part, specifically a manager. Now that Daria's in her midthirties, the teenage protector of her heart, brought back to the surface because of her recent losses, is preventing her from feeling the connection and aliveness—with others but also with herself—that she most longs for.

Even though these protectors may be doing more damage than good now, they're still afraid to leave their posts of duty. They fear that doing so will cause too much pain and overwhelm for us to handle. These protector parts are often young, and they often think that we're still young, too—meaning they assume we're still as helpless as we were when the initial hurt was inflicted. They are often not aware that we have greater emotional capacity and/or that we have the outer support available to us to help us meet and resolve the wounds of the past in ways that feel both gentle and safe.

Some of IFS's greatest offerings are its skillful methods through which we can truly befriend protectors, with compassion and curiosity. Over time, this helps those parts who shield our vulnerabilities to soften, allowing access to the younger ones they've been working so hard to protect. Then, when the protectors soften and we're able to meet these exiled parts and to hear and witness their stories—in ways that no one ever did or could when we were younger—we can help them to release all the frozen, pent-up pain they've been holding onto. In turn, these exiled parts are restored to their initial states of innocence, playfulness, and aliveness. Rather than being burdened with pain from the past, they're free to contribute their unique gifts to our systems.

This makes befriending our protective parts and healing our exiled parts key processes to prioritize along our heartbreak journeys. If protective parts don't soften, we'll stay hardened and stuck in certain areas. And if our exiled parts don't get liberated and restored, the new life that longs to burst forth when the time is right won't be able to.

The Opportunity to Heal Old Hurts

Like Daria's and my stories here demonstrate, present-day heartbreak can be intensified because it brings to the surface all the buried, unhealed hurts in our systems. Thus not only are we grappling with present-day pain but we're also navigating more historical pain. This can be challenging (as it means facing a lot of pain—ouch!), but it also means that this is a potent opportunity to resolve older griefs and heartbreaks that we're still holding onto.

The methods for doing this are fourfold:

1. simply be aware that you're healing both present and past hurts right now;

2. engage in the practice I just shared of metabolizing your pain by feeling and being with it, in small doses over time;

3. befriend the parts of you who are protecting your wounds in order to understand their histories and to get their permission to help heal the ones they are protecting; and then

4. compassionately witness those younger, wounded parts, through a modality like IFS, to support them in releasing their pain from the past and coming into the present.

This latter part of the IFS model—witnessing, unburdening, and helping our exiled parts come into current time—functions within our systems much like a shamanic soul retrieval. In fact, this step was initially inspired by indigenous healing traditions, which IFS helps make accessible for more of us to experience. In an unburdening process, we enter into a meditative state, much like the imaginal realm that indigenous healers work in. From there it's possible to mend past ruptures and create new imprints in our nervous systems, souls, and psyches. When this happens, parts of us who have been frozen in time become liberated, and their soul qualities are available to us once again.

Take an Inventory of Your Unhealed Wounds

Look back over your life and reflect on major, challenging events you experienced—events that don't feel fully resolved or integrated in your system or your life.

- You can write these down in your journal, or if you're a visual person, you can draw a timeline. Mark off the years and events on that timeline where you feel like parts of you are frozen in the past because you didn't have what you needed to help you process those experiences as fully as you needed or wanted to.

- Journaling or recording on your timeline is something I recommend you do in more than one sitting. Keep coming back to it, as more memories may come forward that you want to document on this timeline.

- As you're being with your present-day pain, remember that you're very likely also feeling pain from those past experiences, too.

- If it feels true for you, fortify your conviction to get support in being with your pain, not only for your present-day self but also for all of the past selves who are still hurting.

After you've taken this inventory, you'll have a clearer sense of exiled parts who may need support within you. It's also important to recognize that the bigger the protector in your system is, the bigger the wound they're protecting. So, the presence of a protector shines a light on the exiled parts who need healing.

Signs of Exiled Parts

Here are some examples of signs that there are exiled parts within you who need healing. This list isn't exhaustive, but it can start to give you a clearer sense of what to look out for in your own system.

- You have one or more very strong protective parts who cause you distress, and, if you have done personal development work or therapy, these parts don't seem to be softening despite all of your efforts (for example, a strong inner critic, an addictive part, parts who feel anxious or depressed, a part with suicidal ideation, etc.)

- Sometimes you have emotional reactions to present-day events that overwhelm you even when your rational mind doesn't want them to (for example, lashing out in anger, going numb, feeling like you're leaving your body, getting sleepy, etc.)

- The suffering you're experiencing feels familiar, and you remember feeling that way often as a child or during other times in your life

- Your feelings (like shame, overwhelm, sadness, anxiety, fear) sometimes feel unbearable, and you have a hard time being with them without checking out in some way

- Your nervous system feels dysregulated (either it's revved up or shut down) and you have a hard time coming back to a calm, connected, regulated state

- Certain thoughts or beliefs flood you at times (for instance, self-loathing, the belief that you're not lovable, a fear of being abandoned, etc.)

Do any of these seem familiar to you? If so, this is natural and normal. We all have exiled parts. And heartbreak provides a potent opportunity to heal them, so we can emerge from this experience feeling more whole and worthy. Let's explore the next step in that process together now.

Contacting an Exiled Part

We're going to continue our inventory of our exiled parts, who often live in the deep recesses of our bodies, such as our hearts and our bellies. They also tell their stories though our bodies—through physical numbness, dysregulation, illness, or other symptoms that may be unique to you. They've all been stuck in time because they experienced too much, too fast, with too little support. And, as we've explored, to help keep their pain at bay, protective parts cover up these exiled parts. So you don't overwhelm your system, it's good to move slowly. Baby steps help. In IFS, we say that slow is fast.

Note: Working with exiled parts is very tender territory. If strong feelings start to come up, bring yourself out of the exercise, open your eyes, look around the room, wiggle your fingers and toes, and start to take some deep breaths. It can benefit us to do this deeper healing work with external support whenever possible.

Together we can begin to notice more of these exiles and help them to become aware of us.

I created this meditation based on IFS principles.
Listen to a guided audio version of this meditation at saraavantstover.com/
heartbreakdownloads.

1. Come into a comfortable position, either lying down or sitting up, as if preparing to meditate. If it feels comfortable, you can close your eyes.

2. Notice if there's a feeling right now that's hard for you to be with—one that feels like it has a bigger context and history than what you're experiencing right now. This could be a strong feeling of despair, hopelessness, unworthiness, sadness, overwhelm, anxiety, shame, or something else. Choose one feeling to focus on during this exercise. (I recommend not choosing the most intense one to start with. Select one that has a maximum intensity of five or six on a scale of one to ten.)

3. If that feeling is not present right now, think of a time recently when it was. Then notice where you find that feeling in or around your body.

4. As you locate it in or around your body, feel into your heart. How open does your heart feel toward this part of you?

5. If it feels even a little bit open, extend that openness toward that part. Pause and notice if that part is able to let in the openness. How does it respond?

6. If your heart doesn't feel open, that means a part of you is here, blocking access to your heart. Ask that part if it would be willing to give you some space so you can connect with this younger part of yourself. If it won't, that's fine. Stay with that protective part and connect with it instead.

7. Whichever part you're focusing on now, ask it how old it is. If it's a non- or pre-verbal part, sense how old it is. Abide by the mantra "first thought, best thought" here, so keep thinking and analytical parts aside as you do this exercise.

8. Once you get a sense of this part's age, see if it knows who you are, how old you are, and why you're here with them now. If it doesn't know, go ahead and tell it.

9. Ask this part what it wants to show you or tell you about how things are for it right now.

10. Simply be present, witnessing its story.

11. Continue asking it, "Is there more?" Let it share while you listen.

12. As this part continues to share, keep checking in with yourself to see how you're feeling toward it. If you notice anything other than curious, compassionate connection, another part of you has stepped in. Gently ask that other part to please keep giving you some space; if it won't, turn your attention to hear what it has to share.

13. Once your target part has shared all that it wants to for now, ask it whether and how it wants to stay connected with you. Does it want you to check back in with it? Meet with a guide to help you go deeper with it? Journal about or draw it?

14. Thank this part for all it has shared and ask it if there's a safe place in your system where it'd like to go until you meet with it next. Wait for this part to go to the place it has chosen (it's important that it, rather than you or another part of you, chooses this place).

15. Say goodbye to it for now, and gradually open your eyes if they've been closed and come back into your surroundings.

16. Journal any insights that came up for you through this practice.

I also want to point out that, as Freud first taught through his "repetition compulsion" theory (and which many other trauma specialists have observed since then), our wounds are often repetitive. For example, if your father cheated on your mother when you were young, it's likely that you will be cheated on, too. Or, if you were sexually abused as a child, you're more susceptible to sexual assault later on in life. Thus, if we heal that initial break within ourselves, we can put an end to painful cycles so they don't continue repeating.

Now that we've moved through different protective layers of ourselves and felt into the deeper wounds (some of which are likely repetitive) beneath them, we'll begin to experience a taste of the larger transformation that's coming for us. To help us anchor more deeply into this process of change, let's explore how to create some rituals that will be designed to do just this.

Journaling Prompts

During the vulnerable process of contacting these younger, wounded parts of ourselves, journaling can once again be a steadfast companion. Sometimes, when I'm wanting to give my younger parts more of a voice, I'll journal with my nondominant hand. Above all, simply writing, stream of consciousness, about the topics below can help to open up old memories, drawing links between past and present pains.

Past

- What has been your relationship to pain throughout your life (both to your own pain and to others')?

- What did you learn about being and coping with pain from your family of origin? From your culture?

- What coping mechanisms did and do you lean on when your pain is too great?

Present

- Do you have practices and support resources for meeting your pain consciously?

- What fears, objections, and resistances do you have around doing this?

- Do you notice any wounds that have repeated since childhood?

Future

- During the timeline exercise, what historical pains did you uncover that are in need of healing going forward?
- Are there any next steps for processing your pain that feel right for you now?
- Which wound, if you heal it now, will have the biggest impact on healing your entire system and setting you up for living a life of more peace and wholeness going forward?

Chapter 8

Creating Ritual

"Ritual is an art that requires bringing your own
personal touch, soul, passion and creativity to
the practices, whatever they might be."

— Dr. Daniel Foor

To receive more support with our heartbreak, we need to invite in invisible, universal forces to assist us. At the start of this book, we took some time to define what that means for each of us. This can include your ancestors and your Higher Power as well as the natural forces of the universe that cause flowers to grow in the spring and leaves to drop off the trees in the fall. Aligning more intentionally with your ancestors will expedite your processes. Ritual, which bridges the realms of the human and the Divine, is one of the most potent ways to do this.

Weddings, funerals, bar and bat mitzvahs, and baptisms are examples of common rituals within our culture. These are times when increased focus and intention is brought to a particular event, to help a transition to unfold. Ritual is timeless, existing in eternity yet taking place in a set place and time. It creates a field of possibility where the Divine is invited to enter into and infuse our everyday realities with grace. Through this, rituals help us to feel a sense of relief. They remind us that we're not alone and that we can always invite in larger forces to aid with our hardships. Ritual also provides a container to help us let go and be with our pain.

Plus, ritual invites in the mystery. It helps us remember that we're part of a much larger play of existence, and that whatever adversity we're facing is a part of that and, somehow, will lead us further on our own journeys of becoming. Whatever form or flavor of heartbreak you're experiencing, ritual can help you more deeply process it.

Colorado; July 2, 2017

Christiane Pelmas's house was tucked away at the end of a cul-de-sac in a quiet suburb. The small, brown-shingled, single-story home sat at the edge of open space. The deck, decorated with some worn lounge chairs and a dining table, overlooked a grassy field. Beyond that, the Rocky Mountains rose out of the dry earth like giant spears. I led Sadie through the gate to the left of the house and into the backyard, and there was Christiane, standing next to a wolf, which she'd adopted and raised like a dog. The two of them seemed to shine with an otherworldly power. With her tousled silver hair in a pixie cut and blue-gray eyes that communicated both radiance and wildness, Christiane stood as a modern-day version of the wise woman who lives at the edge of the village. That was why I wanted to do this with her.

Even though we hardly knew one another, Christiane greeted me with a hug and led me into her home for a cup of herbal tea, a dish of raw almonds, and a plate of fruit—plump plums picked from a tree in her backyard. Even though I didn't know Christiane very well, I'd felt called to reach out to her. My therapist at the time, a strong advocate for using ritual to help process major life events, encouraged me to create one to honor the loss of my son. There's no particular formula to follow for such a ritual, she encouraged. Rather, it was important for me to feel into the necessary components myself.

As I did that, I knew there were a few key things I wanted to be part of that ritual: fire, a circle of women, and an emphasis on both letting go and calling in. Before my abortion, I contemplated requesting that my son's remains, however minuscule they may have been, be cremated. But, since abortion is so taboo, I felt ashamed asking for that and didn't know how my request would be received. Plus, I wanted to make the whole thing as easy on myself as possible, and going through the steps for him to be cremated may have brought an extra challenge and complication that I didn't feel up for at the time. So, instead of doing that, I vowed to myself (and to him) that, when I was ready, I'd do a ritual—one after which I could have his ashes, in some form.

After taking a few sips of our tea, we walked back outside. While Sadie darted around the yard, chasing squirrels and sniffing along the fence, Christiane led me to the main thing I'd come to see: her kiva. There was a wide, circular hole in the ground with a few earthen steps that led us down. There, in the center of the kiva, was a pile of ash and a circle of stones where at night the fire would often burn.

"We can fit several people in here," Christiane shared. "How many are you thinking of inviting?"

I paused, silently counting the women on my fingers. "Four or five," I answered, "plus you and me. So about six or seven."

"That'll work." Christiane nodded.

Before parting ways, we sorted out a few more details: Christiane would lead the ritual, opening it by calling in the elements and sharing a prayer. We'd meet the following Friday evening at 8:30 to spend the evening in the darkness, by the fire and under the waxing half moon. To prepare, over the coming week, I would gather supplies for my ritual. My therapist recommended that I consider all of the senses. Did I want any music, singing, or other sounds? Did I want to speak about anything, or invite anyone else to? Did I want any smells present, like incense, flowers, cedar, or sage? Or things to taste, like food or drink? She reminded me that there's no right or wrong way to do a ritual. What mattered was that I listened into what felt true for me and gave myself permission to create the experience accordingly.

When I arrived at Christiane's house on the night of the ritual, it was dusk. I carried a wide basket under my right elbow filled with supplies. White roses for my son. Fuchsia geraniums for the new child I wanted to call in. Tequila for more deeply releasing Jonathan, and a rose potion one of my friends, an herbalist, had made, for calling in sweetness and a new beginning.

Christiane greeted me, and the two of us took our seats in the kiva. I felt nervous and a little awkward; I'd never done anything quite like this before. I acknowledged that all I needed to do was to keep doing what felt true and right, and that both Christiane and the other women present would also be guiding and informing the process.

Once the other women had arrived and taken their seats around the fire, Christiane looked at me to see if we were ready to begin. I nodded "yes," and she asked us all to come into silence. We closed our eyes. Christiane cued us to take some full, deep breaths, to really feel our bodies, our seats on the earth, the warmth of the fire, and the coolness of the evening air. My nervousness started to settle as I felt Christiane's comfort, mastery even, with ritual like this. She invoked the four directions—north, south, east, and west—creating an invisible field that would hold us over the next couple of hours.

When Christiane completed her opening invocation, she looked at me, a silent invitation for me to step in. As she continued to stoke and tend the fire, I welcomed all the women there, thanking them for their presence and contribution, and reminded them of my intentions for the ritual: to release both my past and my son more fully and to invite in a fresh start—and one day, I hoped, a new child. I reminded everyone that the ritual was for them, too. They were welcome to release their grief, and anything else that felt right for them, into the fire.

"Our ritual will follow this arc," I explained, "moving from letting go to calling in." Then, I passed the bouquet of white roses I'd brought around the circle, inviting each woman to take one and to offer it to the fire when and as she felt called. I began by tearing off the silky, ivory petals and slowly releasing them into the dancing orange flames. As I did, we all breathed in the smell of smoke and listened to the pop-pop of the fire as it consumed the petals. As the evening progressed, each woman shared a blessing and a reflection for me, along with an acknowledgment of something she wanted to release and honor. A couple of women in the circle had lost babies themselves, and they invited those souls to be there with us, too.

Gradually, we offered most of what I'd brought in my basket into the fire, which Christiane had stopped tending. The flames were much smaller, and the remaining wood glowed bright orange. When she sensed our completion, Christiane looked at me for a nod of confirmation that it was time to close. Sitting once again in silence for a moment, we honored the experience we'd had, thanked the fire, the kiva, and the four directions for holding us, and then shifted back into ordinary relating.

By the time we put out the fire and I drove home, my basket nearly empty, I felt lighter. I'd been able to express a deep inner process externally. And, since the clinical setting of my abortion didn't allow for a fulfilling goodbye ritual for my son, I felt I was finally able to honor him. Given my tendency is to do things, even rituals, on my own, it felt good to have my process held and witnessed by community.

Create Your Own Ritual

There's no right or wrong way to do a ritual (unless you're given a specific ritual to follow by a spiritual guide or from a beloved tradition, in which case it's important to follow that to the letter). But in cases where you're making your own, invite in your creativity.

1. What is the intention for your ritual? (Are you wanting to let go of a particular person, place, identity, season of life, or situation? Are you wanting to call something in? Are you longing for more support—from invisible forces and/or community?)

2. What is your desired outcome for the ritual? (For example, to feel a greater sense of closure or relate, to be witnessed in your process, to let go of something or someone more fully.)

3. What feels like the right setting for your ritual?

4. Will you do it alone or invite others? If you'd like others to be involved, who will you invite, and why do you want them there? Are there certain roles that you want them to play? Do you want to invite someone to guide this for you?

5. What day and time will the ritual be? (Will you choose a certain date, like a full or new moon, equinox, solstice, special date like a birthday or anniversary?)

6. Will any elements be involved? (Sitting around or putting things in a fire, washing something or releasing it into water, blowing something into the wind, burying something?)

7. Consider objects you want to include. (Smells, like incense? Tastes, like certain foods or drinks? Sounds, like music, words, singing? Things you want to write down or create? Special objects you want to incorporate?)

8. How will you open and close the ritual? Will you do this, or will you invite someone else to?

9. Is there anything else that feels important for you to include?

If you still feel unsure about what kind of ritual you want to create, the one that I shared with my student, Michelle, may spark some ideas for you.

Michelle's Story: A Solo Ritual for Saying Goodbye to Someone You Love

For over a decade, I've led a couple of retreats a year at a Buddhist retreat center in the mountains of Colorado. Originally founded by the Tibetan Buddhist luminary Chögyam Trungpa Rinpoche, the center is built upon land that many feel is auspicious. The land holds an inherent power that led Rinpoche to build his center there, power that has expanded over the years with so much practice, prayer, and ritual happening there on a regular basis.

On the first day of a weeklong retreat at the center one May, one of my students, Michelle, approached me during a break. In our opening circle the previous night, forty of us sat in the main practice hall on square, navy blue meditation cushions arranged in a large circle. The lights were dim and candles flickered on the altar. Each woman took a couple of minutes to introduce herself and share where she was joining us from and what her intention was for the retreat, along with whatever else she felt was important for us to know about her and her life. When it was Michelle's turn to share, she took hold of the talking stick—a thick wooden wand, used to strike the Tibetan singing bowl—and immediately hunched forward, cupping her face in her hands to catch the sudden river of tears. When she felt ready to speak, she shared that she was experiencing a lot of grief. She and her husband of eighteen years were recently separated and in the midst of a divorce. He was the one who had instigated it, and she was having a hard time coming to terms with her new reality.

"I feel like if COVID hadn't happened," she shared, "that we'd still be married. But when we needed to stay at home, just the two of us and our teenage son for many months on end, that showed us so clearly where all the disconnects were in our marriage."

Michelle inhaled deeply and continued, "I had thought that we could work through it. That's what we've always done, and that has always been the larger framework of our marriage. We stick things out. But he told me on Christmas morning this year that he wanted a divorce. I'm devastated and having a hard time accepting this."

She went on to share that her intention for joining the retreat was to have more space to herself, away from the logistics of parenting and working, to process this new reality. And, when she approached me during a break, she asked if there was anything additional she could do to help fulfill that intention.

"Have you done a letting-go ritual yet, around your husband, your marriage, your identity, and your life as you've known them for the past two decades?" I asked her.

Michelle shook her head "no," then added, "But ritual is usually a big part of my life. I do a lot of rituals around the lunar cycles."

"Good," I responded. "Then you might find it helpful to do something similar here, with a different intention. Your intention for this ritual could be similar to the one you have for this retreat—to more deeply let go of your husband and the life you shared together."

I offered her a ritual one of my teachers had shared with me some years earlier, which I had done on that very land to help me let go of Matt.

It included taking a large piece of paper and dividing it into four quadrants. In the top left quadrant, Michelle was to write down all the things that she enjoyed about her time with her husband. In the top right quadrant, she'd list all of her spiritual "ah-hah's" from the relationship, or the ways she'd grown from it, while seeing everything in a positive light. In the lower left quadrant, she'd acknowledge all of her own limits in their relationship and in the ways she'd shown up. And, in the lower right quadrant, she'd write down all the things she cultivated with her husband that she wouldn't and shouldn't trade for the world.

I instructed her to fill out as much of this chart as she could all at once, and then to keep it in a corner for three days, during which she could add more to it if needed. Then, she was to wait another three days, asking herself at that time whether or not it felt complete. Once it felt complete, she was to go somewhere in nature, pour dirt on the center of the chart, and then either bury or burn it. As she did that, she was to visualize her husband, telling him, "I set you free." Her intention would be to set him free of all of his greatest limitations and into his true nature.

Following the afternoon session on our final full day, Michelle completed the ritual at the end of a walk on the land. During our closing circle the following morning, she shared that while she still had a long road in front of her, she felt like the past week had helped her to step into a new phase in her healing process. Before the retreat she had been unable to loosen her grip on her anger and denial about what was happening, but being in a new environment, doing practices each day that supported her wellbeing, and conducting a letting-go ritual catapulted her out of the stuck place she'd been in. She left feeling like she was ready to take the next steps toward her new life, however painful and uncertain they still felt.

The Art & Discipline of Ritual

Ritual can be incredibly simple. It's intuitive, and it connects us to an earlier way of living. Our current cultural model of healing, which emphasizes the individual, is relatively new, for our ancestors knew the necessity of healing in community. Rituals, healing circles, and community gatherings used to be a regular part of life. The more we can weave these ancient traditions into our modern-day healing journeys, the more whole and intact we're going to feel.

You may hold some wounding around religious rituals you've experienced in your life, things like first communion, confirmation, a bar or bat mitzvah, or something else. The rituals we're speaking of here can be inclusive, secular, and without dogma. You can be your own best guide and authority.

To that end, there are several elements of ritual etiquette to consider:

1. Establish your intention.

As in designing the elements of the ritual itself, keeping your larger "why" in mind is helpful for informing both the way you prepare for and how you enact it.

2. Consider your etiquette.

If your ritual involves connecting with the unseen world, be polite, just as you are with those in your material reality. Remember that you are creating a sacred space and time for those from the spirit world to meet you. If you're inviting in elements of nature, acknowledge them as living beings. Prepare that space and moment just as you would prepare your home for a special dinner party or event.

3. Suspend disbelief.

Most of us have been raised to believe we have to "see it to believe it." We've lost trust in our sixth sense of intuition and of the imaginal realm of subtle energy. Ritual requires that we remember our relationship to both of these things. Since the effects of this process are at first invisible, it helps to suspend your disbelief and trust the process, even when you can't (and likely won't) see immediate, tangible results.

4. Invite in protection.

When you open up to the spirit realm, you open up to *all* sorts of spirits. Before you do, invite in a circle of protection around you. This can include your wise and well ancestors, healing guides, and anyone from the living world who would feel supportive to have with you.

5. Share an invocation.

At the start of the ritual, share your intention again and call in any help-ing spirits that may be needed to assist in fulfilling this intention. This could look like calling in the elements, the four directions, nature beings of the land you're on, specific ancestors, the soul of the person you're doing the ritual for, or other helpers.

6. Include prayer.

During the ritual, create time and space for prayer. You've set the stage for deep, divine communication and participation to take place, and prayer will be the channel through which that can happen most effectively. This prayer doesn't need to be religious in nature; it's simply a matter of speaking from your heart to your Higher Power. Let those forces do for and with you that which you cannot do on your own. The more sincere and thorough you are here, the more effective your ritual will be.

7. Make offerings.

Just like we humans appreciate gifts and generosity, those in the spirit realm value the same, through the form of offerings. This could be burn-ing or burying something, placing an item in water or letting it go into the wind, or something else. Again, listen to your intuition and see what feels right.

8. Say thank you.

When your ritual is complete, offer thanks and gratitude for the support and assistance you received, both from humans and the other-than-humans. Intentionally close the ritual space, just as you consciously opened it, before returning to your ordinary life.

9. Be patient.

Rituals work according to their own, mysterious timing. You may notice shifts immediately, or you may not. Trust that the power of the ritual will unfold, over the days, weeks—and even months and years—to come.

Rituals like these can help us acclimate to large, sweeping changes. Microrituals, which we can do each day, can be supportive during our heartbreak journeys as well.

Microrituals to Hold Us Through Transitions

One of the most disorienting things about transition is that our daily routines get decimated. Even our eating and sleeping rhythms are thrown off. This further exacerbates our feelings of disorientation. While we don't want to force a new structure into our lives before we're ready for it, we can start to incorporate small rituals throughout our days to help gradually bring back a sense of order and cohesion.

Here are some examples of what daily microrituals could be.

- Doing a "4 Gs" practice in your journal before you go to sleep at night:
    1. Write down all the things you're grateful for from the day.
    2. Write down all the things you did "good" that day.
    3. Write down all the "glitches" from that day—things that didn't go so well.
    4. Write down your goals for the next day.
    5. I like to add a "J" to this as well: write down all the things that brought you joy today.

- Lying down on your couch to meditate, rather than sitting, if you feel like you need more nurturing.

- Making a special breakfast for yourself on Sunday morning (or a special meal one evening each week).

- Scheduling an outing with a friend at least once a week, even if it's just to go for a walk.

- Taking a hot bath in the evenings.

- Going to the gym, or to a certain exercise class, at an interval that feels right for you, to help you get out of the house.

- Setting up a check-in with a friend or family member once a day, or at certain intervals during the week.

- Decluttering your home once a month, or at certain designated times. Take items from your old life to Goodwill or a consignment shop. Gradually shift your belongings and living space to reflect your new reality, as you feel ready to do so.

- Going on a weekly outing on your own, just for pure pleasure. Maybe it's going to a museum, journaling or reading in a cafe, eating at a restaurant you've been wanting to try, going for a walk in a new area, or something else.

In terms of larger, daily rituals, making it your number-one priority to sleep (or simply rest when you can't sleep), eat well, drink water, and move your body can make a huge difference. Staying connected to our life force during these times of huge upheaval creates a lifeline, for our life force is the part of us that will carry us through. It knows how to navigate messy transitions, and it holds the deep, internal guidance for where we're headed next. So, establishing rituals to nurture your life force in simple ways will be one of the main supports helping you get to the other side of all this.

As you can see, ritual comes in many different shapes and sizes. Above all, it creates the possibility of transformation, helping you to shift from your devastation to your rebirth, your old life to your new one.

Journaling Prompts

The concept of ritual may be familiar for some and foreign to others. Wherever you fall on that spectrum, taking some time to free-write about this topic can help you find a way to integrate ritual into your life, belief system, and heartbreak.

Past

- What has been your relationship with ritual up until this point in your life?

- Have you ever done a ritual of your own before, or attended one for another? (This could include weddings, funerals, and baby showers.)

Present

- Are there parts of you who don't believe in the power and efficacy of ritual? If so, learn more from these parts about their beliefs and why they feel this way.

- What kind of ritual do you feel drawn to doing? Why?

Future

- When you think about doing your own ritual, are there any inner and/or outer obstacles that you encounter?

- How will you work with those obstacles?

- What are your nonnegotiable daily rituals for nurturing your life force? How can you prioritize those even more?

Part III

REBIRTH

REBIRTH

Heartbreak Story:
Career & Finances

Santa Barbara, CA; January 2019

As I set my flip-flops down on a rock, my toes slipped into the silky beige sand. Sadie rushed past me, her floppy ears blowing backward in the wind. I'd made it. I'd finally made it. Here was the beach that I'd envisioned walking on for the past couple of years. In the distance, jagged cliffs housed fuchsia bougainvillea and palm trees at their height and a carpet of sand at their base.

It was an early January evening in Santa Barbara. The tangerine circle of the sun was just about to dip below the horizon. Sadie and I continued to walk the beach, about a thirty minute stretch in each direction that we would come to know very well in the year ahead. I drew in a deep breath and could taste the sea salt, the crisp California winter breeze, the warmth of the setting sun. The taste of arrival, and of survival.

I'd made it. Barely, perhaps, but I'd arrived nonetheless. Sure, I thought I'd arrive with a newly burrowed embryo in my womb, or at least one waiting for me, on ice, for when I'd be ready for it a few months down the line. My first walk on Hendry's Beach was not as triumphant as I'd imagined during all my early morning visualizations. But, still, I'd finally made it. I'd packed everything up, said goodbye to my life in Colorado, given everything I had to trying to have a child, and decided to take the leap to create a new life for myself in Santa Barbara. I'd always wanted to live at the beach. I'd always wanted to live in California. I'd always wanted to live *here*. A feeling of victory pulsed through me, brightening my chest, lifting me up and out of the depression I'd been under for the past many months while living in Chicago.

Sure, it wasn't the new beginning I'd wanted it to be. But it was still a new beginning. Still a chance to start over in an incredible place, a place where no one knew me and I could be anyone. I could create anything. I could start over. Yes, the circumstances that led me here were horrible, but maybe now that I was here, what awaited me would be better than I could have ever imagined.

Then, as I walked on the beach, a voice darted up from deep inside me, asking, *Yeah, but how are you going to make this work? Where's the money going to come from?*

Panic started to spill across my chest, up my neck, and into my head. My deep breaths became shallow, and my gait quickened. As those familiar feelings took me over once more, I was reminded that panic, fear, and anxiety are close companions of loss and heartbreak.

I don't know yet. I don't know yet where the money's going to come from, another voice inside retorted.

It was true. I didn't know where the money was going to come from. I'd just spent all my savings on IVF. Not one round, but two. It all ended up costing much more than I thought it would. Every syringe. Every ultrasound. Every extra visit to the doctor. Every little thing cost much more than I thought it would, or even could.

And, through it all, money stopped coming in through my work. It's like the world could tell, without me telling it, that I was overwhelmed, dog-paddling with all my might to keep myself afloat. I didn't want that to be true. I wanted to feel like I still had it together. I wanted people to *think* I still had it together, but I didn't, and they didn't. And the money kept going out and out and out, without coming in.

I know, in a lot of ways it was stupid of me to come out here, I told the snarky voice, letting it know I wasn't a complete idiot.

This was one of the most expensive places in this country, heck, the world. And moving's super expensive. But what other choice did I have? Stay there, in Chicago, in my mom's spare room, with a tiny window that looked out on a brick wall, to get swallowed up in the gray, bleak Chicago winter?

You heard it loud and clear, I said to the snarky voice. *That morning after I learned the first round of IVF didn't work, when I was waking up and looking out at another dreary Chicago November morning, the voice that told me I would die if I didn't leave there in December. That, even if it was crazy to move to Santa Barbara, I had to come to save myself.*

You need to be realistic, the snarky voice cut in. *You've gotten yourself out of financial jams in the past, but this time you're in too deep. You have the business loan you're paying back. The IRS stuff from the accountant who screwed you over. The credit card debt you've accrued to cover the IVF and to fill the gap for the money that's not coming in. Payroll you need to make. Not to mention covering your usual expenses—business and personal. And now you have to find a place to live and pay for your POD to get shipped out here? It's not adding up. You're in way over your head. Like I've said, you've gotten out of this in the past, but this time it's different.*

My solar plexus pulled into a tight ball, moving my breath higher up, into my throat. My vision narrowed, the vast sea and sand becoming a tunnel of inner haze I trudged through forcefully, hurrying to find my way back to my flip-flops, back to my car.

Screw this, I thought. *I'm not going to let my inaugural walk on the beach end with a near panic attack. I'll figure it out. I always do.*

So, after picking up my flip-flops, rather than stepping over the rocks to make my way back up to the parking lot, I sat down on one of them. Around me were clusters of beach chairs filled with smiling bodies sipping beer from cans. Some people came, wrapped in blankets, to sit on the benches at the end of the parking lot. Others, like me, perched on rocks. Our bodies, and our eyes, leaned toward the western side of the water's edge to where the sun was just about to disappear for the day. To where sprays of lavender, petal pink, and orange spread amongst the clouds.

I can't believe I'm here, I thought. *I can't believe I get to do this every day if I want to.*

Yeah, but . . . the contrarian voice rebutted. *You may need to . . .*

Shhh! I cut in. *Not right now. Let's just be here, enjoying this moment.*

Even though I didn't hear the rest of what that voice was going to say, I'd heard it before. I'd been trying to push the thought out of my mind, to not let it come into being by giving attention to it. But I was past that point. I knew things had gone so far, financially, that it was highly unlikely I'd be able to turn them around without drastic measures.

So while I watched the sunset, like all the others around me who seemed to be living very normal, functional, enjoyable lives, my stomach was gripped with fear. I knew that voice was right. I knew it was time to listen to it. I'd made it. I gotten there. And now I needed to let that voice in and address its concerns.

When I got back to my temporary home, a room I rented on the top floor of a large house in Ojai, I got into bed, propped myself up against the headboard with a couple of pillows and opened my laptop. Then I did it. What the voice had been telling me I needed to do.

Well, I guess it doesn't hurt to at least look, I thought.

So, I Googled "bankruptcy lawyer Santa Barbara."

Seeing those four words, black type against white screen, brought back that punched-in-the-gut feeling—but it didn't feel as scary as I thought it would.

I scrolled through the Google search, clicking on the Yelp page for "Top 10 Bankruptcy Lawyers in Santa Barbara."

So far so good, I reassured myself.

My cursor hovered over the first entry, acknowledging that he shared the first name of both my sister and late grandfather.

Click.

As I scrolled through his description and eyed his picture, he seemed kind, honest. Then I read his reviews: "He was a life saver. He even helped us build up our credit again afterwards to the point where we were able to buy our first home a few years later!"

My belly started to settle. My lower back relaxed more into the pillows behind me. I let my head rest against the headboard.

It won't hurt to just email him, the voice inside said. *It doesn't mean you need to work with him. But maybe just go meet with him. Then at least you'll know what your options are.*

I clicked on his website, entered my name and email into the contact form, and hit "send."

Then, as if I wanted to forget about it, to pretend that what had just happened wasn't really happening, I flipped my laptop closed and shifted my gaze from the screen to the darkness beyond the window in front of me.

Santa Barbara, California; April 2019

I envied my former self. The Sara who got book deals, enrolled hundreds of women in her courses, hired a team, and filled her days doing what she loved while getting paid well for it. I missed the days when my work was *working*. The days when money flowed in, when, even in slower times, there would always be big paydays around the corner. I missed the Sara who had full autonomy and control over her schedule.

Over the past couple of months, since getting clear that I needed to file for bankruptcy and setting the process in motion (even though the full discharge wouldn't be complete until that December), I also got clear on the direction in which life was trying to move me. It was presenting one obstacle after another, not only in my personal life but also in my professional one. Gradually, over the past few years, what had once worked well was no longer working. And, in the process of trying to resuscitate it and make it work, I'd grown more and more exhausted, frustrated, and financially depleted.

While I'd invested the majority of my financial resources in my work over the past decade, I'd also poured my whole heart and soul into it. I was building my dream, following my deepest intuition of what I was born to do. Stepping away from it all felt like another one of my worst nightmares coming true, another heartbreak. I deeply loved my work, and I didn't know who I'd be without my career. I didn't know what I'd do, or if it was even possible for me to get a job. I'd been self-employed for twenty years, my entire adult life. Plus, I'd recently moved to a new town in a new state, where the job market was much more limited than it was in Colorado. For weeks, I procrastinated. I knew I needed to start applying for jobs, and the thought of it all terrified me—and filled me with shame.

Family members and friends coached me through setting up my LinkedIn profile and crafting compelling resumes and cover letters.

I challenged myself to apply to at least one job a day. Taking steady action was helping to minimize my fear. Since I needed to find something immediately, I applied to anything I came across that seemed remotely interesting (or even just tolerable). Some jobs paid a fraction of what I was used to making, so I was going to need to figure out how to live on much less in a town with an extremely high cost of living. Above all, I needed a steady paycheck to help me get back on my feet as I stepped back from supporting others so I could focus on taking care of myself.

In early March, I moved into my new home in Santa Barbara. It had taken me almost three months of intensive house hunting to find, and I'd had to charge the first month's rent to a credit card to afford it. A few days later, I got invited to interview for a job I'd applied for a couple of weeks back. Of the dozens and dozens of jobs I'd applied to, it was the one that felt the most exciting: a leadership position at an organization whose mission I felt deeply aligned with. The office was a short drive from my new home, and they wanted me to come in for an interview at the end of the week.

That Friday morning, I woke up in my new studio cottage, the morning light splashing off the sunny yellow walls and high ceilings. The long rectangular windows at the far end of the room opened out to my private patio, where lavender wisteria wove itself over the iron fence and breathed its perfume inside. As I got out of bed and let Sadie outside, the sound of my neighbor's dog barking and a whirring leaf blower greeted me—sounds that, I soon learned, would be relatively constant in my new hometown. Waiting for the kettle to boil, I brushed my teeth, then my hair, gazing back at my exhausted self in the mirror.

I envied my friends who had partners or husbands to support them financially. Even if they worked themselves, at least they had someone to fall back on during hard times. While I did have the option of staying at my mom's house, that didn't feel aligned with the future I wanted for myself. Still, I wished I too had something to lean into for more financial support so I could, at the very least, catch my breath and get some rest. Yet I knew that stopping wasn't an option. I needed money.

I needed a job. I needed to get dressed and out the door for my interview by nine. I needed to keep going.

Arriving at the interview site, my heart sank. The office was on the bottom floor of a nondescript building in downtown Santa Barbara. During my interview, which lasted ninety minutes, I sat with my soon-to-be boss, the founder of the organization, Claire. She sat across from me while I perched on the couch. I smiled through my exhaustion and the churning in my belly while she asked me why I was stepping away from my own business.

"I'm ready for a change," I told her, "and I want to be part of something bigger," which was true. She wondered how I worked with challenges when they arose, and how I structured my time and my projects.

At the end of our conversation, one that felt resonant and connected, Claire said she needed to step into the other room briefly. She stood up and closed the door behind her, leaving me alone. I sat on the couch, twisting a tissue into spirals, listening to car doors opening and closing in the parking lot outside. Several minutes later, she walked back in, sat down, smiled, and said, "I'd love to offer you the job. When can you start?"

Despite my reluctance to show up at an office and work a nine-to-five job with a boss and limited time off after so many years of setting my own objectives, schedule, and location, relief zinged through me. *I've done it! I've really done it!* a voice inside exclaimed, trying to take in the reality that I'd actually gotten a job. Not just any job, but a job that would be interesting to me. A job where I'd make pretty decent money. A job where I could make a difference in the world. A job that would make it possible to stay in Santa Barbara and live within my means, with some left over to save each month. A job where I would have high-quality health insurance. The first *real* job I'd ever had. We decided I'd start the following Monday, about ten days away, to give me enough time to get unpacked and settled into my new home.

We said goodbye and I made my way back to my car. The late morning sun had warmed the tan seats and dashboard. My hands shook with the exhilaration of the news as I called my mom. Because I felt so much shame about my bankruptcy, she was the only person in my life who knew. Through excited breaths I told her the news. "I got the job!" I exclaimed when she answered. "It's a miracle, Mom," I added. "It truly is a miracle!"

Driving home, even though I felt like life had tossed me a life preserver, I ached. Yes, I had a job, but it wasn't what I ultimately wanted. We don't normally allow ourselves to acknowledge the grief and heartbreak that can come with financial challenges and the loss of careers and jobs, yet, beneath the surface, I felt my heart breaking. Another one of the biggest dreams for my life—sharing my soul's gifts with the world through a business I'd poured most of myself and my resources into for the past twenty years—had been destroyed.

Chapter 9

Finding Forgiveness

"It's one of the greatest gifts you can give
yourself, to forgive. Forgive everybody."

— Maya Angelou

As we move from the fires of transformation to the more solid ground of rebirth, what will determine whether or not we can move forward is the degree to which we've forgiven—others, ourselves, and life itself. Most of us misunderstand what forgiveness is. We think it's something that will, at some unknown point in the future, strike us like a benevolent bolt of lightning, instantly absolving us of all our poisonous resentments. When we hold that misguided view, forgiveness continues to evade us and we stay stuck in our misgivings.

Forgiveness isn't a one-and-done event that either does or does not happen. Rather, it's a process we all must engage in over an extended period of time. This is the only way we can move forward and enjoy our new lives. If you don't know how to do this, that's okay. I'll show you that it's possible for all of us, no matter how atrocious the hurts we've suffered. Forgiveness, when we truly understand how it works and why it matters, can be a gift we not only give but also receive. I learned this through an experience I had in California about a month before I realized I needed to file for bankruptcy.

Santa Monica, California; March 18, 2019

I walked into Jason's backyard, a familiar urban oasis. I'd been there a few times before over the past several years. The first time I met him was back in 2011, when Matt and I visited LA for a work event and he picked us up at the airport. One of my good friends who was overseas for a stretch had left her car at Jason's home in the LA suburbs and said we could use it while we were there. Jason very generously offered to pick us up at the airport to deliver us to her car.

As he escorted us back to his house, he shared with us—once he got a read that we were all on relatively the same wavelength—that he was an urban shaman of sorts. A former Silicon Valley tech guy, he now considered his career to be supporting others to return to their deepest hearts. One of the ways he did this was by growing mushrooms, making his own DMT, securing the highest quality MDMA and LSD, and holding space for others to experience their truths, with his support and the help of these substances.

Sitting in the front seat of his car, I caught Matt's eyes in the rearview mirror as we both listened, intrigued, to Jason's reveal. A voice inside me said: *You're going to do a journey with him when you get to his house.* My rational mind protested that we had to get on the road. The friends we were staying with were expecting us for dinner. I was there for a work event and needed to have a clear head and full presence. Yet, that voice persisted: *Say what you want. You're going to do a journey with him.*

When we got to Jason's house, he led us into his kitchen, offered us some water, handed us the keys to our car for the week, and said, "I don't usually make an offer like this when I first meet someone, but I feel compelled to let you know that you're welcome to do a journey if you want to. I make my own DMT—it's like an ayahuasca journey, only it lasts fifteen minutes max. You'll feel totally fine afterward and it's a very powerful experience."

Queasiness spread through my chest and throat and my palms moistened with sweat. I'd done about a dozen ayahuasca journeys with a Colombian shaman, mostly in my late twenties and early thirties, all of which were very beneficial yet quite intense. It had been a few years since my last one and I didn't feel interested in going down that road anymore, but I did feel intrigued about having the potency of that experience condensed into a quarter of an hour. So, as Jason showed Matt his mushroom collection, I excused myself into his backyard to be alone for some moments. I closed my eyes, felt my feet on the earth, and sensed the gentle presence of the tree in front of me. *You're supposed to do a journey with him*, the voice inside repeated. I followed the guidance of that voice, did the DMT journey, and had an incredibly expansive and healing experience.

Several years later, in March of 2019, a few months after I'd arrived in California, when I stood in that same spot in Jason's backyard I felt how much my life had changed since my first visit there eight years prior. At that time, I was riding high in life. Matt and I were still within the first several months of our relationship, the honeymoon phase. My first book had just come out, and it quickly became a bestseller in multiple places. All signs were pointing toward upward growth and momentum. Now, I was forty-one. I didn't know if I'd ever be able to write a book again, for my life had taken a complete 180 since then. I'd moved to Santa Barbara a few months earlier. My career felt like it was in shambles. Whereas all those years ago I felt sexy and alive, now I felt puffy, tired, and unattractive. *Oh! How naive I was!* I lamented inside. *I had no idea how good I had it!*

In the years since then, I'd returned to Jason's to do a couple of MDMA journeys with him as my guide. With the PTSD I was feeling post-IVF, I felt like I needed some support in shaking things loose and coming back to life. Standing in front of that same tree in Jason's garden, I looked out at the dry leaves that littered the patio and two empty chairs bathing in morning light. Sadie wandered over to the sliver of sun to settle into a pocket of warmth for a while. I heard Jason getting the space ready inside. Drawing the blinds, putting a "Do Not Disturb" sign on the door, laying a futon on his living room floor, making a temporary altar on his coffee table.

I intend to take significant steps in healing from my IVF. I intend to get clarity around what to do with my work. I intend to more fully land here in California. I intend to heal whatever layers are needed for me to feel more connected with myself, I noted internally. And, for good measure, I added the final piece of the intention that I always included: *I intend to heal what needs to be healed, see what needs to be seen, let go of what needs to be let go of, for the highest good of all concerned.*

Walking back inside, I took my place on the futon, my home for the next several hours. I swallowed my first dose, a small capsule filled with a fine white powder, washing it down with a shot of orange juice. Jason sat to my right and talked with me until, about forty-five minutes later, the medicine started kicking in.

"I'm starting to feel it," I told him, as the light in the room pixelated slightly and my sense of hearing intensified. "I think I need to get up and move around a bit."

Jason nodded as I threw the blue fleece blanket off my lap, stood up, and started to walk slowly around the room. I bent my knees, bringing a slight bounce to each step, to help move the intensifying, warm energy in my sacrum higher up my spine. After a few minutes, I was ready to sit down again. Remaining quiet, I started to turn my attention inside. I felt a prick, then a punch in my lower abdomen. Tears started pouring down my cheeks, my ovaries releasing the pain from my two egg retrievals. My body began to shake, discharging the invasion I'd felt from my IVF doctor, though I hadn't realized it at the time. I rapidly twisted my head and torso side to side, side to side, exhaling strongly through pursed lips. I felt Jason sitting quietly beside me, witnessing and holding all I was seeing and releasing. Rocking back and forth, my body processed how violated it felt by all the hormone injections, the ultrasound wands in my vagina, the foreign sperm in my womb. Then, I saw a larger, more pervasive darkness inside me.

"There are dark energies in my body. This isn't mine. None of this is mine," I moaned, clenching my fists and still shaking my spine.

"This is Matt's stuff, oh my God. None of this is even about me," I continued, whispering, "I'm willing to release this. I'm willing to release this. I'm willing to release all of this."

"I was so naive, I didn't know," I said after a few moments. "I didn't understand. I thought there was something wrong with me, since nothing was working. I felt like I had to get rid of this thing."

I shifted from sitting to lying down. Jason helped me to place a mask over my eyes, draw the blanket over my body, now moist with sweat, and slip some headphones over my ears. As sounds flowed down my ear canals and filled my being—flute, deep drums, soft, feminine voices—more inner guidance became unlocked, and the armor around my heart began to fade.

"My career is like a shoe that doesn't fit any more. There's nothing wrong with that. It just doesn't fit me, and it's too painful to live inside something that doesn't fit me anymore. Life will show me my next step. Everything is going to be okay. Everything is okay. This is all going to be worth it—it's all already worth it."

I continued breathing deeply, curling onto my right side in a fetal position.

"IVF was never meant to happen. It wasn't right. I'll know when or if it's right. I don't need to be afraid."

Jason stayed sitting beside me, his iPad in his lap, recording all of my words.

"There are so many good things about to happen. All I have to do is open my heart. That's all I need to do. Open my heart and know that I'm worthy to receive. Inhale it all the way in."

"I really loved Matt. We had a true love. That was real. Deeper than either one of us had ever experienced. I want him to be happy. Matt, I want you to be happy. I want to be free of our past. I have forgiven you. You are a powerful being and my wish for you is that you can use that power in the direction you most long for."

"Matt, I'm really grateful for parts of me that you helped me wake up. A truer version. I feel myself in a way I hadn't before. I will always value that and take it with me. Thank you for seeing that in me and for being willing to dance with it. We worked a lot of big shit out together. We agree on that."

"I forgive myself for all the ways I didn't show up fully for myself. For ways I settled for less because I thought that's what I deserved."

"Jonathan, you are such a wild man. You are too big for this world. You really are larger than life. That's why I fell so hard for you, one of the reasons. I give myself permission to be all that."

"All this time, life is trying to make love to me, dance with me. I've been wanting that too. I really want to be in love with life. It's okay. All of it's okay."

Later that evening, when the highs of the medicine began to wane but its residue remained, I felt like I'd finally arrived in California. It was as if I'd been hovering above the surface of my life over the past few months, just trying to survive. Sitting outside in Jason's garden as the sun set with Sadie at my feet, despite all that had happened, despite how much I'd been fantasizing about taking my own life, despite the fact that the medicine had instructed me to step away from the career that I'd so lovingly and painstakingly built, I knew it was all truly, deeply okay.

Before we continue on, I want to offer a gentle disclaimer first: While psychedelics can offer profound insights and healing, it is important to note that they have the potential to be dangerous when not used properly. Many of these substances are not only free of government regulation, but they also may be illegal in some areas. Therefore, I don't recommend trying this on your own. If doing a journey like this appeals to you, I strongly recommend seeking the guidance of a qualified professional, ideally someone who honors the indigenous roots of many of these practices. This may include a therapist or other healthcare provider who is trained in psychedelic-assisted therapy, or a shaman or spiritual guide who has extensive experience working with these substances.

Heidi's Story: Spontaneous Self-Forgiveness

"I've been having a really powerful experience this past week," Heidi shared when we met over Zoom for an IFS session. Tears started dripping down her cheeks. She wiped them away with her sweatshirt sleeve, and she added, "I've been needing to cry. This feels good."

Heidi and I had been working together regularly for just over two years, and during that time she'd undergone a huge transformation. She had come to me with a long history of sexual abuse beginning with her father when she was a little girl and continuing on occasion through her adult life, including at the hospital after the birth of her first child when she was under anesthesia. This left her in a constant state of PTSD. She was unable to create her life in the ways she wanted, like keeping her home and finances orderly or caring for her body with appropriate food, movement, and sleep. Since her father had sexually abused her in her bed in the middle of the night when she was young, she had trouble falling asleep. Being alone in the dark felt terrifying, and a recent divorce, which left her living on her own for the first time, was bringing up such strong feelings of depression and overwhelm that she struggled with suicidal ideation.

In our early sessions, while getting to know some of these parts—the part who wanted to die, the part who was afraid to go to sleep at night, and the part who was depressed—oftentimes other protective parts, like a foggy part or a sleepy part, would come in, preventing us from going to deeper layers. As we spent time getting to know each of these protective parts, they gradually relaxed, allowing us to connect with the young, exiled parts who were at the root of all those extreme behaviors and beliefs.

"I don't know how to explain it, Sara," Heidi shared, "but I just feel this sense of surrender inside. This sense of softness. I see how I've treated myself in the ways that those who abused me treated me, just because I didn't know any better. Just because that was how those parts were protecting me." She paused, her bottom lip quivering with emotion, and placed her right hand over her heart. "I feel like I'm finally forgiving *myself*. And, before, I didn't even know I needed to do that. I thought I had to forgive all these other people. I thought I had to forgive God for giving me all of these challenges, for giving me a life like this. But, somehow, I've gotten to a layer in myself where none of that even matters. None of that really even makes sense. It's all about me forgiving me. I forgive *me*. I forgive *myself*."

IFS teaches us that our Self is always innately whole and healed, regardless of what we've experienced in our lives, just as the sun is always here, even on a cloudy or stormy day. When we align with our own Self energy—as supports like IFS and MDMA help us to do—we eventually arrive in a similar place as Heidi. We realize that while we experience injustices at the level of relative reality, at the level of absolute reality, all is always well. The healing journey invites us to be aware of and live at this absolute level of reality first and foremost. From here, the balm of forgiveness can pervade us, softening our armor and healing our hurts.

The Process of Forgiveness

Before we talk about what forgiveness is, let's first get clear on what it is not. Forgiveness is not about forgoing boundaries; you can forgive someone even as you commit to never speaking to them again. It's not about letting another person off the hook for their wrongdoing. Forgiveness is not about feeling completely okay and openhearted about what you experienced. And it's not something that happens instantly and spontaneously. Rather, forgiveness is a process of recognizing the inherent goodness at the heart of all things and of letting go of one's inner opposition to what has happened. But, before we get into that process, let's take a step back to really understand why forgiveness is so crucial.

One of the practices that I added to my morning rituals early on in my heartbreak journey was to read a lesson from the *A Course in Miracles* workbook each morning. One of the key lessons in this book is that forgiveness is the key to happiness. Let's unpack that together. From the perspective of nondual spirituality, there's always only one of us here. The true nature of reality is that there are no separate selves, no individual you and me. We are all one being, one existence. Until our inner, spiritual eyes and heart open to this truth, our physical eyes will continue to see separate, physical bodies and continue to believe that is all that exists.

Yet, when we abide by this deeper truth of nonduality, we know that if I harm you through my words, actions, or thoughts, I'm also harming myself. When I love and support you, I'm also loving and supporting myself. In terms of forgiveness, if I'm sending ill will toward another, I'm sending ill will toward myself. And, when I do that, there's absolutely no way I can be happy.

This is how and why forgiveness is the key to happiness. First we need to resolve to experience happiness and to recognize that forgiving another, life itself, God, or ourselves is the key to that. We forgive first and foremost for our own benefit. We've likely all heard the saying that resentment is like drinking poison and expecting the other person to die. So, be clear that by forgiving whomever or whatever you need to forgive, you are making yourself stronger and more whole.

If you're struggling with self-forgiveness and don't believe you have the right to forgiveness or happiness, that's okay, too. From an IFS perspective, that means that there are protective parts of you present who don't believe you deserve to be forgiven or to be happy. If this is true for you, you can do the "Get to Know a Protective Part" exercise in chapter 4 as well as the following forgiveness practices, directing them toward yourself.

Another misconception about forgiveness is that you need to feel good about it. Not so. Forgiveness is a *practice*. Just like it's important that we brush our teeth, drink water, and go to the gym even when we feel resistance, it's important to do forgiveness practices even when we don't feel like it. It's the doing of it that allows things to shift and change. Even when you feel closed-hearted, rageful, resentful, and stuck, keep practicing forgiveness. As you do, know that this is not about bypassing your feelings. Remember all the terrain we've covered so far and the importance of honoring and validating whatever your current experience is. This is a "both-and" practice. Honor how you're feeling—and still do the forgiveness practice.

There will come a time when grace enters and the burden will be lifted. We need to consistently show up, putting the work in, and things will shift according to their own divine timing. You'll likely also notice that as forgiveness starts to flow, other things in your life begin to flow, too. When love, the divine force and fabric of the universe, is blocked in one place, that impacts its flow in other places.

The Practice of Forgiveness

This is a forgiveness practice that I created, inspired by Marianne Williamson's teachings on *A Course in Miracles*. Now that we've looked at the "what" and "why" of forgiveness, it's time to explore the "how."

Here are some simple steps you can take to deepen in your own forgiveness practice. As always, feel free to adapt this in any way that feels true and right for you. The most important thing is that you do it, and regularly. I invite you to try five minutes a day.

1. You can do this practice lying down, in a seated position, or even while you're doing other things (walking, taking a shower, cleaning your house).

2. Envision the person or situation that you want to forgive and see them (or yourself) in front of you. If that feels triggering for you, ask to see this person without their parts—to experience them in their essence.

3. Feel yourself drawing all of the love of existence into your heart—the love from the sun, the plants, the people in your life.

4. Next, extend that love to the person or situation in front of you, bathing them in Divine love.

5. You can stay with that, or, if you'd like, you can layer some phrases on top of this visualization. Some options: "I forgive you and I release you to the Holy Spirit" or "May you be blessed, happy, and loved."

6. Stay with this for up to five minutes.

7. If there are multiple people or things you need to forgive, start with one at a time, asking your inner guidance to show you who or what to start with.

8. Remember, it doesn't matter how you feel when you're doing this. Just keep showing up and doing the practice, and grace will take care of the rest.

Now that we have a clearer understanding of forgiveness and how to practice it, we're ready to move to the next stage of our journey: reestablishing trust (in ourselves, others, and life itself).

Journaling Prompts

Since the perspectives I've shared in this chapter about forgiveness may be new to you, let's take some time together now to really let them sink in and be applied to your unique circumstances. In addition to the prompts below, it can also be helpful (if you haven't already done this) to write letters to people you're holding grievances toward. You don't need to send the letters. You can bury or burn them if you want. But, as we've seen, writing can be a potent form of releasing things so we don't need to carry them inside of us anymore. In addition to writing letters, here are some journaling prompts to explore:

Past

- What has been your experience of forgiveness (either at the giving or receiving end) up until this point in your life?

- Whom or what do you need to forgive? What do you need to forgive within yourself?

Present

- Which elements of forgiveness that I've shared here stand out for you the most?

- Are there parts of you who feel resistant to the process of forgiveness?

- If so, can you give them some air time and hear what their reservations and concerns are?

Future

- Is there a particular time of day when doing the forgiveness practice would work best for you?

- Can you commit to trying the forgiveness practice with one person for the next thirty days?

Chapter 10

Restoring Trust

"'What is the secret of your serenity?' Said the Master,
'Wholehearted cooperation with the inevitable.'"

— Anthony de Mello

Reintegrating ourselves into the fabric of life after heartbreak requires more than forgiveness alone. Because heartbreak can leave us feeling a deep sense of betrayal—by our partners, life, God, and the friends and communities that couldn't handle our heartbreak and turned their backs to us when we needed their support the most—it can create a rift, a brokenness. We may have also lost trust in certain parts of ourselves. Thus we need to rekindle trust and faith not only in ourselves, but also in life.

As we start to feel more ready to take the first steps toward our new lives, we need to trust our instincts (especially if we've been gaslit in the past). We also need to be bold and courageous in reshaping our lives rather than playing it safe in order to avoid future hurts. During this stage of our journeys, it's essential that we befriend uncertainty, let go of control, and trust not only the process but also the larger plan for our lives. A few unexpected twists in my own life, starting in March 2020, forced me to do all of this in an even bigger way.

Santa Barbara, CA; March 6, 2020

Chimes rang from my phone, signaling my 7 am wake up. Shifting from the hazy space of dreamtime into the light of the morning, a part of me sighed in relief. Friday. I didn't have to go into the office on Fridays.

I glanced at my reflection in the computer screen on my desk, across from my bed, and tried not to look too long into my own eyes. They held pain. Pain from hating my job. From breaking up a couple of months ago with a man whom I had dated briefly and fallen pretty hard for. Pain from still feeling incredibly lonely and like I was going backward, not forward, in my healing process, which was now stretching into year number five. I was continuing to wonder if I was cursed and my life was going to be one long, winding, dark tunnel of despair.

I had a couple of hours ahead of me before meeting with Claire. She'd requested a 9 am meeting to go over the organization's budget. Just the thought of sitting through another meeting with her tightened my intestines. Over the past few months, our relationship had become increasingly strained. I was growing more and more unhappy and frustrated in my position, and some disturbing, long-standing dynamics in the organization were becoming more apparent to me. At a couple of recent meetings Claire had snapped at me, leaving me feeling increasingly unhappy, unseen, unheard, and alone. To help with this, during my free time, I'd been applying for other jobs. A plan was beginning to crystallize: I'd get a new job to serve as a bridge until I could build up my own work again to the point where it could sustain me. In the meantime, I felt trapped. *I have to get out of this job. I have to get out of this job,* I said to myself on repeat.

When I sat down at my desk and logged into Zoom for the meeting with Claire, she wasn't there. Two minutes passed, then three. She still wasn't there. As I stared at the white box on my screen that said, "Waiting for host to start the meeting," the clenching in my intestines intensified. My heart raced faster. Picking up my work phone to text Claire, I saw a text from her had already come in:

"Where are you? We're at the office waiting for you," she wrote.

Fuck, I yelled into the silent space around me.

"I thought we were meeting on Zoom," I quickly texted back, my hand shaking.

My mind raced back over the details of scheduling the meeting. *I always work from home on Fridays, and she knows that. I put the Zoom link in the calendar when we scheduled the meeting. She never told me we were meeting in the office. I would have remembered if she'd said she wanted to meet in the office. First, because that would mean I wouldn't get to work from home that day, which would have been a bummer. And second, because that would have seemed strange.*

"Give me a minute, I'll log onto Zoom," Claire texted back.

Feeling like a little girl about to get in trouble by a parent—*again*—I sat at my computer, waiting for her to join the meeting.

A few minutes later, Claire appeared. Stress hormones ricocheted through me, as if my entire body was a pinball machine that wouldn't stop firing. Her face was stern.

"I'm sorry," I shared. "I thought we were meeting over Zoom."

She stayed silent for what felt like too long, and then she revealed what our meeting was really about.

"I've been looking over our numbers since the year-end campaign," she began, "and I'm realizing we need to streamline and make some budget cuts. I need to let you go. Your last day is next Friday, and I'll offer you two weeks' severance. You can work from home next week and meet me in the office next Friday afternoon to return your computer, phone, keys, and sign your final paperwork. I've enjoyed meeting you and wish you all the best."

My mind went blank, like an old TV screen that fuzzes out unexpectedly when the signal cuts out. Over the past few months, I had remarked to some friends (mostly jokingly) that I needed to reign myself in from quitting on the spot because I'd rather wait to be fired so I could receive unemployment. But I didn't think it would actually come to that. I was stunned.

"You can take the rest of the day off," Claire added.

When we both left the Zoom meeting and my computer screen went dark again, my body started to numb. Thoughts raced: *This is so humiliating. How am I going to share this with people? How am I going to pay my bills until I find a new job? Is this really happening? Did I really just lose my job?*

The wise part within me interjected, adding its perspective on top of the rush of anxiety and shame: *You know by now that if this is happening, it's what's meant to be happening. There's no use arguing with reality. Somehow, in some way, you will get through this, and it will be okay.*

Julie's Story: Heal Your Mistrust in Life After Devastation

In early December of 2017, Julie stood outside her home, which overlooked the Ojai Valley and was nestled up against the Topatopa Mountains. Orchards and clusters of small homes filled the view in front of her. Behind her, the presence of the triangle-shaped mountains stood firm and assuring. Yet, farther in the distance, the first flames of the Thomas Fire were beginning to burn. Then, luckily, the fire moved away from her. *Phew, I'm okay,* she thought.

Julie had put a lot of love into her home. She'd designed and built it from the ground up, using the inheritance she'd received when her grandfather died about ten years earlier. Every corner held something special: a painting she bought in Nepal, seashells she'd picked up on the beach in Costa Rica, dishes from Italy. She had once shared her home with her former husband, but since their divorce she lived there alone. To invite a feeling of more connection and warmth into her home, she'd adopted a crew of three rescue dogs. You could often find them curled up at the far end of a couch, sprawled out on the deck in the sun, or roaming through the vast yard in search of an interesting scent.

As Julie stepped inside to cook dinner, she got another text message from the local emergency services. A second fire had started. This one was not far from her house. The Santa Ana winds were also starting to pick up, moving directly toward her part of town at sixty miles per hour. Her heart started to beat faster as she rushed around her house, throwing a few of her most valuable items into her bag before fleeing her house, her car packed with a single suitcase and two of her dogs. Sadly, she couldn't find her third dog, and she risked losing her other dogs and possibly her own life if she spent more time looking for him. Within a matter of hours, her entire home and everything inside it had burned to the ground.

In the days and weeks following, Julie went into "get shit done at all costs" mode. She needed to secure some basic essentials—new clothes, a temporary place to live, paperwork from her insurance agency to begin the process of building a new home. She bonded with neighbors and the larger community of Ojai to help get the town back on its feet. Having tangible, tactical things she had to do each day helped give her life some structure. Then, at the end of the day, she'd give herself time to feel her feelings. Turning on some music, closing her eyes, and letting her body move in whatever ways it needed or wanted to—sometimes making sounds, sometimes through tears, sometimes with silence—helped her as she began to process the different layers of grief, anger, and sadness that were overtaking her.

About a month after the fire, once the shock and acute stages of grief had passed, a huge sense of feeling betrayed by life started to overtake Julie. *What kind of a god burns your entire home to the ground and leaves you with nothing?* she lamented. *What did I do to deserve this? Why is this happening to me? I was just getting back on my feet after the divorce, and now this?!* It was at that time that Julie and I began working together. She was having a hard time moving forward to build a new life since she feared that would be taken from her, too.

When Julie voiced these fears, I encouraged her to continue with the daily practice of moving and giving sound to her feelings, an evening ritual that had become a new lifeline for her. It's important not to make any of these feelings or parts of you wrong, I told her. I encouraged her to resuscitate her prayer practice, one she'd had as a little girl but had abandoned later in life after she felt duped by her childhood religion of Catholicism.

"If you need to call it something other than prayer," I encouraged her, "do that. You could call it divine communication, a conversation with your heart or your highest self, or a connection with the universe. It doesn't really matter what you call it. But you need to open that channel of communication between you and your Higher Power.

That will help you to move forward and navigate during times of fear and not-knowing."

With some resistance, Julie revived her prayer practice. After meditating each morning, she'd sit with her journal and a cup of coffee, writing to the universe, sharing how she was feeling and what she needed tangible, practical help with, and also asking for guidance about bigger things that she wasn't sure how to navigate or make sense of. The combination of meditating and journaling in the morning, taking tactical action during the day, and doing her embodiment practice in the evening was helping Julie to find the courage each day to keep putting one foot in front of the other.

"During times of devastation like this," I shared with Julie during one of our sessions, "it's not so much about what you're doing, but that you just do. Just getting up in the mornings and feeding your dogs can be a lot of work. So it's the doing of one thing after another, without putting any value judgment on what those things are, that helps to build forward momentum. That movement will build and build, creating a current that carries you from all this uncertainty into the stability of something new."

I also reminded Julie that, since we have free will, our Higher Power can't intervene and offer support without us first asking for that. Nothing is too mundane or too practical to ask for help with, I told her. "Don't shy away from asking for very specific support. Whatever you need, ask for it," I urged.

Letting Go & Trusting Something Bigger

As was true for Julie, you may have parts of yourself who cringe when I use the word "prayer." Those parts are welcome. I invite you to hear their stories and what burdens they're holding that have led them to feel this way about communicating with your Higher Power. And, if that word is just too triggering for you, like I advised Julie, call it something else. The most important thing is that you do it.

When we hit these rock bottoms, the capacity of our own personal wills to navigate our lives usually bottoms out, too. We can feel as if life has backed us into a corner without an exit. When we don't know how we'll live through a situation, much less take our first steps in a new direction, it's time for us to call on something much deeper and vaster than our individual egos. For some of us, it takes a lot of adversity to bring us to this place of true surrender. That was certainly the case for me. I was used to living according to my personal will. And I was very good at it! If I hit a wall, I used my tenacity, cleverness, and resilience to help me pivot in a new direction. And, over the several-year span I'm writing about in this book, when I kept hitting one wall after another, I finally reached the point where my personal will had no choice but to give up. I needed to fully turn my life over to the higher power of my understanding, which I call God.

While prayer and handing things over to God had been a central part of my life for many years, when I lost my job during the first days of the COVID-19 pandemic, my mind started short-circuiting. I had been trying to rebuild my life in a new place after bankruptcy, on top of everything else I'd been through. Any trajectory that I envisioned for my life kept blowing up. When that had happened enough times, I realized I needed to let go of any vision, any trajectory, any plan. I had no idea how I was going to move forward, so my only option was to deepen my connection with, and trust in, God.

During my MDMA journey at Jason's the previous year, I remembered a story about surrender that I'd heard before and that I share a lot in my teachings. When fishermen are out on their boats and their nets get tangled up into knots, they don't sit down and start to try and pick apart every single little knot. That would be incredibly time-consuming, frustrating, and, likely, futile. Rather, they throw the tangled net overboard, letting the knots loosen through the constant rocking motion of the ocean's waves. The same is true for us when we're mired in a problem. Our whole lives feel like a giant, tangled fishing net. Can we throw it overboard, allowing the natural movement of life's currents to untangle it?

I also remembered something I'd heard once: that we can't solve life's big problems. They always solve themselves when the time is right. Looking back at the track record of my life, even over the past few years, I could see that was true. The more times I experienced this truth, the more my trust in life (and, in turn, myself) deepened. If I had gotten through all that and had come as far as I had, certainly whatever had helped me do that would help me in this new scenario—unemployed during a pandemic. I didn't know how, but I knew it would work out.

When I could stay close to that knowing, I could start to feel how trust could be restored. I also knew that wholeness, peace, and love are the central organizing principles of the universe. Life, and our own bodies and psyches, are always leading us toward wholeness. They're always wanting to move us in the direction of healing. If staying close to my source had led me through everything up to that point, and had kept me moving, still alive and intact, toward a state of greater healing (albeit not at the rate I wanted it to), then if I could stay intimate with Source, that would be my thread through this situation—and every other situation I would navigate in my life.

Cultivate a Prayer Practice

Maybe you feel let down (at best) and betrayed (at worst) by your Higher Power. You may often ask, "Why me? Why would a benevolent god or universe ever do this to me?" or "How could God possibly allow such destruction, violence, pain, and suffering?" I've asked those questions too, and while many of these questions might not ever be answered, deepening your own connection to your Higher Power will help you to continue on amidst the uncertainty. Here are some ways to do that.

1. Choose a time of day when your environment is relatively quiet and you have some moments alone.

2. You can include this as part of your meditation practice or do it as a standalone practice—either through internal dialogue or in the pages of your journal.

3. If you choose to write in your journal, you can address your Higher Power, "Dear Universe," "Dear God/Goddess," or whatever feels best.

4. Begin by speaking or writing whatever you feel called to. You can share your struggles, fears, worries, concerns. You can ask for help with specific things. You can share what you're grateful for. And you can ask questions about what your next steps are.

5. Once you feel complete with speaking, leave space to receive guidance. This step is important.

6. Start to attune yourself to the response—through hearing or receiving images or a felt sense. If you're journaling, you can switch to write the response from your Higher Power in your nondominant hand, or you can continue writing with your dominant hand and just change the channel to write from that wider perspective.

7. If it feels right, you can see yourself placing your problem, your question, your future, even your Life into the hands of your Higher Power.

8. Do this until you feel complete. End with a statement of gratitude.

Like any relationship, the one you have with your Higher Power will only grow stronger, more trustworthy, and more fulfilling with time. Show up for it every day and it will show up for you in greater and greater ways. Gradually, you can start to turn to prayer in any moment when you feel fear, uncertainty, or stress. I'm grateful that now, when I'm faced with a big decision or tough situation, rather than letting parts of me jump in and feel like they need to be the ones to figure something out, I remember (most of the time) to give myself space. To take the question or situation and put it into God's hands. I ask God to please resolve the situation, and I remember that it's not my place to do that. I am merely here to follow through on the guidance I receive.

Just as it takes time for trust to erode, so too does it take time for that trust to be restored. Showing up at least once a day for this divine connection will, over time, begin to restore trust at the root. For all mistrust stems from our mistrust of the Divine. All unhappiness stems from our disconnection from our source. Especially when you reach rock bottom and don't know how you're going to move forward, it's time to let go into something deeper. There, you'll find the support and direction you need to move forward when the time is right.

Heal Your Mistrust of Yourself

Since our aim is to heal heartbreak at every dimension of ourselves—physical, mental, emotional, and spiritual—we also need to address how to restore psychological wholeness after we've been betrayed or gaslit. This was a huge part of my healing process, and the same is true for many women whom I support.

While we're inside the experience of being gaslit, and in the early months (or even years) following, at times we can feel like we're going crazy. We saw an example of this in chapter 3 with my client Tasha who left a twenty-year marriage to a sociopath. In the first year after leaving him, she struggled with beliefs that she was the one in the wrong, that she was the one who caused her ex-husband's sociopathy, and that she was the one who couldn't be trusted. In the aftermath of my relationship with Matt, when I realized that I had been engaged to a man who gaslit me in numerous, damaging ways, I felt as if a major wire in my inner circuitry had been cut. That wire, I sensed, was the one that linked my intellect and sense perceptions to my gut instincts. With this core wire clipped, I had a hard time trusting my choices and my instincts, which was a huge part of why and how I got into a relationship with Jonathan soon after my time with Matt. And it was a big part of why I was having a hard time ascertaining what my truth was around whether or not I should have an abortion.

About two and a half years after Matt's and my separation, I spoke to a woman who had been married to a narcissist. She counseled me that it would likely take up to seven years to heal from that level of mind control. As I write these words, it's now nearly seven years to the date of the night I wrote about at the start of this book. While I'd hoped my healing journey wouldn't take so long, she was right. It takes a long time to heal from this kind of abuse. It takes a long time to not only rewire ourselves, but also to rebuild all the outer structures in our lives that are often decimated by these kinds of relationships.

From an IFS perspective, one of the most potent ways to do this is to first identify the parts of ourselves that were impacted by the manipulation, and then to restore their connection to our own Self energy. Doing this reconnects that core wire between our gut instincts and our minds. As we explored previously, Self energy is already whole and healed. It's the divine spark within each of us that always knows our true, right path.

Map Your Mistrusting Parts

This is a meditation I created following IFS principles.
To listen to a guided audio version of this practice, go to
saraavantstover.com/heartbreakdownloads.

For this exercise, you'll need a piece of paper and some markers, crayons, or colored pencils. If those aren't available, a regular pen will be fine. First, a few words of encouragement: you don't need to have any artistic ability to do this! Scribbles, sketches, or even just words on the page are fine.

Now, I'm going to invite you to get to know some of your parts who are in relationship to one another around this experience of being betrayed or gaslit (if those experiences don't apply to you, you can choose another experience that does, like being disappointed by life, or being heartbroken in a larger or more general sense). At the top of your page, write down your intention for this exercise (for example: "I intend to heal my experience of being betrayed/gaslit," "I intend to heal from heartbreak," or "I intend to heal my mistrust in life/my Higher Power").

Now, close your eyes and recite this intention to yourself internally. As you do, notice the first part who comes forward in response. Remember, parts can present themselves as bodily sensations, thoughts, voices, images, a felt sense, or something else. Stay with that first part, just noticing. Sense: where do you find this part in or around your body? Are there any words, actions, feelings, or messages associated with this part? Once you get a sense of that, open your eyes and represent this part on the page in whatever way feels right. Once you complete that, repeat this process four or five more times, seeing which parts come forward each time, until you have several parts mapped out on the page.

Now, pick up your page, extend your arm, and hold your page at arm's length. As you do, what do you notice from this perspective? Which parts are bigger? Which are smaller? Which ones are closer or further away? How do you sense these all relate to one another? Are there any parts who feel more protective or more hidden? Do any of these ones fight with one another, or, conversely, have an alliance? Are there any other parts who want to chime in, in response to the intention written at the top of the page? Did your inner wisdom, or Self, weigh in on this topic at all? If so, how? As answers arise, take some moments to write your insights down on the page.

Last, look again at the parts represented here. Feel your heart, and notice how open your heart feels toward each of these parts. What do you sense this cluster of parts, this mini-system within you, needs from you right now? Is there any one part on this page whose healing could have the biggest impact on your entire system? If so, you could bring that part into one (or more) of the IFS exercises I've shared previously to get to know it better.

This practice can help us begin to bring more space into what can feel like a muddled jumble of parts. Doing so can bring more clarity to what's happening inside of us around a complex issue. Externalizing our parts in this way is an effective method for helping us to get more space from them, seeing that they are merely parts of us. In IFS, this is called "unblending." When we blend with parts, we see the world through their beliefs and perspectives. Unblending, on the other hand, allows us to come into deeper relationship with our parts. We can do this through any of the IFS exercises previously shared here. When we unblend, we can relate "to" rather than "from" our parts, for we're resting in the seat of inner wisdom and clarity, our Self.

Once we begin to restore our inner circuits of trust with our own parts, our Self, and our Higher Power, life shows us that we're ready to experience the first buds of spring after what may have been a very long, dark winter. Yes, it's almost time to come alive again.

Journaling Prompts

I invite you to take some moments to reflect more deeply on how these themes of trust and mistrust impact you. While the larger themes of our healing journeys may be similar, the specifics are unique to each of us.

Past

- What is your experience of hitting rock bottom at different times in your life?

- How have you found your way forward from there? (Does it ring true for you that life is the one that always solves our problems, not us?)

- Have you ever been gaslit or betrayed (in little or large ways)? How did you wake up to the truth of that, and how did that impact you?

Present

- How much do you trust yourself right now? How much do you trust your life right now?

- What is your relationship with source, or your Higher Power?

- How do you feel about prayer? Surrender? Faith? Trust? Patience?

Future

- Which of your parts who is associated with your mistrust of yourself/others/life is in greatest need of healing and attention?

- From here, what are your next, right steps, sourced from a place deeper than your personality?

Chapter 11

Coming Alive

"You let time pass. That's the cure. You survive the days.
You float like a rabid ghost through the weeks. You cry
and wallow and lament and scratch your way back up
through the months. And then one day you find yourself
alone on a bench in the sun and you close your eyes and
lean your head back and you realize you're okay."

— Cheryl Strayed

We can't rush our rebirths. This stage of our journey comes at the
end of this book for a reason. We need to meet and give ourselves over to everything we experience prior to this point: our rage,
grief, anxiety, shock, sleepless nights, confusion, resentment, depression,
loneliness, despair. All of it. We need to rail against God, against life,
lamenting, "Why me? Why is this happening to me?" We need to sit
in the not-knowing of what's next and in the pain and unfairness of it
all. When we show up for all of this, there comes a point in our healing
journeys when grace steps in. Actually, it's been here all along, but it's
been letting us do the heavy lifting, for it knows that it's only through
the doing and feeling of all of these things that we'll grow—as human
beings and also as divine souls.

You could say that, at this stage of the process, grace arrives in
the ways we've wanted it to all along. It delivers an acceptance of our
circumstances—however atrocious, unfair, or unrelenting they may have

seemed. Neither a "yes" nor a "no," acceptance is a holy and neutral state of allowing all things to be exactly as they are. Especially in cases of injustice, this doesn't mean that we don't act. This is a "both-and" approach. We take the outer steps we need to, and we simultaneously do the inner work of accepting that what is happening is what is happening. And this acceptance is no small thing. It's a doorway to freedom—freedom to feel and experience anything and everything, without preference.

When this grace of acceptance blesses us, our perspective on both our lives and our heartbreak begins to shift. With enough distance from our rupture and the support of Dr. Time, we can even begin to experience the blessings our devastations have brought us—what is often called post-traumatic growth. Our new identities and lives start to take form more and more, and with this, we can see that we could never be who we are now without having endured those dark nights. As we slowly come alive again, we do so with eyes more able to see blessings in unexpected places and hearts more softened by compassion and humility. For me, these first signs of coming alive again appeared during the early days of the COVID-19 pandemic.

Santa Barbara, California; March 13, 2020

In the week between when Claire shared the news of my release and my final day of working with her, I grappled with coming to terms with my new reality. Yes, I'd receive two weeks of severance and some unemployment benefits, but that wouldn't be nearly enough to live off of. While I had been deep in the process of applying for new jobs over the past couple of months, nothing had panned out yet. Plus, news about the new virus—the coronavirus—was starting to intensify. By the time my last day of work came, the entire world seemed as if it was about to end.

Since my meeting with Claire the previous week, we had all woken up to the severity of the virus. It had impacted our organization greatly, causing it to shut down most of its operations (coincidentally, I would have lost my job there anyway). Before going into the office to do the final handoff, I stopped to stock up on groceries. As I waited in line, which wrapped from the registers all the way to the back of the store, my heart thumped in my chest and my mind raced. I longed for the normalcy of my life, even just ten days ago, when I could pop in and out of the grocery store and feel excited about the upcoming weekend. Now, each time the line crept forward, the man in front of me opened a new door of the freezer section we stood beside to throw piles of frozen vegetables, pizzas, whatever he could find, into his overflowing cart.

What the hell is even happening right now? a voice cried inside. *I lost my job. I'm going to be stuck at home alone for who knows how long. I have no idea how I'm going to pay my bills. And now it looks like I may not even have food to eat and, oh, by the way, the whole world is falling apart right now, too.*

In the coming days, while I did feel a sense of relief that I didn't have to work at a toxic job anymore and could sleep in and stay home, I lamented that I couldn't do all the things that I finally got to do now that I didn't have a nine-to-five job. I couldn't go to yoga classes in the morning, hang out in my favorite coffee shop, or go out to lunch with a friend. Instead, I stayed home, doing yoga over Zoom and frantically continuing my job search. One freelance position that I'd applied for in February that looked like it was about to come through was cancelled when the frenzy of the pandemic kicked in.

Even amidst all the uncertainty, a new normal started to settle in for me. I'd let myself sleep in and then enjoy long mornings to myself—meditating, journaling, and practicing yoga—all of which helped me to decompress from a tumultuous past few months. In addition to my job stress, I was still aching from a breakup with Steve, the first man I'd dated since Jonathan.

Steve brought up some yellow flags that I had vowed I'd stay away from. To stay committed to the new life I was building for myself, I knew I needed to walk away. Still, being with him was a gift in many ways. It reignited dormant parts of myself. While I had kissed Ryan (very passionately!) that one night two years before, I hadn't had sex with anyone since Jonathan. That was the longest I'd gone without intimacy (or a relationship) since losing my virginity in high school. Sadie and I spent weekends at Steve's home. He and I would take long baths, drink coffee on his couch, and get lost in deep conversation at some of the town's nicest restaurants. Having someone with whom I could connect so deeply and enjoy Santa Barbara felt like a huge gift after having had so much solitary time there.

The combination of ending things with Steve and hating my job had started to send me into a downward spiral. In desperation, I researched hypnotherapists in town. I was discouraged that, despite all the intensive work I'd done on myself, the first guy I'd fallen for in years had a similar track record as my past partners—a pattern I was trying to get away from. Still, somehow, my subconscious mind was attracted to that kind of man. I thought maybe hypnotherapy could help me get to the bottom of that attraction to rewire it and lift me out of my funk. Also, I knew I wanted to train in a new healing modality to help me revive my work, and I thought that becoming a hypnotherapist could be a viable option.

That January, I'd made an appointment with a hypnotherapist who had an office on the top floor of a historic building on downtown State Street. I laid back in a leather recliner, the hypnotherapist sitting next to me, and she began inducting me. While I descended into deeper and deeper relaxation, a random memory popped up: my freshman year at Barnard, being invited to a party at a popular social club at Columbia; being downstairs in the living room under a crystal chandelier, wearing a light blue cashmere cardigan; being served a drink; waking up the next morning, fully clothed, in the bed of a guy I'd had a major crush on, feeling shame and shock, having no idea how I'd gotten there or what had happened; hurrying out and never thinking about it again. While I didn't linger on that memory in the hypnotherapy session, it resurfaced again a few days later when I was walking on the beach with a friend. She was sharing the story of how she'd been drugged and raped in college, and as I listened, alarm bells started ringing inside of me: *That's what happened to me! That's what happened to me!*

Over the next couple of months, I had that memory to reckon with on top of everything else. It explained a lot of things: why I started smoking nearly a pack of cigarettes a day during my freshman year of college, why I nearly had a nervous breakdown on my eighteenth birthday, why my bulimia got so out of control that year and my hair started falling out. Now, twenty-five years later, I was starting to feel that way again, and when I washed my hair, unusual amounts would fall out. Given my limited income, I felt frustrated that I couldn't afford the help I needed, such as more regular therapy and modalities like bodywork and acupuncture. That was a reality I was trying to contend with since I started IVF. Even though I needed a lot of support, I couldn't get it. I know this is a position many find themselves in.

Once the pandemic began, though, many other people were in a similar position as me. (I also want to acknowledge that many people—parents, teachers, those working in retail and health care, for example—were unable to stop working or to receive government benefits.) More and more people, from therapists to car insurance agencies to cell phone companies, started offering financial breaks to many who were in financial need. Gratefully, I could begin doing more therapy again at a reduced rate—namely IFS and EMDR to help me process the trauma from college as well as the more current stressors of the pandemic, losing my job, and sheltering in place alone.

About a week after my final day of work, I heard news about expanded unemployment benefits and stimulus checks. Unsure if I qualified for either, I did more research and found that, in fact, I did. *Yes!* Euphoria flowed through me. My panic and fear about having the financial foundation I'd created for myself over the previous year being wiped out dissipated. And I realized that life was giving me an incredible gift disguised in an unexpected package. Now, for the first time in my life, I could take my foot off the gas pedal. A semi-sabbatical, of sorts. And get paid for it. Yes, I would still work at piecing together my next steps as I was going to need a long runway to revive my career, but I had some funding to begin to do that. For the immediate future, I had resources to help give me more space to rest and breathe more deeply for the first time in years.

Once that good news (and the first check) arrived, I started to slowly rekindle my own work again. Doing that helped me tap back into an essential dimension of myself while feeling like I was sharing some inspiration and support with the women in my community during a challenging time. Helping others was helping me. While continuing to let myself have more space to rest, I started sending occasional emails out to my list, recording some podcast episodes, and posting on social media. While my life—and the world—looked nothing like how I wanted (or expected) it to look, I was starting to feel like I was being taken care of, like there really was a larger force out there guiding me toward something. Even amidst the adversity, I was beginning to taste the gifts from my experience and to let go and relax into the twists and turns of my path. I was beginning to feel the very nascent stages of coming alive again.

Zina's Story: Post-Traumatic Growth Through Chronic Illness

Zina Mercil, a body-centered psychotherapist and a director of coaching, was diagnosed with a chronic, rare autoimmune liver disorder in the spring of 2011. With that news, Zina's entire life and identity as she'd known them were turned upside down. She was heartbroken. During those early days and months, she struggled to figure out how to live within her new reality. Almost instantaneously, her identity shifted to "a person with illness," and this filled her thoughts constantly.

Today, Zina notes that her illness has receded much further into the background. So much so that she marvels at how she never thought she'd be in a place where it feels so integrated with her life. She feels much more vibrant than ever before. While her illness is always a prominent part of her life, it's invisible, and she passes as normal most of the time.

Shortly after her diagnosis, Zina remembers her therapist sharing that often artists, and others living with illness, remark that they wouldn't give their illness back if they had the option. At the time, Zina thought that was the craziest thing she'd ever heard. Yet she's come to realize that this is absolutely the case for her, too. A self-proclaimed workaholic, Zina remembers how, before her illness, she had a "power over" relationship with her body. "I would burn the candle at twelve ends," she remembers, all the while demanding a lot of her body both physically and aesthetically. Having this core coping mechanism break down felt scary for Zina.

Now, however, she reflects that she lives in greater partnership with her body, relating to it with deeper listening and curiosity. While this is hard for her at times because she doesn't always like what her body needs, wants, or has to say, she feels that she's in a relationship with it now, which includes both ruptures and repairs. Other unexpected blessings from her heartbreak of living with chronic illness are that she's learned how to set boundaries in relationships. Whereas she perpetually overextended herself in the past, now she's very aware of how she schedules things and what she's attracted to, both in her personal and professional lives.

Overall, Zina recognizes the post-traumatic growth she's experienced as a result of her illness. Post-traumatic growth (PTG) is the process of positive change that can occur for any of us who have gone through a traumatic event, such as heartbreak. This can take the form of heightened personal strength, improved relationships, and a greater appreciation for life. PTG is not a return to a previous state of well-being but rather a move beyond it to a new level of experiencing ourselves and our lives. PTG shows us that a trauma, such as heartbreak, can lead us to tremendous positive change.

Playing the Hand of Cards We're Dealt

In the early stages of Zina's diagnosis, she struggled to accept her new reality. It's normal and natural to have times along your heartbreak journey when you're railing against life, God, someone who wronged you, and people you know who seem to have it so much better than you. I did that a lot, too. Sometimes I still do. And it's good to let yourself express that sometimes. At a certain level (or perhaps at many levels), you are a victim. A victim of hardship. A victim of adverse circumstances and societal inequalities. A victim of people you thought you could count on who turned their backs on you, and maybe also a victim of someone else's hurtful behavior.

Yet, at some point, we won't move forward and heal if we don't look at the context of our heartbreak, including where we are victims, and decide to take responsibility for how we respond. We may not be able to control our circumstances, but we can more fully claim agency within how we move forward with our lives.

Life deals each of us a hand of cards. Everyone's hand is different. No two are the same. And, once that hand is dealt, that's all that we have to work with. Sure, it's easy to envy someone else's hand, yet envy isn't going to change the fact that they have what they have and you have what you have. So, the empowered way forward is to accept: This is the hand of cards I've been dealt. How can I play this as skillfully as possible? How can I make the very most out of what life has handed me?

We each come into this world with a specific curriculum. While we are all ultimately here to learn the same soul lessons, like forgiveness, patience, perseverance, trust, humility, generosity, compassion, honesty, and so on, we each learn these lessons differently. Unique relationships and life situations unfold throughout our lives to help us to grow into these qualities. No two people learn in the same way. So, even if the hardships you're experiencing seem random and don't make any sense to you, we can, when the time is right, lean into the understanding that if life has dealt us this particular hand of cards, then it's up to us to play them well. Ultimately, there's no use battling with reality, because life is always right.

Looking back over the past several years of my life, I have no idea why I experienced so much adversity in such a short period of time. Maybe it was a curse. Maybe it was a soul initiation that had been building for many lifetimes. Maybe it was random. Or maybe it was all of the above. All I know is that that level of adversity quite nearly killed me, on multiple occasions. It was adversity so strong that it took several additional years of dedicated, concentrated, hard work to rebuild every single aspect of my life, inner and outer. And I know that these things didn't happen to punish me. I didn't do anything wrong, and I have no idea whether or not they happened for a reason. No one knows why they happened. All that we know is that they happened. And, if you're in the midst of something right now, all that you know is that this is what is happening. This is what's real.

So, if this is what's so, the most helpful thing we can do is get on board with reality. To do this, we drop our defenses against life, and we start to allow our lives to be exactly as they are. This doesn't mean we hate them. This doesn't mean that we love them, either. We simply allow them because they are. How do things shift for you when you recognize that? It doesn't mean that you don't do anything to better your situation, but it means that you first acknowledge your hand of cards before you start playing them. Full acceptance of your circumstances is what opens the door to your new life, so this step is important. To help you get a felt sense of what this is like, I want to lead you through a meditation practice that has been helpful for me, which I learned from Miranda Macpherson in her book *The Way of Grace*.

Opening, Softening & Allowing Meditation

This is adapted from the teachings of
Miranda Macpherson. To listen to the guided audio version, go to
saraavantstover.com/heartbreakdownloads.

1. Come into a comfortable seated position, with your hips higher than your knees. If sitting up feels challenging, you're welcome to lie down. Close your eyes if that feels comfortable for you.

2. Now, invite in an overall disposition of relaxation. That word, "relaxation," takes on different meanings to us at different points along our spiritual journeys. See what it's like now to relax not only physically but also emotionally, mentally, and even spiritually.

3. Have the intention to be present, feel everything, and do nothing. To help with this, say to yourself, *Opening, softening, and allowing*, and feel the ripple effect these words have on your inner being. Repeat this to yourself a couple more times if needed.

4. Become aware of your breath. Notice the parts of your body that move as the air flows in and out. Stay with this for a couple of minutes.

5. As you stay with your breath, you don't need to try to stop thinking; instead, see if you can let go of following your thoughts. Meditation isn't about stopping your thinking; it's about becoming more aware of the present moment.

6. Once you feel more settled, relaxed, and present, you can drop a self-inquiry question into your mind by asking: *What's it like in my body, heart, and mind when I allow my experience to be exactly as it is?*

7. Don't try to think of the answer; just wait and see what you notice. If you find yourself in a spiral of anxious thoughts, see if you can notice what that feels like. What sensations are present in your body? What emotions are here? What are the thought loops moving through your head? Of course, if the anxiety is too strong to continue to sit in meditation, consider getting outside and going for a walk. There are times when the storms inside of us are too great to close our eyes and sit still.

8. Over the next ten minutes or so, ask yourself that question a couple more times: *What's it like in my body, heart, and mind when I allow my experience to be exactly as it is?*.

9. When you are ready, gradually open your eyes and come back into your space.

Bringing the Practice of Allowance into Your Life

Formal meditation is a good place to begin this practice of opening, softening, and allowing your experience to be exactly as it is. When we engage in meditation in a contained place and time like this, it's easier for us to learn the technique and to notice the impact it has on our systems.

Then, it's helpful (even crucial) to take this practice off this cushion and into more and more of life's ordinary moments.

When you go on a walk, you can ask yourself, *What's it like in my body, heart, and mind when I allow my experience to be exactly as it is?* Then, in hard moments, when you're feeling something you don't want to feel or you're experiencing something you don't want to be happening, your mind will be better trained to drop in that inquiry question. All of these practices, then, are helping us to reverse our usual responses to agonizing moments, which are to defend, deflect, and run. This practice asks us to do the opposite.

This undefended, relaxed state of acceptance is a holy state. It doesn't mean we condone another person's actions. It doesn't mean we don't feel all of our feelings. It doesn't mean we don't have any boundaries or that we don't communicate our anger. What it does mean is that we're willing to meet life on life's terms. We accept what life is presenting to us, and from there we have the agency to move forward and choose what the next, best step is.

Remember Humor

As we start to feel less and less like we're backed into a corner by life, we may start to feel more glimmers of smiles, and even laughter. This is a good thing, for both humor and laughter help to counter the negative effects of heartbreak. For example, laughter triggers the release of endorphins, the body's natural feel-good chemicals, which can help to reduce pain, improve mood, and create a sense of overall well-being. It also increases the release of dopamine, a neurotransmitter associated with pleasure and reward, while decreasing the levels of stress hormones like cortisol and adrenaline, which can help to reduce feelings of anxiety and stress. Humor can also decrease inflammation in the body and boost the immune system.[1]

I can probably count the number of times I laughed on one hand during my years of heartbreak. Those brief reprieves came when watching comedy specials (I remember laughing out loud with Seinfeld, Ellen, and Ali Wong). During the short spell that I was dating Steve, my smile and laughter started returning. Bit by bit, I felt like I was starting to emerge from a long, dark tunnel.

Certainly laughter comes more easily for some of us than others. Maybe you hide behind humor to avoid your pain. Or maybe, like me, you need to make a deliberate effort to include it. Wherever you fall on this spectrum, it's good to notice your relationship to humor and laughter and to explore ways that you can seek it out, when the time is right, to help bring more levity again.

Here are some ways you can use humor to help heal your heart:

- Watch a comedy show with someone you know you find funny

- Start a series that you've heard is lighthearted

- Play with a child or an animal

- Practice laughter yoga (you can search for an instructional video on YouTube to help guide you)

- Spend time with someone who makes you smile, or even laugh

- Make an effort to smile more often—as you're reading these words right now, doing things around the house, driving, etc.

Once we're in touch with more acceptance and humor again, we know that we've passed through the treacherous tunnel of heartbreak and are about to come out on the other side. We know that we've learned a lot, and very deeply. And, for many of us, this may mean that we feel ready and inspired to look back, extend a hand, and support others on their own heartbreak journeys. We'll explore what that looks like in the next chapter.

Journaling Prompts

The process of coming alive again also invites us to reflect on the blessings within and around us that are becoming more apparent after our time of strife. Take some moments to reflect on these blessings, as well as the other themes from this chapter, in your journal now.

Past

- Looking back, do you have a felt sense of what it's like to accept what feels unacceptable?

- What are you proud of about how you've played the cards you've been dealt?

- What has your relationship to humor been throughout your life?

Present

- What is hard for you to accept about your life right now?

- What soul lessons (like trust, patience, perseverance, humility, forgiveness, compassion, etc.) have you learned and cultivated throughout this heartbreak journey so far? How are you aware of those?

- Do you see any unexpected blessings in your hardships?

Future

- What's needed for you to come to a place of greater acceptance?

- How do you want to bring more laughter and humor into your life again, when the time is right?

- What do you feel your post-traumatic growth is leading you toward, in yourself and in your life?

Chapter 12

Supporting Others

"It is through weakness and vulnerability that most of us
learn empathy and compassion and discover our soul."

— Desmond Tutu

My second book, *The Book of SHE*, depicts the heroine's journey for modern women. True to the original archetypal blueprint for this path of becoming, such a journey always ends with a homecoming. Returning home doesn't necessarily mean that we return to an actual place (though it did for me in this heartbreak journey when I ended up, unexpectedly, returning to Colorado). Rather, it can be a metaphorical return to our lives. Grace has decided that we've passed our tests and learned the required lessons of heartbreak. Refreshing levels of normalcy, stability, and goodness start to return to our daily realities. No longer are we struggling to simply stay alive starting the moment we open our eyes in the morning. No longer do we feel debilitated from doing regular, daily tasks because of the depth of the emotional agony we're in. No longer do we feel like we're living on the outskirts of our own lives.

We may go for days without thinking about what happened to us. New people and experiences come into our lives. We may become aware of people close to us who are going through challenging times, and we may feel like we have the energy and capacity to show up for them, perhaps in ways we wished others had shown up for us. We're not fully back on track yet, but even the fact that we could consider supporting another signals that we're very close. In this final chapter, we'll explore how to be of the best support to others' heartbreak journeys now that we are nearly on the other side of our own.

Colorado; November 29, 2020

Standing at my kitchen counter, I gulped half a quart-sized Mason jar of warm water with lemon. Outside my new front door, with square glass panes bordered by bright red trim, cars were starting to park along the otherwise empty, tree-lined street. I'd been in my new home for almost three months, and that November morning, I had just completed a ritual to help anchor me in it.

The previous July, my landlords in Santa Barbara, a married couple who lived in and owned the main house that stood on the same property as my cottage, informed me that they were about to start a massive, multi-year construction project. Since my cottage had no insulation and was right next to their home, I knew that would mean years of bulldozers, saws, and workers everywhere. A highly sensitive person who was now not only working at home but also home pretty much 24/7 because of the pandemic, I knew that level of disruption was going to be untenable.

With my recent unemployment, the pandemic, as well as everything else I was still healing from, the realization that I needed to move yet again—after having lived in my new home for only fifteen months—stirred inner waves of panic. I knew the first—and sanest—thing I needed to do upon hearing this news was to turn inside and pray. When I did, the guidance I received was even more shocking than my landlord's news. My inner voice said: *Move back to Colorado.* I asked, *Are you sure? I said I would never move back to Colorado. I thought I was done with that place, forever.* And the voice responded again, and again, and again: *Move back to Colorado. Move back to Colorado. Move back to Colorado.*

While I sat with that guidance and took it into consideration, I simultaneously explored my options in Santa Barbara, though the project nauseated me. Finding a workable home within my price range in Santa Barbara—with a dog and now bankruptcy on my credit history—required a medium-sized miracle. My plan upon moving into my cottage the previous spring, while applying for bankruptcy, was to stay there for as long as I possibly could. With this new development, I could move in with a friend in Santa Barbara temporarily while I looked for a home, but the thought of that made me feel uneasy, too. I had put my things in storage and lived out of a suitcase for nine months the previous year. I didn't want to do that again. Whatever my next move was going to be, I wanted it to bring me more stability and security, not less.

The more I thought about returning to Colorado, the more it made sense. While housing would still be expensive there, it would be much more affordable than in Santa Barbara. I could get a two-bedroom home instead of a studio. I had more friends and community. It felt familiar. And, especially with everything having shut down due to COVID, halting my attempts to forge stronger connections in Santa Barbara, all of that really appealed to me. In the middle of the night a couple of days after I'd received that inner guidance, I looked through Colorado rentals on Zillow. Buried a couple of weeks back in the listings was my soon-to-be new home.

I emailed the owner, and he responded that it was still available. Plus, he was willing to rent it to me, sight unseen, even though I had bankruptcy on my record. Two other places that I really wanted had turned me down because of this, but, luckily, he was willing to take a chance on me. The lights continued to turn green. So, over the next couple of weeks, I got to work reserving a POD and movers, selling a lot of my belongings so everything could fit into the smallest container possible, saying my goodbyes, and preparing to move back to Colorado in a couple of weeks.

Never before had I made a decision so quickly, so unexpectedly. While I was sad to leave the paradise of Santa Barbara and the dream I had for myself there, I was grateful for its gentle beauty and how being there had helped strengthen me. Near daily walks on the beach with Sadie, hikes in the foothills and to hot springs, and simply walking around amidst palm trees, succulents, flowers, the ocean, and blue skies most every day were balms for all my bruises. Still, I couldn't deny that things just weren't clicking for me there. Yet another vision for my life crumbled unexpectedly, and all I knew was that moving back to Colorado was my next, right step.

So, on that late-November morning in Colorado, when I stood in the kitchen at 7:30 am after I'd been living in my new home for almost three months, I'd already been up for two hours. Swallowing my last gulp of water, I was thirsty. I wasn't allowed to eat or drink anything until after I'd finished my ritual. I felt relieved that I'd completed it. Somehow, in ways I didn't understand, that ritual felt like the conclusion of the incredibly challenging chapter of my life that had begun in 2015. Just ten days earlier, I was inspired to do the ritual after receiving a cowry shell divination over Zoom—a birthday gift to myself—with Malidoma Somé (the West African elder and teacher whom I mentioned in chapter 2).

Cowry shell divination, widely practiced in many African and Afro-Caribbean cultures, involves the use of small, white, egg-shaped shells that are considered to have spiritual significance. They're tossed onto a mat, and the way they land is interpreted to provide insight into personal issues, such as relationships, health, career, and finances, as well as to gain guidance from ancestral spirits or other spiritual entities. My divination revealed that part of what had been haunting me over the past several years had been the acceleration of an ancestral curse. Malidoma Somé's reading for me detailed the following:

"The challenges you've been encountering that put you in this constant transitional, threshold state are an ancestral curse, like an ancestral wound that keeps being passed on to you. You've chosen in this lifetime to be the medicine woman, the carrier of the healing that particularly addresses this issue. The overall message is that the success of what you are called to do is measurable within the context of your capacity to deal with this issue in the family line that has been affecting relationship, abundance, belonging, anchor, and all of that. You are the one who came in this lifetime to heal all of that. Until this is removed, challenges are always going to be popping up. Challenges have been there all along, expressed in a smaller fashion, but reaching an increasingly loud format, as if this is the way of the ancestors to remind you of the promise you made that as a healer you came into this world to put an end, to purify the line that connects the dots of the family as part of your purpose. This work needs to be done. This has to happen sooner than later."

At the end of the reading, Malidoma Somé prescribed a ritual to remove obstacles in my life and to clear the ancestral curse. He urged that I needed to undertake the ritual with my full passion and power and that I was to do so before the sun rose and on an empty stomach. The morning I decided to do it, I set my alarm for 5:30. Leaping out of bed in the dark, I said goodbye to Sadie and gathered my supplies in a backpack. I drove through dark, empty streets to the base of my favorite hiking trail—one that had held me through countless iterations of myself, and that I wanted to share this new leg of my journey with.

My assignment was to smash four fertilized eggs along various designated points on the trail—eggs that I'd spoken to, prayed over, and slept beside the night before. The first egg landed at a street crossroads, close to the hiking trail. The second, in a dry riverbed. The third, on the trunk of an old tree. When I reached the top of the trail, standing at my favorite lookout point, my eyes soaked in the town from above. The orange light of dawn was starting to peek over the horizon, and my heart swelled with gratitude that somehow, mysteriously, after all of my ups and downs, twists and turns, I'd made it back to where I'd started from. I'd made it back to the place that felt like home—the place I least expected to call home. Taking in the view as wonder tingled through my body, I smashed the final egg on the ground in front of me, symbolizing abolishing any obstacles that stood in the way of my vision of the future.

As I made my way down the mountain, a few early morning joggers shared the trail with me. I smiled and almost skipped my way down, feeling a lightness and an aliveness that I hadn't felt in I didn't know how long. I could feel the shift in energy, like a liberation from some dark spell I'd been under. My hiking shoes crunching gravel and dirt beneath my feet, I felt a nod from the universe and a message from my ancestors, saying, "You passed the test. You showed up fully. You listened deeply. Well done, Sara."

That month, not only did I receive Malidoma Somé's counsel and ritual to dismantle my ancestral curse, but other things in my life began to palpably shift as well. I met my now partner. Just prior to that, I'd received the news that I'd been accepted into an IFS level-one training, with a scholarship, no less. I knew this would be a significant step toward turning my energy outward once again, supporting others who were going through similar dark valleys. I was starting to feel more space—and fire—to support others again. For the past several months I'd taken initial steps to rebuild my business, but I resolved that, starting in January, I'd take that on full time. I knew that I had so much more to share—so much more compassion, so much more *me* to offer—than ever before.

Healing and Giving Back: Our World Needs More Compassionate Caregivers

One of the appreciations I receive most often from my clients is that they feel zero judgment from me. Whether they're stuck in a painful, addictive cycle that the "wellness world" would condemn as being unhealthy, have had a few abortions, have struggled with urges to cut or kill themselves, have been unfaithful to a partner, declared bankruptcy, or experienced challenging side effects of past sexual abuse, they feel that I don't even flinch when they reveal their deepest, darkest secrets to me.

And it's true: I don't judge them. Having been through all that I have, and having had the felt (and often unspoken) experience that many around me were judging me, I know how painful that can be. And I know that there's nothing to judge. We all make mistakes at times. We all experience falls from grace. We all are victim to adverse childhood conditioning as well as life circumstances that don't necessarily make any sense. No matter how self-aware and intelligent we are, we're all vulnerable to psychological and emotional manipulation. We all do what we can to keep going in the face of it all. Living in a culture that's grief, death, hardship, and failure phobic, there's so little room for anyone of us to make even the tiniest misstep without being socially ousted in some way or another.

The bright side is, once you've experienced this and made it through to the other side, you recognize the limitations in living this way—for you, for society, and for those who are suffering. Being a real citizen of this world means living through the experience of heartbreak, patiently taking the steps to heal, and, as a result, harboring much deeper, truer levels of compassion than would have been possible otherwise. As I sit with my students and clients now, I'm able to go to much deeper places with them than I ever was prior to the heartbreaks I've shared with you in this book. I hadn't accessed those deeper layers within myself despite over a decade of intensive inner work. It took what it took for me to fully crack open. And the serendipity of finding IFS along the way and becoming trained in it at the tail end of my heartbreak journey is that it has equipped me with the precise skills and psychospiritual technology I needed to be a steady, loving presence for many women whose lives and identities were (and are) crumbling.

You've met some of these women in the pages of this book, and many are beginning to come out the other side of their heartbreaks as well. As they're starting to stand on firmer inner and outer ground, they too are feeling the impulse to serve and support others. Heidi enrolled in an online graduate program in counseling psychology. Tasha has begun a training in psychedelic-assisted therapy to support others. Daria is planning to take an IFS level-one training with hopes of using it to support children. Julie weaves the lessons she learned from her home burning down into embodiment workshops that she leads, offering hope to others who are struggling with unthinkable losses.

Just as plants know to start growing again in the springtime after the dormancy of winter, our souls also know when to start reaching and branching out again. There's a divine timing to this process. We'll know when we're ready, and we'll be guided, through external coincidences and internal direction, toward where we're meant to share our new strengths and capacities. There were many times during my heartbreak journey when I tried to hurry or force things out of impatience or fear that I was going to fall too far behind in my career or miss out on doing what I'm here to do. Whenever I acted from those motives, things didn't work.

Throughout it all, there was a calm, steady presence inside telling me to wait. To trust. To listen for when the time was right. It took a lot of trial and error for me to finally give in and trust that inner guidance in a bigger way—especially when there was nothing to hold on to. Yet, ultimately, it's that steady presence that helps lead us all to the other side.

Ideas for Supporting Others

I've compiled this list as a result of noticing what felt good to me when people showed up to support me—and by noting what didn't feel good when people didn't show up (or didn't show up in ways that I found helpful). It's not exhaustive, so please add what feels right for you—to give or to receive.

- Remember that it's not about what you say or do when you're with someone who's in pain. It's about where you're coming from inside yourself. Arrive in the presence of someone who's struggling in an open, present, nonjudgmental state within yourself. Come with zero agenda other than to be fully present. If it helps, you can ask any judgmental or agenda-oriented parts of yourself to step aside and give you some space for a little while.

- Be the presence of love for this other person. See what you're inclined to say or do from there. Remember, just this love is one of the greatest gifts we can give someone.

- Don't give advice unless you're asked for it.

- If you're not sure what to say, recite a prayer internally, which is one I learned from Miranda Macpherson: *Bring the thoughts to my mind and the words to my lips that will be most healing and helpful.* Then do or say what you're guided to, even if that's nothing.

- Check in, regularly. Send texts asking, "How are you doing today?" Call them. Invite them to do things with you.

Times of heartbreak can be incredibly lonely and isolating, and an invitation to join you for a walk or to come over for a meal can mean the world to someone.

- Bring over some food, for this is such a primal way of connecting with people. When you're going through heartbreak, a lot of times you're eating all of your meals alone. Helping someone feel a sense of community or connection around food can be so healing.

- If you know someone who's experiencing heartbreak around others, consider offering childcare for a few hours, or offering your home as a quiet, private space for them to be away family or others.

- Reach out on birthdays, holidays, and anniversaries. These can be especially hard times for someone who's heartbroken. And with the holiday season touted as being such a "family time," those without families, or whose families have undergone change or pain, can feel even more estranged and alone during these times. Ask people if they need anything, or even if they want to join you for your festivities. Consider stretching yourself to be more inclusive and generous than is often modelled in our culture.

- Above all: no matter how busy you are, don't turn your back on your grieving friends. They need you during this time more than ever, even if their process is taking longer than you think it should or looks different than you want it to.

- Know that by showing up in these ways, you're modeling for others (and our culture at-large) a healthy and helpful way to be present for those who are in pain. Rather than ignoring and turning your back to them, you're turning toward them and making them an important part of your life and daily awareness. In this way, we can hold the intention that no brokenhearted person will be left behind!

- You could also explore supporting others on a larger scale by joining an organization or volunteering, like Ari in chapter 4. Perhaps there's a population of people who could benefit from the wisdom and compassion you've gained from your heartbreak journey.

I also want to acknowledge that there may be times when it's best not to reach out to someone who's in distress because your presence may cause more pain. When a friend of mine, Jamie, was pregnant with her son, one of her best friends, who lived nearby, shared the same due date with her. It was Jamie's first pregnancy. They were both giddy that they were going to have children together. They threw baby showers for each other and often shared their pregnancy milestones with one other.

Jamie's son was born first—and her friend and her husband came to visit them a day or two after that. They were so ready to meet their child too. It would be any day. Yet when their baby, also a son, was born, he was born still. Jamie remembers that she had never witnessed grief like her friend's. As part of that, her friend could not see Jamie or her son for years. Throughout, Jamie understood why that was so. Still, she kept sending messages to her friend, telling her that she loved her. But seeing Jamie and her son was impossible for her friend. It was just too painful because she did not have a son in her arms, too.

That was fifteen years ago, and Jamie's friend has since moved to another state. They're close again now, and Jamie visits her. While her friend is able now to see Jamie's son, her friend's husband is not (during her last visit he made himself scarce—Jamie and her son were too much of a reminder for him). So, while one of Jamie's closest friends went through an unimaginable loss and she wanted to be there for her so badly, she ultimately had to accept that she was not the person who could be there to help. Still, she's glad that she didn't let go. Even though they couldn't see one another for years, Jamie sent her messages of love. As Jamie's story demonstrates, supporting a friend can be very hard and needs to be in service to what the heartbroken person needs.

Our Next Steps

As nature's cycles teach us, after a dark night, the dawn always comes. Always. Whether you're in the very early days and weeks of heartbreak or you're months or even years in, I hope the path outlined in this book will help you make it through. It has helped me through. It has helped so many of my students and clients through. If you stick with it, it will help you through, too. I know that there can and will be (many) days when you don't think that's possible. You'll wonder if you'll ever feel like yourself, open your heart, experience love, or feel joy again. You'll wonder if you'll ever be able to lay your grief (or shame, or regret) down. I had too many days like that to count, so I get it.

I don't have special superpowers that helped me to get through this time in life—I'm human, just like you. But I know that when you dig deep, stay with yourself, keep reaching out for support, and connect with your source, you will make it to the other side of this. When you do get to the other side, you will feel much more whole and intact than you did before this all started.

While I wish I didn't have to experience all that I did over the past several years, I am so proud of the woman I've become on the other side of it. As someone who has experienced a certain level of outer success during other seasons of my life, I can say very confidently that what I'm most proud of in my life is how I showed up for myself and my life circumstances over the past years. I'm proud of how I turned fully toward the challenges presented to me, how I learned to hold myself through it all, and how I played the very shitty hand of cards I was dealt as skillfully as I could.

My friendship with myself, as well as my trust in God and my life's path, has been fortified. When the world went through the pandemic together, a part of me felt relieved that now so many others around me were feeling the same level of distress and disruption that I had been feeling over the previous several years. It made me not feel so alone, so outside of the flow of daily life. And, within that, I could feel that for me, the challenges presented by the pandemic were much more manageable in comparison to the hardships I'd faced in the previous years.

My capacity had grown. I'd learned how to be resilient and tenacious in the face of adversity, and I'd learned how to keep showing up courageously and resourcefully amidst high levels of uncertainty and seemingly never-ending unfavorable curveballs.

You too may be noticing new strengths coming online for you. Maybe you're more able to stay with hard feelings, or you feel more adept at showing up at work even when you're under extreme distress. If you can now place a hand on your heart in hard moments, letting yourself feel your own compassionate presence, that's enormous. Perhaps you too are now seeing the truth about heartbreak. That it's not a failure. In fact, it's the exact opposite! Heartbreak, ultimately, is an initiation into warriorship, heartfelt service, and a deeper, more mature humanity. Congratulations on saying a conscious "yes" to this initiation. It's a courageous act, and one that I hope you can now see will forever change your life in increasingly wondrous ways (even if you can't quite see those yet).

Journaling Prompts

I invite you to take some moments now to reflect on this theme of support, even if you don't feel like your journey is over yet.

Past

- What are some ways that people in your life showed up for you during your heartbreak journey that were healing and supportive?

- What are some ways people didn't show up and you wished they had? Or that you found to be unhelpful?

Present

- Do you or have you judged people who are in pain or have experienced falls from grace?

- Rather than pushing your judgment away, can you instead turn toward it to explore what it was about and where it came from?

- What do you consider to be successes along your heartbreak journey? What are you proud of? Who are you now that you weren't before?

Future

- How do you feel called to support the heartbroken, in small or large ways?

- What do you feel your inner compass is leading you toward next on your healing journey?

Conclusion:
Preparing for Our Ultimate Heartbreak

"And once the storm is over you won't remember how
you made it through, how you managed to survive. You
won't even be sure, whether the storm is really over. But
one thing is certain. When you come out of the storm
you won't be the same person who walked in."

— Haruki Murakami

When we continue to put one foot in front of the other, we eventually arrive in a new season of our lives. Despite my many doubts that this would ever be the case for me, the season of my aloneness and heartbreak has indeed passed. Inside my new life, a few days after my forty-fifth birthday, at the tail end of a relaxing Thanksgiving weekend, I settled onto the couch, my partner to my left and Sadie to my right. An early-winter wind whipped outside, stirring the ashes behind the glass doors of the fireplace. Sadie sighed as she felt my hand land on her back, and I turned up the volume on the TV as the opening credits began to flash across the screen.

We were settling in to watch a documentary that a friend and Buddhist teacher, Tory Capron (whom I mentioned in Carolyn's story in chapter 2), had created. After months of experiencing strange symptoms—tingles in her left leg, a little numbness in one of her hands—she began traveling around the country, undergoing testing to figure out what was wrong.

When diagnoses still came back inconclusive, someone advised her to visit the Mayo Clinic. It was there that Tory was finally diagnosed with ALS.

During a retreat I attended with Tory shortly after her diagnosis, she sat on a black, square meditation cushion on the floor in the front of the room. From there, she led us through an opening meditation, listening to the sounds in the room and feeling our diaphragms move like jellyfish as we breathed in and out. When she closed the meditation with a ring of the singing bowl and a bow, she stood up slowly, faced the altar behind her, and reached for a small brown item. Turning around to face us, she shared, "If I'm to leave you with one practice, the most important practice to do, it's this one. The offering of the torma."

She went on to explain that the offering of the torma is a Buddhist tradition of placing a small piece of cake (or any sort of sweet) on one's altar in the morning. As we do so, we imbue the offering with all that is transpiring in our lives—internally and externally, from the most horrible to the most sublime, and everything in between. Into the torma we offer our despair, our fear, our gratitude, our self-doubt. We offer it all as sacred expressions of the miracle of life. By placing it on our altars, we are handing it all over to something greater. We're letting go of controlling, holding onto, resisting, or identifying with any of it.

"Imagine setting a big banquet table and inviting every single thought and emotion you're experiencing to take a seat at that table with you," Tory continued. "This is the power of the torma. At the start of each day, offer it all up on your altar. And, later, go outside and offer that torma to a tree, or to the Earth."

Shortly after her diagnosis, Tory began working on the documentary. She had recently led her last in-person retreat and had wanted the film to be her final offering. Over the past months, the calf muscle on her left leg had eroded to the point that all that remained was skin over bone. Her voice tired easily, her words slurring slightly. She often needed to use a ventilator to breath, and it was hard for her to zip zippers, tie shoes, walk up and down stairs.

To help prepare her students for her death, Tory reminds us all: transitions are messy and hard. She then restates what you and I have come to know very deeply through the pages of this book: different rules apply during these transitional times. Heartbreak does thrust us out of our normal lives. We feel different, and our days look different than they used to. And, "It's not a problem," Tori reassures. A hallmark of the Buddha's teachings is that uncertainty, change, loss, suffering, old age, sickness, and death are part of life. There's no escaping them. They will come for each of us, usually in many different ways throughout our lives, all the way up until our own death, which will be our ultimate heartbreak.

Toward the end of the film, Tory describes a dream she had one night. She was in a house, saying goodbye to every room. Each room, she felt, held special memories and certain identities. Each room required her full presence to be with and bid farewell to it. When she was complete with that and made her way to the front door of the house, it came time to say goodbye to the house itself. As she stood in front of it, she knew that, once she said that final goodbye, she couldn't look back. All she could do was look forward, moving toward her next adventure. As Tory shares about this dream, her deep blue eyes twinkle and the deep creases on her cheeks tell the story of a life well lived.

Tears began to well in my eyes, and I squeezed my partner's hand a little tighter. I knew that moment she was speaking of, the one when you know you need to break your own heart. When you know it's time to take that one last look—whether it's at an actual home you've loved and need to move on from, a partner whom you'll never be with again, a baby nestled inside your pregnant belly, or a loved one you'll never see again. You know that life isn't giving you a choice. You must keep taking steps in a new direction, even though your vulnerable human heart and body truly don't believe that you'll ever be able to survive the pain, much less move on.

Yet, we all know that, with the help of time, we do move on. And my life in a new home, with a new partner, on a new couch, watching Tory's film, proved this to me. Not only was I alive, but I was arguably the most well I've ever been. Healthy, in a wonderful relationship, doing the work I love, living in a beautiful home, writing a new book. Many times over,

I'd said goodbye and walked toward my new adventure—one that looked nothing like I thought it would. Yet, in witnessing Tory's decline, I know very tangibly that more heartbreak awaits me: the deaths of my parents, Sadie, my partner, and, ultimately, myself—whenever and however that will come.

Everything we get from external sources will go away, and all we can do in the face of that is to keep letting go—both in times of heartbreak and in times of stability. We need to continue stepping into uncertainty, feeling and allowing everything in our experience to be as it is. We must hold tight to all that we love while at the same time be willing to hold on to nothing and stay in a place of not knowing.

I'm sharing Tory's story at the end of our heartbreak journey not to scare or discourage you. I'm sharing it to be real. Yes, it's incredible that you made it through what you did and are here now, in a new place in life and within yourself. Yes, this is worthy of celebration. After so many months (or years) of struggle and challenge, it's so important now to play, to enjoy, to really LIVE. And yet one of the greatest lessons that heartbreak teaches us is how to be more human, and more soberly aware of the truths of this human existence. No, this heartbreak won't be the last one you'll experience. If we're to be really honest with ourselves, as we get older, we can expect the frequency and intensity of our heartbreaks to increase. In the midst of this, the heart of the world will continue to break. With the effects of climate change and political unrest continuing to ramp up, we must anticipate and prepare for challenges that perhaps none of us have ever experienced before.

Your heartbreak has a purpose. It's not some random, horrible thing that you experienced. Well, yes, maybe it was that too. But remember that to truly emerge empowered from any life experience, we need to make meaning of it. Can you sense that part of the meaning of your heartbreak was to prepare you for future heartbreaks? Not just your own, but others, and the world's? Can you sense how much more available you are to be with your own darker states, and therefore are more available to be with others in theirs? Do you see how much more available you are for joy and aliveness now that you have allowed yourself to fully experience grief and death?

Can you feel how much more willing and able you are to meet life on life's terms rather than forcing it to meet you on your own?

Each day moving forward from here, I invite you to heed Tory's advice and to offer the torma in your own life. Maybe it's not a physical cake that you place on your altar each morning, but it could be an acknowledgment that everything you're experiencing is holy. Everything you're experiencing will come and go. Everything you're experiencing is valuable. The excruciating experience of heartbreak trains us for this. To feel it all, no matter how painful or bewildering. We humans have such a desire for life to be problem-free. And this is an impossible wish. We'll never arrive in a place where we're free of problems. There's no finish line of perfection and orderliness. That's not how life works. That's not what life is about.

As one of my friends has tattooed on his forearm, "This is it." Yes, this is it. This is what life is. As we move forward, then, let's do so with greater maturity and a spirit of radical inclusivity, welcoming everything. While our problems will continue to be here, we can view them as opportunities to continue to grow. Like water smoothing out stones over the course of many years, our problems, when engaged with consciously and wholeheartedly, level out our sharp edges and reveal the innate sheen within us.

To close our journey together, we'll engage in a final ritual.

Closing Ritual

- Choose something that will be your torma. It could be a piece of chocolate or candy, a cookie, a slice of cake, or something else that's sweet and delicious. Consider getting something special for this rather than just grabbing something that's lingering in your kitchen (although that will work, too!).

- Also gather a small bowl of water, ideally from a local water source (like a river, pond, lake, or ocean). If that's not available, water from your tap is fine.

- Place these items, along with a lit candle, on your altar.

- Sit in front of your altar with your journal and write down all the ways your experience of heartbreak has helped you grow, and the lessons you've learned from it. (Some examples: you learned how to trust and be patient with life, that you can be very depressed and overtaken by grief and still grow happier than you've ever been before, how to ask for help, how to take better care of yourself, how to set boundaries and higher standards for yourself in terms of what kind of relationships you'll tolerate, etc.)

- When you feel complete with the journaling, sit quietly with a feeling of gratitude in your heart for your experience. If you have a prayer practice, you can speak out loud or internally in appreciation for the unexpected gifts that your heartbreak has brought you.

- To close, offer into the torma whatever is happening in your life currently. The parts who are hard, confusing, wonderful.

- When you're complete, offer the torma to a tree or plant outside, along with the water from your bowl.

It's been an honor to be a part of your journey. Thank you for letting me into this very sacred and tender time in your life. In many ways, you were part of mine all along, too. I vowed that if, or when, I made it through these heartbreaks, I'd write this book for you. Knowing that I might have the chance to help another woman get through what I did helped me keep going. Sharing my journey with you now in this way has offered me a deeper level of healing. We are meant to heal together. We need one another. You are not alone. There is nothing wrong with you, and you are absolutely not in the wrong life. You are exactly who you need to be and where you need to be. From the bottom of my scarred, triumphant, and resilient heart, I bow to you, in thanks for your courage and companionship.

Above all, I believe in you. You will make it to the other side of this. When you do, you will be so proud of the person you've become. Keep going!

Acknowledgments

This heartbreak journey spanned several years, and, along the way, many extended helping hands. First, thank you, Mom, for being a steadfast companion throughout. I offer a deep bow to Sarah Powers for her mentorship over the past two decades, as well as for making my initial introduction to Internal Family Systems. I appreciate the ways that my father and sisters supported me around the time of my abortion procedure. And thank you to the other healers and mentors who, at various stages along the way, helped me be with my pain and, in time, glean wisdom from it: Susan Aposhyan, Nancy Wonder, and Mirah Love. Magie Staedler, I'm grateful for how you helped support my body throughout, always holding a safe space to heal.

I also appreciate the various friends and community members who met me in ways I needed at different points along the way. Thank you, Holly Cook, for being such a generous friend and cheerleader in Santa Barbara and beyond. Emma Teitel, I'm grateful for your steady presence and thank you for being in the room with me. Some others moved in and out of my life, offering care and support at various stages: Carolyn Flyer, Christiane Pelmas, Merryl Rothaus, Christine Vladick, Beth Walker, Melanie Elkin, Jill Emich, Tracey Holderman, Jennifer Lee, John Bodine, Ross Hostetter, and Jamie Mantey. Ali Kole and Lucy Wallace, your dance classes helped uplift me during a very dark time. I'm grateful to the IFS trainers I've had the privilege to learn from and work with, namely Elizabeth Taeubert, Chris Burris, and Rina Dubin.

Thank you to Julie Artz for your support in writing my proposal and pitching it to agents (and to Jennifer Louden for the referral). Lisa Jones, I loved being part of your writing circle, as that was where I wrote the bulk of the personal stories in this book. Thank you, Haven Iverson, for your wise and compassionate feedback on both my proposal and the first draft of this manuscript. Thank you to my agent, Wendy Sherman, for partnering with me to find the perfect home for this book, and to my editor at Sounds True, Sarah Stanton, for saying such an enthusiastic "Yes." Big thanks to Sahar Al-Nima, Joe Sweeney, Evelyn Hampton, Christine Day, Jeff Mack, Mike Onorato, and the entire team at Sounds True. Also, I appreciated the feedback I received from my test readers Emma Teitel, Holly Cook, Zina Mercil, Téana David, and also Jennifer O'Sullivan, who focused on the IFS portions of the book.

Thank you to Hendry's Beach, Yoga Soup, and the beautiful nature of Santa Barbara for helping me heal. I'm grateful to all the women who've shared the tenderness and vulnerability of their own heartbreak and healing journeys with me over the years. Thank you also to Miranda Macpherson, Daniel Foor, Tory Capron, Malidoma and Sobonfu Somé, and Marianne Williamson, whose work provided important lifelines at various points along the way. Above all, I thank God for my life and the capacity to continue to heal and grow and Sadie girl for her ongoing sweetness. Chris, you were an incredible gift waiting for me on the other side of all of this! Thank you for your unconditional support, kindness, and love. I appreciate all the ways you see, love, and encourage me in little and large ways every day.

Recommended Resources

You can find all of my offerings on Internal Family Systems and women's spiritual entrepreneurship (including online programs and in-person retreats) on my website at saraavantstover.com.

The resources here—certainly not exhaustive—are ones that I offer to others and that helped me during my process, and I wanted to pass them on to you, too.

Grief & Loss

- *When Things Fall Apart: Heart Advice for Difficult Times* by Pema Chödrön
- *The Wild Edge of Sorrow: Rituals of Renewal and the Sacred Work of Grief* by Francis Weller
- *It's OK that You're Not OK* by Megan Devine
- *Heartbreak: A Personal and Scientific Journey* by Florence Williams
- *Falling Out of Grace: What We Learn from Life's Challenges* by Sobonfu Somé

Relationships

- *How to Spot a Dangerous Man Before You Get Involved* by Sandra L. Brown
- *Women Who Love Psychopaths* by Sandra L. Brown

- *Facing Love Addiction* by Pia Mellody
- *Your Brain on Love* audiobook by Stan Tatkin
- *Calling in "The One"* by Katherine Woodward Thomas
- *Getting the Love You Want* by Harville Hendrix, PhD

Finances

- *I Will Teach You to Be Rich* by Ramit Sethi
- *Get Good with Money* by Tiffany Aliche
- *The Path to Wealth: Seven Spiritual Steps to Financial Abundance* by May McCarthy
- *Rich Dad, Poor Dad* by Robert T. Kiyosaki

Abortion

- *Life Choices: The Teachings of Abortion* by Linda Weber
- *The Healing Choice: Your Guide to Emotional Recovery After an Abortion* by Candace De Puy and Dana Dovitch

Childlessness

- *Living the Life Unexpected* by Jody Day
- *Women Without Kids* by Ruby Warrington

Internal Family Systems

- *No Bad Parts: Healing Trauma and Restoring Wholeness with the Internal Family Systems Model* by Dr. Richard Schwartz
- Find an IFS therapist or practitioner at ifs-institute.com/practitioners

Miscellaneous

- *Ancestral Medicine: Rituals for Personal and Family Healing* by Daniel Foor, PhD

- *When the Body Says No: The Cost of Hidden Stress* by Gabor Maté, MD

- *The Way of Grace: The Transforming Power of Ego Relaxation* by Miranda Macpherson

- *The Dance of Anger* by Harriet Lerner, PhD

Notes

Chapter 2

1. Florence Williams, *Heartbreak: A Personal and Scientific Journey* (New York: Pushkin Industries, 2021), 5, 49.

2. Williams, *Heartbreak*, 51.

Chapter 3

1. Amita Health, "5 Common Autoimmune Diseases that Affect Women," accessed December 12, 2022 (amitahealth.org/blog-articles/womens-health/5-common-autoimmune-diseases-that-affect-women#:~:text=Estimates%20indicate%20the%20number%20of,with%20autoimmune%20diseases%20are%20women).

2. Gabor Maté, MD, *When the Body Says No: The Cost of Hidden Stress* (New Jersey: John Wiley & Sons, Inc., 2023), 85–86.

Chapter 5

1. Gabor Maté, MD, *When the Body Says No: The Cost of Hidden Stress* (New Jersey: John Wiley & Sons, Inc., 2023).

2. Samuel Brod, Lorenzo Rattazzi, Giuseppa Piras, and Fulvo D'Acquisto, "'As above, so below' examining the interplay between emotion and the immune system," *Immunology* 143, no. 3 (November 2014), 311–318, ncbi.nlm.nih.gov/pmc/articles/PMC4212945/.

3. Brod et al., "'As above, so below.'"

Chapter 11

1. Amita Health, "5 Common Autoimmune Diseases that Affect Women," accessed December 12, 2022 (amitahealth.org/blog-articles/womens-health/5-common-autoimmune-diseases-that-affect-women#:~:text=Estimates%20indicate%20the%20number%20of,with%20autoimmune%20diseases%20are%20women).

Index

abortion, 17, 27–38
Abraham-Hicks, 69, 70, 71
addiction, 9, 11, 90
allowance, practice of,
   216–217
ancestors, 21–22, 64, 92
Angelou, Maya, 181
anger, 67
   allowing, 18, 113–117
   feeling and relaxing into,
     119–120
   finding healthy ways to
     express, 120
   getting curious about,
     120–121
   giving it somewhere to go,
     118–121
   speaking for, not from,
     your parts, 119
   taking a pause, 119
   tending to the rage that
     hurts others, 116–117
   understanding its messages
     and power, 117–118
anxiety, 118
asking for help, 18, 83–96
   difficulty of, 90
   ways to ask for help, 91–93

awareness, 49
Ayurveda, 12

betrayal, 1–5
body, grief and, 60–62
breakups, 1–5, 7–8, 9, 30–31,
   62
Brown, Sandra L., *How to Spot
   a Dangerous Man Before You
   Get Involved*, 31
"Buddha nature," 14
Buddhism, 14, 129–130,
   162–163, 236

calm, 133
Cameron, Julia, *The Artist's
   Way*, 20
Capron, Tory, 59, 235–239
career, 9, 173–180
caregivers, compassionate,
   226–228
Center for Somatic Grieving,
   54–55
Chinese medicine, 12
Chödrön, Pema, 139
chronic illness, post-traumatic
   growth (PTG) through,
   212–213

clarity, 133
closing ritual, 239–240
coming alive, 19, 207–219
community gatherings, 164
compassion, 133
confidence, 133
congestive heart failure, 61–62
connectedness, 133. *See also*
     connection
connection
     need for, 83
     tapping into, 133–134
courage, 133
COVID-19 pandemic, 8, 53,
     128, 199, 200, 208, 211,
     221, 223, 231
cowry shell divination,
     224–225
creating ritual, 157–162
creativity, 133
curiosity, 133

death, 9, 45–46, 146, 226,
     236–237, 238
De Mello, Anthony, 193
depression, 67, 69–70
devotion, 15
disease, 9. *See also* COVID-19
     pandemic
     chronic illness, 212–213
     congestive heart failure,
          61–62
     stress and, 74–76
Dispenza, Joe, 70–71

divination, 224–225
the Divine, 157
divine timing, 227–228
DMT, 182, 183. *See also*
     psychedelic-assisted therapy

EMDR (Eye Movement
     Desensitization and
     Reprocessing), 211
emotions. *See also specific*
     emotions
     emotional support, 94
          (*see also* support)
     immune system and, 118
     repressing, 90
     stigma surrounding
          "negative," 76–77
     validating, 67–68, 76–77,
          79
essential goodness, 14
exiled parts, 95
     contacting, 151–154
     signs of, 150–151

fertility journey, 103–111
finances, 9, 173–180
finding forgiveness, 181–188
firefighters, 95–96, 142
Flyer, Carolyn, 57–60
foods, nourishing, 20–21
Foor, Daniel, 157
     Ancestral Meditation, 21
forgiveness
     finding, 181–188

practice of, 189–191
process of, 188–189
self-forgiveness, 186–188,
    189
Freud, Sigmund, 153

gaslighting, 29–30
Gilbert, Elizabeth, 83
greatness, 16
grief, 18, 67, 226
    allowing your grief to be
        witnessed, 57–60
    bowing to, 17, 53–63
    creating a container to
        grieve well, 63–65
    "death" phase of, 39
    grief rituals, 54–57
    impact on health, 62–63
    physical movement and,
        63–64
    talking and, 63
    your body and, 60–62
grieving. See grief
growth, suffering and, 7–8

Hafez, 123
healing, 20
    collective, 164–165
    creating a healing cocoon,
        20–21
    healing circles, 164
    healing cocoons, 20–21, 22
    healing immersions, 120
    heartbreak, 146–147

holistic approach to, 14–15
mistrust in life after
    devastation, 196–198
mistrust of yourself,
    202–203
old hurts, 148–149
ritual and, 164–165
self-doubt, 72–74
spiritual dimension of, 15
"unburdening" and, 95
health. See also disease, impact
    of grief on, 62–63
heartbreak
    approach to, 13–15
    examples of, 8–9
    future, 238–239
    healing, 146–147
    healing from, 10
    initial and subsequent, 10
    kinds of, 8–11
    navigating early weeks of,
        47–49
    preparing for our ultimate,
        235–240
    purpose of, 238–239
    reframing, 7–23
heartbreak altars, 22
heartbreak journals, 20, 22. See
    also journaling
heartbreak journeys, 9–10,
    16–17
    preparing for, 20–23
    ways to navigate early
        weeks of, 47–49

heartbreak stories, 17
  abortion, 27–38
  career and finances,
    173–180
  fertility journey, 103–112
help, asking for, 18, 83–96
Hicks, Esther, 69, 70, 71
Higher Power, 15, 21–22, 63,
  64, 92, 157, 198, 200–202
Hoffman Process, 120
homeopathic remedies, 49
Honarvar, Ari, 87–89
humor, remembering,
  217–218
hyper-individualism, harms
  of, 90
hypnotherapy, 210

immune system, emotions and,
  118
inclusivity, radical, 239
inner wisdom, 15, 204. *See also*
  Self energy
inquiry, 15
intentions, setting, 22
Internal Family Systems (IFS),
  11, 14–15, 19, 72–74, 94,
  121, 130–131, 133, 186–
  187, 211, 227. *See also*
  meditation(s)
  meditations, 203–204
  mistrust and, 203–204
  pain and, 147–148, 149
  on the Self, 187–188

self-forgiveness and, 189
speaking for, not from,
  your parts, 119
suicidal ideation and, 142
training in, 226, 227
two kinds of parts, 95–96
visualizations, 77–78
women's circles, 116

journaling, 20, 22, 198
  prompts, 50–51, 64–65,
    80–81, 98–99, 121–
    122, 137, 154–155,
    169, 191–192, 205,
    219–220, 232–233
judgment, lack of, 226

katabas, 1
Kissen, David, 118
Kübler-Ross, Elisabeth, 67

Lerner, Hannah, 113
letting go, 162–164, 198–200
letting yourself off the hook,
  47
Lewis, C. S., 39
life experiences, as greatest
  teachers, 12–13
loneliness
  fearing, 131–133
  living with, 18, 123–128
  resource lonely parts with
    Self energy, 134–136

ways you cope with,
130–131
loss, 9. *See also* breakups; death
LSD, 182. *See also* psychedelic-
assisted therapy

Macpherson, Miranda,
215–216
The Way of Grace, 215
managers, 95–96, 142
mantras, "One breath at a
time," 47
Maté, Gabor, *When the Body
Says No*, 74–75, 118
MDMA, 182, 183, 187, 199
meditation(s), 15, 96–98, 198,
236
allowing, 215–216
contacting an exiled part,
151–154
to feel and relax into anger,
119–120
getting to know a
protective part, 96–98
inviting all of your parts
to the banquet table,
77–79
mapping your mistrusting
parts, 203–205
opening, softening and
allowing meditation,
215–216
practice of allowance,
216–217

a practice to feel your pain,
144–145
resource lonely parts with
Self energy, 134–136
tonglen, 129–130
Mellody, Pia, *Facing Love
Addiction*, 30
Mercil, Zina, 212–213
microrituals, 167–168
"mind over matter," 70
mirth, 118
mistrust. *See also* trust
after devastation, 196–198
mistrusting parts, 203–205
of yourself, 202–203
"Morning Pages," 20
Murakami, Haruki, 235

National Institutes of Health,
118
Nat Mur, 49
nature
being in, 48
living in harmony with, 12
next steps, 231–232
numbness, 49

obsessive thinking, 42, 48
opening, 215–216
others, supporting, 19,
221–233

pain
feeling your, 144–150

healing old hurts, 148–149

processing, 18, 139–143

taking inventory of
    unhealed wounds,
    149–150

Palmer, Amanda, *The Art of
    Asking*, 91

Palmer, Parker, 92

parts

    behind our pain, 147–148

    contacting an exiled part,
        151–156

    exiled, 150–156

    inviting all of your parts
        to the banquet table,
        77–79

    mistrusting, 203–205

    protective, 96–98, 143–144

    protective parts who
        can keep you stuck,
        143–144

    resourcing lonely parts with
        Self energy, 134–137

    two kinds of, 95–96

physical movement, grief and,
    63–64

playing the hand we're dealt,
    213–215

post-traumatic growth (PTG),
    through chronic illness,
    212–213

practices. *See also* meditation(s)
    of allowance, 215–217

allowing meditation,
    215–216

closing ritual, 239–240

contacting an exiled part,
    151–156

creating a container to
    grieve well, 63–65

creating your own ritual,
    161–162

cultivating a prayer practice,
    200–202

to feel your pain, 144–145

of forgiveness, 189–191

getting to know a
    protective part, 96–98

giving your anger
    somewhere to go,
    118–122

ideas for supporting others,
    228–234

inviting all of your parts
    to the banquet table,
    77–82

mapping your mistrusting
    parts, 203–205

microrituals to hold us
    through transitions,
    167–168

opening, 215–216

prayer practice, 198–201

resourcing lonely parts with
    Self energy, 134–137

softening, 215–216

tonglen, 129–130

ways to navigate early
  weeks of heartbreak,
  47–49
prayer practice, 198–200
  cultivating a, 200–201
protective parts, 96–98
  who can keep you stuck,
    143–144
protectors, 95–96. *See also*
  protective parts
psychedelic-assisted therapy,
  183
psychotherapeutic modalities,
  14

radical inclusivity, 239
rage, 116–117
rebirth, 18–19, 181, 207–208
refugees, support for, 87–89
reintegrating, 193
relaxation, 118
restoring trust, 193–205
Rinpoche, Chögyam Trungpa,
  162–163
rituals
  art and discipline of,
    164–167
  being patient, 166
  closing ritual, 239–240
  considering etiquette, 165
  creating, 18, 157–160
  establishing your intention,
    165
  grief rituals, 54–57

healing and, 164–165
including prayer, 166
inviting in protection, 165
making offerings, 166
microrituals to hold us
  through transitions,
  167–168
for saying goodbye to a
  loved one, 162–164
saying thank you, 166
sharing an invocation, 166
suspending disbelief, 165

sadness, 18, 67
saying goodbye to a loved one,
  9, 162–164
Schwartz, Richard (Dick), 14,
  121
self-care, 20–21
self-doubt, healing, 72–74
Self energy, 14, 15
  identifying presence of,
    133–134
  resourcing lonely parts with,
    134–137
self-forgiveness, 186–188, 189
self-trust, taking a vow of,
  79–80
self-validation, 18, 67–77
  learning to validate yourself,
    76–77, 79
  signs that you're
    invalidating yourself,
    74–75

sexual abuse, 186–187
shock, 49
    coming out of, 43–45
    facing, 45–46
    navigating, 17, 39–46
    symptoms of, 43
sleep, elusiveness of, 48–49
softening, 215–216
Somé, Malidoma, 224–226
Somé, Sobonfu, 55
staying in motion, 47
Stover, Sara Avant, 12
    approach to heartbreak,
        13–15
    The Book of SHE, 12, 221
    privilege and, 13
    *The Way of the Happy
        Woman*, 12
Strayed, Cheryl, 207
stress, disease and, 74–76
suffering, 12
    growth and, 7–8
    value of, 7–8
suicidal ideation, 142
support, 49, 79. *See also*
    supporting others
    asking nonphysical realm
        for, 63
    circle of, 63
    emotional, 94
    emotional support, 94
    receiving support as a
        refugee, 87–89

supporting others, 19,
    221–233
    ideas for, 228–230

talking, grief and, 63
therapy. *See specific kinds of
    therapy*
Tibetan Buddhism, 129–130,
    162–163
the torma, 236, 239, 240
transformation, 16, 18
transitions, microrituals to
    hold us through, 167–168
trauma, 9, 62
    disease and, 74–76
    processing, 42
trust
    restoring, 193–205
    trusting something bigger,
        198–200
Tutu, Desmond, 221

unburdening, 95, 149
unhealed wounds, taking
    inventory of, 149–150

validating yourself, 18, 67–77
Van Derveer, Krista, 45–46
visualizations, 129–130. *See
    also* meditation(s); practices

walking, 48
warmth, comfort of, 49
Weller, Francis, 53

Williams, Florence, *Heartbreak*,
62
Williamson, Marianne, *A
Course in Miracles*
workbook, 188, 189–190
wisdom, 12, 15, 79, 121, 204
wounds, repetitive, 153–154

About the Author

S ara Avant Stover is an author, certified Internal Family Systems
practitioner, and teacher and mentor of women's spirituality and
entrepreneurship. After graduating Phi Beta Kappa and summa cum
laude from Columbia University's all-women's Barnard College, she had
a cancer scare and moved to Thailand, where she embarked on a decade-
long healing and spiritual odyssey throughout Asia. Since then, she's
devoted her life to helping women embody their full potential, in business and in life, and has gone on to uplift the lives of tens of thousands
of women worldwide. Her previous books include *The Way of the Happy
Woman* and *The Book of SHE*. Learn more at saraavantstover.com.

About Sounds True

Sounds True was founded in 1985 by Tami Simon with a clear mission: to disseminate spiritual wisdom. Since starting out as a project with one woman and her tape recorder, we have grown into a multimedia publishing company with a catalog of more than 3,000 titles by some of the leading teachers and visionaries of our time, and an ever-expanding family of beloved customers from across the world.

In more than three decades of evolution, Sounds True has maintained our focus on our overriding purpose and mission: to wake up the world. We offer books, audio programs, online learning experiences, and in-person events to support your personal growth and awakening, and to unlock our greatest human capacities to love and serve.

At SoundsTrue.com you'll find a wealth of resources to enrich your journey, including our weekly *Insights at the Edge* podcast, free downloads, and information about our nonprofit Sounds True Foundation, where we strive to remove financial barriers to the materials we publish through scholarships and donations worldwide.

To learn more, please visit SoundsTrue.com/freegifts or call us toll-free at 800.333.9185.

Together, we can wake up the world.

sounds true
WAKING UP THE WORLD